EMPLOYMENT AND CITIZENSHIP IN BRITAIN AND FRANCE

For Bridget as ever

and for Marie-Cecile, Guilène and Sylvia

Employment and Citizenship in Britain and France

Edited by

JOHN EDWARDS
Royal Holloway, University of London

JEAN-PAUL RÉVAUGER
Université de Provence and Université de Antilles et de la Guyane, France

Ashgate

Aldershot • Burlington USA • Singapore • Sydney

Published by
Ashgate Publishing Limited
Gower House
Croft Road
Aldershot
Hampshire GU11 3HR
England

Ashgate Publishing Company
131 Main Street
Burlington
Vermount 05401
USA

Ashgate website: http://www.ashgate.com

British Library Cataloguing in Publication Data
Employment and citizenship in Britain and France
  1. Labor mobility - Great Britain - Congresses 2. Labor
  mobility - France - Congresses 3. Labour policy - Social
  aspects - Great Britain - Congresses 4. Labor policy -
  Social aspects - France - Congresses 5. Labor market - Great
  Britain - Congresses 6. Labor market - France - Congresses
  I. Edwards, John, 1943- II. Revauger, J.-P. (Jean-Paul)
  331.1'27941

Library of Congress Catalog Card Number: 00-131629

ISBN 0 7546 1294 5

Printed and bound by Athenaeum Press, Ltd.,
Gateshead, Tyne & Wear.

Contents

PART II: EMPLOYMENT UNCERTAINTY AND ECONOMIC SECURITY

PART III: CITIZENSHIP RIGHTS AND EMPLOYMENT SECURITY

List of Tables

List of Contributors

John Edwards is Professor of Social Policy at London University. He has published widely in the field of minority rights and affirmative action and was recently Visiting Professor of Human Rights at the University of Utrecht.

Jean-Paul Révauger is Professeur de civilisation britannique at the Universities of Grenoble, Aix en Provence, and Antilles-Guyane. He conducts comparative research in the fields of social policy and political science. Together with Professor Edwards he has been running a programme on the transfer of policies and concepts in the field of social policy.

Jean-Louis Meyer is Maitre de Conférence in Sociology at the Université de Nancy 2. His research work bears mostly on employment and training. He is in charge of a vocational MA programme (DESS) on 'the management of employment-based social integration schemes (emplois d'insertion')'. His latest publications include a book on employment schemes designed for young people, *Des Contrats Emploi Solidarité aux Emplois Jeunes*.

Antoine Capet is Professor of British Studies at the University of Rouen. Most of his publications are devoted to the debate on the Second World War as a social and political watershed, and he has recently edited a collection of essays on British Society in the Second World War. He is currently engaged in compiling a comprehensive Bibliography on Britain in the Second World War.

Laurence Dreyfuss is Chercheuse en sciences politiques, Université Paul Valery, Montpellier III.

Alain Marchand is Professor in Economics at Montpellier III University. His fields are the economics of the cooperative and non-profit making sectors and labour market economics. He is the director of a research centre (ARPES: Analyse, recherche en politique et economie sociale). In 1993 he edited *Le Travail Social à L'Epreuve de l'Europe*, (L'Harmattan).

Tony Cutler is Reader in Sociology, School of Social Science, Middlesex University, co-author of *Keynes, Beveridge and Beyond* (1996) (with J. and K. Williams), and *Managing the Welfare State* (with B. Waine) (1994) and (1997).

Phillip James is Professor of Employment Relations at Middlesex University Business School. He has researched and written extensively within the fields of industrial relations and occupational health and safety. His latest book, *Regulating Health and Safety at Work: The Way Forward* has recently been published by the Institute of Employment Rights.

Susanne MacGregor is Professor of Social Policy at Middlesex University. She has published widely on urban issues, social problems and the politics of social policy. Publications include *The Politics of Poverty* (1981), *Tackling the Inner Cities* (edited with Ben Pimlott) (1990), and *Social Issues and Party Politics* (edited with Helen Jones) (1998).

Barbara Waine is Principal Lecturer in Social Policy, School of Social Science, Middlesex University, author of *The Rhetoric of Independence* (1991) and co-author (with T. Cutler) of *Managing the Welfare State* (1994) and (1997), and has written extensively on pensions policy in the UK.

Elaine Jaoui-Pylypiw is Maître de Conférence de civilisation britannique at Université de Paris I Pantheon Sorbonne.

Ruth Hancock is a Senior Research Fellow in the Nuffield Community Care Studies Unit at the University of Leicester. She is an economist with interests and expertise in pensions and long-term care financing, financial resources in later life and the economics of ageing. Recent publications include *Home Ownership in later life: financial benefit or burden?* (with J. Askham, H. Nelson and A. Tinker) (1999), 'Older couples and long-term care: the financial implications of one spouse entering private or voluntary residential or nursing home care', *Ageing and Society*, (1999).

Claudine McCreadie is Research Fellow in the Gerontology Department at King's College, London. She has a long-standing research interest in social policy issues, recently contributing to research commissioned by the Royal Commission on long term care. Her special research interest is in the abuse/ill treatment of older people. Her recent publications include 'Elder Abuse' (with A. Tinker) in R.C. Tallis, H. Fillitt and J. Brocklehurst (eds) *Brocklehurst's Textbook of Geriatric Medicine and Gerontology*, (1998) and contributions to the Royal Commission on Long Term Care.

Michael Hill has been Visiting Professor in the Department of Social Policy, Goldsmiths College, University of London since 1998. He is Joint Editor of the Journal of Social Policy 1999-2003. He was Professor of Social Policy, University of Newcastle upon Tyne 1986-97 and appointed Emeritus Professor from October 1997. His publications include *Understanding Social Policy* (2000), *Social Policy: A Comparative Analysis* (1996) and *The Policy Process in the Modern State* (1997).

Alan Gordon is Senior Lecturer in Social Policy at Royal Holloway, University of London. He is the author of *The Crisis of Unemployment* (1988) and a number of research reports for the Department of Education and Employment on such topics as youth employment strategies, local labour markets and economic assessment reports. His main research concern is with the linkages between education, training and employment.

David Middleton is Senior Lecturer in Sociology at London Guildhall University. His main research area is in the field of social justice, but he has also been involved in research in the fields of health care, communications, and crime policy.

Anthony Rees is Senior Lecturer in Social Policy at the University of Southampton. He is the author of the completely revised fifth edition of T.H. Marshall's classic text on *Social Policy* (1985) and in recent years has published a number of articles on citizenship and related subjects in academic journals and edited books. He is a member of the Council of the National Association of Citizens Advice Bureaux.

Ina Doornweerd is a PhD student in the Department of Social and Political Science at Royal Holloway College, University of London. In 1996 she completed her Masters degree in General Social Sciences at Utrecht University in the Netherlands. Her doctoral thesis focuses on a comparative analysis of welfare states and conceptions of social citizenship rights across Europe.

Preface

This is the second volume to be published in the 'policy transferability programme'. Like the first, it represents a selection of the contributions made at a 'transferability' conference held in Aix-en-Provence in September 1998 – just seventeen months after the first conference.

The purpose of these gatherings is to bring together (mainly) French and British academics from a diverse range of disciplines and fields of study who have an interest in social and public policy. Each conference focuses on one policy topic (the first was on inequality – the next will concentrate on policies in respect of minority groups; this volume takes as its theme increasing employment flexibility).

The purpose of the transferability programme is not to undertake comparative analyses of policy topics between France and Britain (in fact, one of its aims is precisely not to). Rather, so far as possible, the purpose is to examine cultural, social, economic and linguistic factors which might facilitate the transfer of policy ideas and policies between the two countries and those factors which act as a constraint.

As the chapters in this volume demonstrate, whilst the Luxembourg meeting on employment flexibility in 1997 generated a good deal of consensus on the nature and value of increased flexibility, the effects are likely to be very different as between France and Britain. And this for a variety of reasons that have little or nothing to do with policy or policy effectiveness. Indeed, what the contributors also show is that employment flexibility and its consequences raise quite different concerns in the two countries such that no commonality of policy response would make any sense.

Whether social and public policies can transfer between countries clearly depends on a large number of extraneous factors but learning about these – and especially about differences in meanings and cultural and social contexts – will at least be of some assistance in understanding which policy ideas and policies will transfer.

John Edwards   Jean-Paul Révauger
St Jean D'Aulps   Schoelcher, Martinique

Acknowledgements

Our first debt of gratitude must be to all those who participated in the second conference on transferability and who made it such a rewarding experience. Thanks especially to those who have contributed to this volume. The fact that this volume has taken longer to publish than the first is due entirely to the absence of one of the editors in the Netherlands for an extended period.

Thanks are due to the following for contributing so much to the success of the conference:

- The Université de Provence under whose auspices the conference was organised.
- The Observatoire de la societé britannique.
- The Centre de Recherche et d'Etudes en Civilisation Britannique.
- The MIRE for financial support
- The Comité Regional du Diologue National sur Europe.
- The Mairie d'Aix-en-Provence for kindly making available one of its beautiful salons.
- Royal Holloway, University of London.

Sheila Sweet typed the entire volume and prepared it for publication – which for camera-ready copy is a mammoth and intricate task. Very special thanks are due her.

1 Introduction

JOHN EDWARDS

The European Employment Summit held in November 1997 in Luxembourg, formulated for the first time, a European employment agenda. The product (as no doubt was the intention) was less of an employment policy than an attempt to formulate a common approach (or perhaps even more loosely, 'flavour') to the way in which increasingly inter-connected employment markets might develop. Since national markets could no longer operate in isolation from one another, the direction that enforced inter-connection took them ought at least (so it was felt) to be given some steer.

If there was one core theme to the new employment approach, it was that of 'flexibility'. This may have been an acknowledgement of the inevitable insofar as elements of flexibility had been entering national (and international) employment markets for more than a decade but what the summit did was to articulate these trends for the first time and to attempt some more coherent approach and some agreement on what aspects of flexibility were 'desirable' and which were not.

'Employment flexibility' can mean a multitude of things, and comes in a variety of forms from 'lifelong education' for a workforce that needs constantly to adapt its skills to changing demands, to the use of interchangeable skills, an increase in contract employment, short-term employment, self employment, low paid and marginal employment, and more intra- and inter-state mobility for employment purposes.

Change is gradual but the social and economic consequences of growing employment flexibility whether integrated and harmonised or left to the free play of the employment market are likely to be considerable. And they constitute as yet uncharted territory. We know something of the economic imperatives behind the development of more flexible labour markets (but we need to know more), and, as some of the essays in this volume show, we have some understanding of the changed nature of the relationship between people and state that the idea of flexibility has brought about. But what is of equal concern (and is reflected in the following essays) is the nature and extent of social and economic insecurity that comes in the wake of employment flexibility. Most

1

employees in all fifteen EU countries still hold long-term jobs with steady pay and make only relatively infrequent job moves during their working lives. However, an increasing number and proportion (but with large variations between countries) are either self-employed or hold jobs that do not last for long – having been engaged to fulfil a particular task or been given a fixed term contract. Their employment experience (and their livelihood) is often tenuous and uncertain and the future may have a habit of drawing-in, so that it stretches no further than the sight of the next job. The situation is ameliorable of course. Those capable of doing so can retrain (and re-retrain), gaining a bigger portmanteau of skills so to be more marketable (flexible or adjustable). Or they can be more mobile and widen their job search area, crossing national boundaries if necessary.

The consequences of this increasingly common pattern of employment are heightened levels of social and economic insecurity. Foremost among the economic (or more exactly, financial) consequences will be the increased difficulty of accumulating pension rights through a multiplicity of jobs and employment. Socially, there is the personal and family insecurity that follows from short-term futures and the inability to plan (both financially and socially). And much of this (along with the psychological effects of enforced shortened horizons) is as yet scarcely known or understood. Some of the territory that the following essays encroach upon has been partially surveyed and there are data and some information to draw on; other parts allow of only conjecture. The essays reflect this variable terrain, some speculative, others analytical, but together they throw some light on a phenomenon which will almost inevitably have a telling impact both on individual and family life and, at a different level, on the relationship between citizens and states.

The essays brought together in this volume began life as contributions to the Second Conference on the Transferability of Social Policy held in Aix-en-Provence in September 1998, organised jointly by Royal Holloway College, University of London and the University of Provence Aix-Marseille 1, the focus of which was the nature of, and the problems created by, employment flexibility and the appropriate policy responses. As with the first conference on policy transferability, the emphasis of the chapters in this volume is on policies and problems in Britain and France. They are not, however, and nor are they intended to be, *comparative* as between the two countries (though comparisons are, on occasion, inevitable). The underlying theme of policy transferability is better served not by (often mechanistic) comparisons using terminology that frequently has no common meaning or sense, but by gaining a better understanding of what flexibility – but more particularly – the consequences of flexibility mean in the two countries. The point here is that descriptively speaking, the impact of increased flexibility may appear to be quite similar in France and Britain, whereas, *how* it is felt by individuals and families may, for a variety of reasons (but not least cultural ones), be different. (Community, extended family, friendship networks, church membership for example, may provide reassurance and support in times of financial and social insecurity in one country but their relative absence in another may expose those who have experienced employment flexibility to heightened levels of insecurity and isolation). Likewise, when we consider policy in relation to flexibility and its affects, we need to recognise the social and political milieu in which these policies are formulated and implemented. At the most basic level for example, we have no reason to assume that the same value is attached to flexibility in both France and Britain and insofar as flexible labour markets can be promoted by public policy, this different evaluation may result in quite different perceptions of the need for a policy response. And policy to ameliorate the effects of employment flexibility (by, for example, creating new ways of accumulating pension rights that take account of the increasingly fissiparous pattern of employment over a working life) will be affected, in the earnestness of their inception and in their content, by the relative weighting that each country puts on the benefits of flexibility on the one hand and the amount of insecurity created on the other. If for example, it is thought acceptable or inevitable that the costs of economic and technological change should lie where they fall, any ameliorating policy response may appear to be otiose. It may on the other hand, appear to be a matter of some importance, and urgency, if value is placed on the welfare and security of individuals and families or if the consequences of flexibility are such as to alter the nature and status of citizenship and the relation between state and citizen in a way that appears deleterious to the worker and his or her dependants.

All these dimensions of flexibility and its consequences are such as not to be easily amenable to comparison between countries. Comparison *is* possible of course but what the ensuing chapters recognise is that it must be multi-dimensional and must recognise the cultural and linguistic differences within which the phenomenon and policy responses to it, are embedded.

3

The substantive chapters that follow have been grouped into three sections, though by their nature, they do not easily conform to any precise categorisation. The first section, covering topics under the rubric 'State, Society, and Employment' contains five chapters, most of which by happenstance, are by French contributors.

Révauger begins the substantive chapters with a broad canvas approach to flexibility in which he sketches the increasing trend of employment flexibility and its consequences as generating a process in which a number of players including governments, the European Union, political parties and trade unions are engaged in searching for, and establishing a new 'social settlement' or set of arrangements for negotiating the varied interests at work in the labour market. Employment flexibility for Révauger, is more than a shift in employment relationships from (relatively) long term allegiances between employers, employees and unions to short-term de-unionised and fragmented employment relationships. Rather, it is part of a longer term trend which may result in a very different settlement between the parties in the labour market and, in consequence of this, a re-alignment of political allegiances and interests. It may not happen soon, but if flexible labour markets were to become the norm, the emergence of new social settlements drawn along new lines would appear to be entirely plausible.

As a means of structuring the argument, Révauger identifies a number of components or types of flexibility. The principal distinction lies between internal and external flexibility where the former refers to changes within a company or organisation and the latter to changes in the outside employment market environment. A second level of distinction is that between qualitative and quantitative flexibility. External flexibility can only ever be quantitative whereas internal flexibility can be either quantitative or qualitative. Three general types of flexibility therefore result : external quantitative, internal quantitative and internal qualitative. This typology (which seems to have gained a fairly general recognition) is of value in trying to make sense of the forms that flexibility takes but more importantly in clarifying the complex interaction between flexibility and the complex of interacting components not just in the employment market but in employment structures and sectors more widely. It is this more complex set of interactions that Meyer takes up in his chapter which also brings a number of different countries into the frame. Employment flexibility, Meyer argues, is not a process that affects employment markets, sectors and structures in a uniform and passive manner. Rather, it interacts with them in complex ways and in ways that differ from one country to another. For example, it impacts on male and female workers differently in different countries; its impact will vary as between different employment sectors (service, managerial, manufacturing, administration) and these in turn will differ from one country to another. And, to the extent that greater flexibility is deemed desirable (as, for example, a counter to increasing unemployment), the relative balance that it takes between its three forms will also vary from one country to another. And these differences are nowhere more noticeable says Meyer than between Northern and Mediterranean European countries. The outcomes of increasing employment flexibility therefore, whether intended or by happenstance, will nowhere conform to the Luxembourg Summit pattern, and the idea that there can be a uniform or even common policy response to it is wholly unrealistic. Flexibility may be a common phenomenon in European employment markets, but the consequences of its interaction with employment sectors and structures will be highly varied.

Capet examines the idea of flexibility (in its more general sense) in historical terms taking in the work of Adam Smith, Malthus and Ricardo. He shows that whilst there are no precursors in any precise sense to the modern idea of employment flexibility and its intended and unintended consequences, the idea itself has long had standing in economics. The meanings and nuances have changed but the basic idea of a tenuous and fragile link between the employment market and those who seek work in it is of long standing. In bringing his story up to date, Capet traces the idea of employment flexibility through post war Conservative and Labour government policies in the UK and then, concentrating on Labour party manifestos during post-war years, he demonstrates how rhetoric has changed as the party has come to accept the idea, to the present day when 'new' Labour appears to have embraced flexibility in the service of a modern competitive economy.

If there is one sector of employment that is less well known and less well researched than any other, it is what in France is referred to as the cultural occupations or industries. It is a sector unlike most others and though its nature and composition vary greatly between countries, its main peculiarities are common as Dreyfuss and Marchand illustrate. It is a sector of employment (and self-employment) that is more varied than any other (being as broad as the arts themselves and with all the accoutrements of business added on). Its product takes many forms - some quite tangible such as paintings or photographs and sculptures; others, of a transient nature as in the case of performance art. And most distinctive is the relationship between the producer and the product. In no other sector can the maker of a product be so intimately involved in, identified with, or connected to, the product itself (indeed, they are, on occasions, indistinguishable). Given these peculiarities of the cultural occupations, it is not surprising that they tend to get relatively little attention as sectors of employment and self-employment to be compared with manufacturing, the service sectors, education, banking and so on. Yet, many people do earn their living in cultural occupations and they are as subject to the vicissitudes of the employment market as workers in any other field (indeed, as Dreyfuss and Marchand show, they are more at risk than people in most other sectors).

Fragility and insecurity of employment have also been a feature of the cultural occupations for longer than other employment sectors (as the history of the search for patronage attests), but the nature of this insecurity has changed in a manner that has often been dictated by the way in which the product of 'cultural' activity is marketed and as Dreyfuss and Marchand argue, the manner in which the cultural product is marketed may be such as to 'alienate' the producer from the product of his or her creative activity. There may therefore develop a complex interaction between the creation and marketing of a cultural product and the 'quality' of the conditions of employment and self-employment.

There is another theme that the authors of this chapter develop which attempts to link the nature of employment flexibility and insecurity in the cultural occupations, to the development of complex sets of allegiances and social movements including the taking of proxy social action (such as street demonstrations) on behalf of other groups of workers. There is, so the argument goes, little allegiance on the part of cultural workers to the job as such (which may be a tenuous, short term, and poorly paid arrangement offering little or no security). Such allegiances as cultural workers have therefore are more likely to be to the cultural product and to ideas and ideologies. And hence the link to new social movements. As Dreyfuss and Marchand argue the case, and despite the fact that some of their data derive from fieldwork in Great Britain, it is clear that this is a very 'French' analysis and that the picture they draw relates more directly to France than to Britain (or indeed, most other European countries).

The chapter by Cutler and his colleagues focuses on Britain. Their concern is with the relationship between labour market flexibility and deregulation on the one hand and welfare state retrenchment on the other.

The combination of these, the authors argue, will lead to greater 'modernisation' in social and economic policies. The question that this development then poses is whether 'modernisation' will, in its turn, deliver more security or alternative routes to more security (alternative that is, to long term employment) or whether it will in effect create yet more insecurity. Flexibility and insecurity create new welfare demands (and not least of course, in the field of pensions); response to these will require changes in the welfare system and if this system proves to be too rigid to deliver welfare in modified forms, then a more radical re-alignment many be necessary. Hence the move towards modernisation with its emphasis on private sector involvement in welfare delivery. Cutler and his co-authors focus their analysis on two areas of welfare provision - pensions and health care and on policies in respect of both by Conservative and Labour governments. They argue that 'modernisation' in welfare policies shows no political or ideological divide and that both Labour and Conservative agenda bear close similarities (as evidenced for example by Labour's formulation of citizenship as being increasingly tied to work and by the growing emphasis on 'welfare to work'). Whichever party was in power, therefore, the prospects for insecurity would look very similar. And the prospects of modernisation the authors show are an increased potential for insecurity in both pensions and health care. When employment flexibility is located in a context of welfare state retrenchment therefore, its negative effects appear to be exacerbated.

The four chapters that make up the second section focus more narrowly on the question of economic security and how it can be maintained or created in circumstances of employment uncertainty that is the product of flexible labour markets.

One significant component of employment flexibility that perhaps gets less attention than others is the geographic mobility of workers to find employment or improve their employment prospects. When such movement involves cross-national boundary flows within Europe - as is increasingly the case - it creates complications for the social security standing of migrants. Nationals of one country who move to another may find their eligibilities for benefits of a variety of kinds changed or eroded - or made less definitive. This is the territory that Pylypiw explores in her chapter on the transfer of entitlements. One might be forgiven for assuming, says Pylypiw that in a single market with (in theory at least) free movement of labour, social rights would be transferable across national boundaries, that benefit levels would be standardised and that cross-boundary movement for employment purposes would not compromise either entitlement or amount of benefit. Such, of course, is not the case. Pylypiw identifies national differences between member states of Europe on two dimensions. Firstly, there are variations in social rights and entitlements and levels of benefit as between member states. Secondly, there are variations in entitlement (and in entitlements in different countries) as between different categories of employment migrant. In combination, these variations in entitlement make for a very complex and bureaucratic system of benefit transfers such that, as Pylypiw shows, employment mobility even in the single market, can put migrants at considerable risk of insecurity. The picture therefore, is contradictory. If the vaunted benefits of employment flexibility are to be a reality, then employment mobility, as one of its key components, must play its part. But employment mobility it seems, contains in-built disincentives; to be mobile is to increase your welfare insecurity in the present and into the future.

Common to several of the contributions in this volume that include some coverage of flexibility and related matters in Great Britain, is some mention of the manner in which the (present) Labour government has put an increasing emphasis on the status of work (being gainfully employed) as the basis of citizenship. It is being in work or having spent a lifetime in employment that is becoming the defining characteristic of the citizen. Being 'unnecessarily' on welfare on the other hand is to be less than a fully participating citizen. The same set of ideas form the defining context for Hancock and McCreadie's chapter on the function and efficacy of pensions in the domain of employment flexibility. The main thrust of their contribution is an examination of the relationship between increasing flexibility and the efficacy of different types of pension provision in ensuring economic security in old age. New proposals for pensions in the UK to replace or supplement occupational pensions which are becoming increasingly difficult to sustain with the growth of flexibility, put more emphasis on what are known as 'stakeholder' pensions, provided by the state in (increasing) partnership with the private sector. Purchasing stakeholder pensions of course requires the ability to purchase (some proportion) of the pension in the private sector which in turn requires a steady income stream - just what might not be forthcoming in a flexible labour market. As Hancock and McCreadie note therefore, the new proposals reinforce a lifetime's paid work as the route to an adequate retirement income and as such are ill-conceived to meet the demands of flexibility.

Hill's chapter is a complement to that of Hancock and McCreadie, dealing as it does with pension reform and its compatibility (or non-compatibility) with an adaptation to employment flexibility. He scouts slightly different territory however in using as his starting point the World Bank's model of pension provision, identifying the three pillars of pensions management in the public, private and voluntary sectors where both public and private pillars would be mandatory (which is not the case at present in either France or the United Kingdom). Hill also, however, turns his sights on the 'demographic time bomb' debate and the manner in which it has been conducted. He is sceptical of some of the claims made in this debate, particularly as they have been made to relate to the question of dependency rates and pension provisions and more especially as the threat of the demographic time bomb has been used to press the case for the mandatory use of the private pillar of provision.

Hill makes a three-pronged attack on 'time bomb' arguments. He cites data to show that the case has been much exaggerated. Secondly, he argues, even if the demographics were to be correct and we *are* indeed facing a serious dependency problem, it is far from clear that mandatory private sector pension provision is the appropriate answer. And thirdly, it is not, says Hill, an age imbalance that is the obvious problem but rather the availability and distribution of work that will most influence the dependency problem.

In the last chapter in this section Gordon focuses on one further component of labour market flexibility - minimum wages as an instrument of labour market policy concentrating on the United Kingdom and taking as the focus of active labour market policy, the Low Pay Commission report of 1997 and he examines the impact of the minimum wage on labour market flexibility, active labour market policy, and on social exclusion. Two components of the National Minimum Wage proposals are of particular significance to Gordon's analysis - the lower rate set for 18-21 year olds and the complete absence of a minimum wage for those aged 16 and 17 years. The intention of the Commission in this treatment of younger workers was to try to minimise the negative employment consequences often attached to setting minimum wage rates for these groups.

Gordon's analysis concludes that minimum wage legislation is likely to reduce labour market flexibility in the UK (and increase unemployment at some levels) and that the social exclusion of the young (already affected by a variety of factors) would be increased - because of their further exclusion from work - by the imposition of a minimum wage. Measures to exclude them from minimum wage regulations, or to impose a lower minimum rate, he argues, are therefore sensible precautions against greater social exclusion.

The third group of four chapters examines a different set of questions relating to flexibility. These are questions concerning the impact of flexibility on the moral standing of workers and their dependants in terms of their citizenship status, their rights, and their self-respect. The underlying rationale of these chapters is that employment flexibility represents an important shift in the socio-economic environment in which people live and that such a shift will impact not only (and most immediately) on people's finances but also on their security, well being, and their position as citizens.

Middleton examines the complex relation between the insecurity induced by flexibility, the self-respect of those who might be affected, and the conditions for social justice in society. The creation of an insecure workforce through employment flexibility is inimical, says Middleton, to the basic requirements of (his chosen schema of) social justice. Rawlsian contract theory, he notes, demands the preservation of the basic social goods amongst which are the 'bases of (self) respect'. Flexibility, in other words may represent a direct threat to one of Rawls's key primary social goods. Of all the things that contribute to, or make up, our self-respect, paid employment ('being gainfully employed') is one of the most important in market societies. To lose a job is to suffer a blow to self respect, particularly if the next job is not easily come by. But just as important, says Middleton, is the damage to self respect that can be occasioned by the *fear* of losing ones job, and it is just this sort of insecurity that is generated by employment flexibility. Losing a job is something that may happen. Fear of doing so, *will* be an ever present condition.

There is at least a *prima facie* case that the insecurity generated by employment flexibility may violate our social rights. It *is* only a *prima facie* case, however, and in his chapter, Edwards examines some of the moral questions involved in trying to put flesh on what starts as only supposition. That flexibility generates social and financial uncertainty and insecurity is fairly certain ground. Whether this insecurity violates any rights we may have is debatable. The root of the problem lies in the question of whether, in modern western societies (and, a somewhat separate issue, amongst humanity at large as a *human* right), we have a right to social and economic security. Edwards examines the case for such a right as a component of universal articles of rights but more importantly, and foundationally, as a necessary condition to being able to plan lives - of individuals and families. Do we have a right (and would it be a social right) or are we only justified in holding a 'reasonable expectation' (with none of the attributes of a right with its correlative duties) to plan our lives (the purchase of houses, planning childrens' education, having a reasonable idea of the state of our finances) over the medium or long-term? There are, Edwards concludes reasonable grounds for arguing so but the answer is not (yet) conclusive.

Both Rees and Doornweerd consider the question of citizenship and how it might affect and be affected by, questions of employment flexibility. Rees considers recent critiques of citizenship and its associated package of rights and duties that have argued the need for more emphasis on duties. Citizenship has been seen by some to consist of too many 'dutyless rights' with the result that citizenship itself has become distorted. Rees therefore examines the nature of citizenship when more duties are placed on citizens to complement the rights they wish to claim and whether this new 'duties perspective' has influenced social policy in both France and the United Kingdom. Like other contributors to this volume, he notes that the obligation to work or to seek for work is foremost among the new 'duties', satisfaction of which have become a prerequisite to the receipt of benefits. (And it is worth noting in this respect that if 'rights' to benefits become conditional on fulfilling other requirements, it becomes questionable whether they can be rights at all). In the context of flexibility, Rees notes that if employment is spasmodic and short-term and if new jobs are not always readily available, then the duty to work becomes hard to fulfil. 'Citizenship' Rees notes, as a legal, contractual concept, contains few real rights and few entitlements and benefits because receipt of them is always made conditional on other requirements. Citizenship then becomes devalued if it consists in large measure of duties that are hard to perform in the employment market place.

Doornweerd focuses on the rights components of citizenship and, taking a fairly broad canvas, she is concerned to identify a variety of conceptions and dimensions of citizenship and then to explore how employment flexibility impacts on these dimensions. Her main concern

11

is to examine whether there can be any citizenship right to employment security. Like Edwards, she pursues a line of argument in terms of the standing of a right to security (if there is one) and how such a right may be founded. Her approach leads her to examine the International Covenants to the Universal Declaration (The International Covenant on Economic, Social and Cultural Rights) and the International Labour Organisation Employment Policy Convention. In none of these does she find firm grounding for anything like either a human or citizenship right to employment security, if this is taken to mean a right to uninterrupted employment. But even if we were able to construct such a right as a citizen right, she notes, it would in practice (in Europe at least) turn out to be a *residents'* right rather than a right of citizens.

12

PART I
STATE, SOCIETY
AND
EMPLOYMENT

2 Flexibility: In Search of a New Social Settlement

JEAN-PAUL RÉVAUGER

That the term 'flexibility' has several different meanings is by now a commonplace. However, this is often presented either as a linguistic problem or as an instance of the differences between the so called 'liberal Anglo-Saxon model' and other models. In this particular debate, the frontier between the 'liberal model', the 'continental corporatist model' and the 'Scandinavian social democratic model', to use the classical categories of Esping Andersen, is far from clear (Esping Andersen, 1990). My intention here is to offer a different construction of the debate, based on the notion of social settlement, or compromise. Editorial collections such as this are not intended to change the meaning of words, or decide on correct interpretation. Only Louis XIIIth could invent the Académie Française, and this is not an example that late 20th century European academics would wish to emulate. The term does lend itself to different interpretations however and our primary task is to be aware of this, not to wish things out of existence.

From Dilution to Flexibility: the Frontier of Control

Flexibility has a flexible meaning. In the same way, 'adaptability', which has increasingly come to replace 'flexibility' in European documents, is equally adaptable to the needs of its users. We are faced here with borderline cases, or rather with a twilight zone with terms used to describe disputed territory, frontiers in the American sense of the word rather than borders of the Oder-Neisse type. A historical comparison could be suggested with the notion of 'dilution', used in the UK at the beginning of the Fordist era, in particular during World War I, to describe the gradual melt down of traditional crafts and the replacement of skilled workers by untrained, unskilled, unorganized, badly paid employees (Hinton, 1973; Gallacher, 1936; Coates and Topham, 1977; Révauger, 1986 and Harris, 1993). Dilution was feared and sometimes fiercely resisted. Its introduction led to an intense process of bargaining, and, eventually this laid the ground for a social settlement and enormous steps forward in living standards. A historical assessment of 'dilution' would probably have to take on board both aspects: it was a process designed and implemented by employers, intended to steamroll, in the name of efficiency and productivity, the flimsy protective/restrictive practices erected by workers and, at the same time, a rather liberating development, making, at least for a few decades, waged work the linchpin of social organization, with momentous consequences in terms of individual prosperity and freedom. The work contract, the employer/employee relationship replaced the old deferential, master/servant bond, as waged work gradually replaced inherited status as the legitimate matrix of social identity . This ultimately led to authority being challenged in other areas, but this was not just due to technical progress and the sheer implementation of dilution. It resulted from the process of bargaining between social groups which went along with dilution, and which was one of its by-products, for complex historical reasons. Dilution, the generalization of the scientific organization of labour was by itself not necessarily liberating: a number of nations, including the USSR, adopted pathways towards industrialization which were certainly not conducive to human liberation. The early Marxist militants who refused to oppose dilution in the name of 'the development of productive forces', the new version of 'positivism', did so for the wrong reason. Economic and technical efficiency alone are not necessarily liberating. Conversely, poverty and economic failure make democratization a very difficult exercise indeed.

'Flexibility' today has a very similar function to that of dilution during World War 1. Its historical significance, at the end of the day, might well depend on historical factors, especially the balance of social forces at the time of its implementation.

No option can be ruled out at the moment. Flexibility is both necessary, or at least helpful, from an economic point of view, just as dilution was, and highly contentious, socially speaking. The central point developed here is that its significance can vary widely and that the interpretations of the term refer and lead to contradictory forms of social organization and philosophy.

Flexibility can be construed as a relationship between employers and employees, as well as a way of adapting to change: the introduction of new technologies, new forms of organizations in firms, new types of demand, new constraints for response and delivery, new markets, new competitors. 'New' includes, here the time factor, as well as a geographical dimension. Opposition to or advocacy of flexibility, systematically alludes to globalization at the same time. We are faced with a three dimensional figure. What we are dealing with here is an ideological construction, a discourse, not necessarily hard realities. The extent to which 'globalization' is more a myth than a reality is debated and challenged by serious economists, such as Paul Krugman in the USA.[1] In France, anti liberal thinkers from the Left and the Right sides of the spectrum, as well as dedicated supporters of the conservative version of economic liberalism, such as Alain Madelin, put forward the view that liberalism, globalization and labour market flexibility are part and parcel of the same reality, and imply a fundamental shift of the balance of power away from 'working people and their families', to mis-quote the 1973 Labour party programme.

As for the emphasis on newness, it is not terribly original, as the economic system has been dominated since 1918 by the need for permanent productivity gains and growth. What is certainly new is that this can now be achieved without the drafting of ever growing numbers of workers, since production no longer requires vast numbers of employees, and that the linkage between growth and domestic demand is no longer as essential as it used to be, because of globalization. The positive by-products of Fordism - vast numbers of wage earners, the need for reasonably affluent consumers - which gave some credence to the 'trickle down theory', are now a thing of the past.

British Conservatism

It is no wonder then that the concept of flexibility has been so central in political debates and discourses in the recent past. Flexibility was at the heart of the 'conservative restoration' which dominated the 1980's in the Western world. Deregulation, the containment and rolling back of trade union power, the abolition of protective legislation under Margaret Thatcher, the abolition of Wages Councils, the development of non-standard jobs, the deliberate encouragement of new types of economic activity in areas where trade union organization was low or non existent,

17

and the scuppering of the country's industrial base where it was a significant force were not the outcome of inevitable historical change (*Annales de l'Université de Savoie,* 1994; Johnson, 1991). The 'invisible hand' was activated by a very coherent brain, which accompanied, accelerated, and encouraged historical change, wiping out the areas dominated by traditional industries and the pluralist industrial relations that went with them. British coal mining did not vanish into thin air by magic. It was deliberately and joyfully dispatched. Thatcherism was quite open about this. In the eyes of arch liberals, the real, fair and just value of labour is what employers are prepared to pay, and any regulation, any distortion of the market is bound to bounce back and reduce the efficiency of the whole system, the amount of wealth created in society, and the volume of the trickle down.

The conservative version of flexibility lays the burden for modernization quite clearly on the shoulders of the employees.

Laying the Burden on Employees

Academic descriptions usually distinguish external from internal, and qualitative from quantitative flexibility (Brunhes, 1989; Join-Lambert, 1997).

External flexibility, which is exclusively quantitative, consists in resorting to part time work, relaxing regulations on dismissals, and systematic subcontracting. Of the three types of flexibility, it is the most primitive. In the short term, it is rather easy to practice, provided the political conditions are met and the legal framework is sympathetic, as it was in Thatcher's Britain. It lays the burden exclusively on the workforce, and ultimately on the community, that foots the bill in terms of unemployment benefits and social exclusion.

Internal flexibility can be either quantitative or qualitative. Quantitative internal flexibility allows some space for negotiation. It consists in modifying the duration of work and the cost of labour within a firm. It is therefore open ended, since the outcome depends totally on the balance of forces at the time of negotiation.

Qualitative internal flexibility is focussed on changes in the organization of work, and the allocation of tasks. It also requires the agreement of the workforce - just as dilution did - and is predicated on the idea that people can learn and are willing to do so and that firms are prepared to invest in

18

training. A rather extreme version of this is put forward by the human resources school and the proponents of life long learning.

Qualitative flexibility is usually presented in a very favourable light, and sometimes described as 'offensive' (in French), and forward looking (Boyer, 1986).

In the eyes of British Conservatives then, the question appears to be clear. Flexibility means deregulation of the labour market, ie quantitative flexibility. The following analysis, based on a number of primary sources, mostly relevant speeches in the House of Commons and House of Lords made in 1997-1998 puts flesh on these bones but makes clear that the nature of Conservative views on labour disposability differs not greatly from that of Labour.

I believe in an economy that creates employment and prosperity, as our economy has during the past 20 years, by not having undue restrictions on the labour market (Hansard, House of Commons, 20.1.1998, Mr Green, MP).

The idea that flexibility is imposed on us by globalization is not only found on the Conservative benches. Ian McCartney, Minister of State at the Department of Trade and Industry presents flexibility as necessary within the European and global framework:

The new agenda is based on the recognition that Europe's labour markets need to become more flexible in adapting to ever more rapid change. With global competition intensifying, we need the flexibility that allows businesses to respond effectively to economic change and which equips people to do a range of jobs as demands vary (Hansard, House of Commons, Employment Law debate, 3.12.1997, Mr Ian McCartney, MP).

In this respect, the Thatcherite heritage, as messianic as ever, is still very much cherished:

On flexible labour markets, we must take our message and our experience of policies that really create jobs to every corner of Europe...Conservative members have a vital duty to the nation and to the people of Europe who have languished too long under high unemployment to explain what real flexible labour markets are all about. We shall carry on doing that while we have breath in our bodies (Hansard, House of Commons, 4.12.1997, Mr Streeter, MP).

19

Britain must spread the word on flexibility, and make sure its benefits are extended to the whole of Europe. For Conservatives, this is part and parcel of British identity. One may wonder to what extent Esping Andersen has been taken in by the official Conservative discourse on flexibility. It may be the case that the gap between the 'Anglo-Saxon model' and the other models is wider in theory than in practice. Shadow boxing does not seem to have disappeared with Conservative government, since New Labour prides itself in arguing the case for flexibility in European arenas.

My right honourable friend the Prime Minister was instrumental in ensuring that the new employment chapter agreed at Amsterdam explicitly recognized the importance of labour market flexibility (Hansard, House of Commons, Employment Law debate, 3.12.1997, Mr Ian McCartney, MP).

Nevertheless, when it comes to nationalist posturing, France is the ideal bugbear for Conservatives.

We have seen the effects of (other economies') failure to create jobs in actions such as the current civil unrest in France (Hansard, House of Commons, 15.1.1998, Mr Green, MP).

Once again, France's robust negotiation procedures, involving mass demonstrations and fiery rhetoric instead of quiet bargaining, are mistaken for the first shots of a civil war, threatening European stability. The French situation is portrayed as beyond redemption:

Is it not true that many of the inward investors from France are escapees and refugees from the high wage levels that are wrecking the French economy? (Hansard, House of Commons, 15.1.1998, Mr Green, MP).

Even allowing for House of Commons rhetoric, this rather rash rhetorical question owes a lot to the 'Scarlet Pimpernel interpretation of history', typical of Thatcherism.

Sharing Costs and Benefits: the Inception of Social Europe

The British Conservative approach could only lead to a major conflict with the proponents of European integration. The Bruges speech in November 1988, marked the apex of the conflict between British Conservatism and

Europe. 'We have not rolled back the frontiers of the State here in Britain to see them reimposed by some sort of European Super State in Brussels', as Mrs Thatcher said at the time (see also *Annales de l'Université de Savoie,* 1991). This set the tone for the next ten years, and explains Britain's refusal of the Social Charter and the provisions on overtime, parental leave and working hours. The debate within Europe was in fact rather more complex. Should the Union be about the creation of a deregulated single market, which could compete, and come to terms with the rest of the world (i.e. the US) thanks to its sheer efficiency, or should it be aiming for a different kind of society, the 'social market economy', based on consensus and negotiation between social partners? The social market economy, sometimes described as a corporatist nightmare, is in fact quite liberal if one refers to Dahendorf's views on the subject (Dahrendorf, 1996). Some saw European integration as a way of getting rid of national regulations, and a path towards productivity and efficiency.[2] They could point out that, from the start, mobility within Europe (i.e. labour market flexibility) had been central to the European project. Indeed, the only provisions of the Rome Treaty from a social point of view were intended to facilitate mobility. Others, such as the French Socialists, presented Europe as a means to an end. Europe alone could pursue the reflationary, Keynesian policies which dismally failed in France in 1982. This was accepted by Labour in opposition in 1984, when under Neil Kinnock, it took the European turn. Europe alone could pursue a real industrial policy, in the footsteps of the Airbus consortium, whereas national governments had neither the technological muscle nor the market for large scale projects. Needless to say the two arguments have been somewhat sidetracked, and replaced by a new one. European governments certainly paid lip service for a time to the notion of European industrial policies. Investment in infrastructure, especially transport, was even adopted and offically supported, in the last months of Jacques Delors' presidency. This was music to the ears of the French government, and of French politicians in general, since it combined perfectly well with the French tradition of Colbertisme. The embryonic European State was taking over from governments, and embarking on a real reflationary, industrial policy. This 'narrative' as British academics would call it, came to an abrupt end when the convergence criteria for the single currency were adopted. Governments were expected to adopt painful restrictive budgetary policies at home, and

21

were certainly not prepared to devote vast amounts to common long term projects whose benefits would be shared with other Europeans, but whose costs would be borne by individual governments.

The European 'narrative', in the field of social policy, changed. On the one hand, competitiveness must be pursued at all costs. This was the basis for the white paper on competitiveness, and jobs published in 1994 (European Commission, 1993). This emphasis had the usual limits of the exercise, in the sense that it seemed to imply an acceptance of the 'trickle down' discourse - set the economy right, and social problems will dissappear. Besides, the rhetoric of 'competition' and economic warfare is politically fraught with danger in terms of foreign relations and might encourage anti-liberal mercantilist tendencies which experts, whose dominant culture is inherently liberal, were keen to avoid.

A specific approach was needed, in order to demonstrate that the march towards the Euro would not lead to social regression. A specific social policy discourse was needed, quite distinct from the economic one. This culminanted in the Employment summit, held in November 1997 in Luxembourg. It defined the specific European approach to the labour markets, focusing around four policies, and mostly advocating qualitative flexibility.[3]

European Policies

Europe alone could set social targets and force the social partners to come to terms with them. Both the state and the social partners are therefore involved. This is no doubt the outcome of a compromise between the culture of corporatism and the practice of collective bargaining in Northern Europe.

The four sets of policies emerging from Luxembourg can be summed up by four concepts: employability, entrepreneurship, equal opportunities, and, most importantly for us, adaptability.

The type of flexibility which the EU advocates is rather more complex than the British one. It is indeed absolutely comprehensive and it does include the more conservative interpretations, ie labour market, external flexibility (European Commission, 1997d, p.1) but cannot be reduced to it. This is probably due to the political constraints weighing on the EU whose policies must be acceptable to all governments. The construction is rather baroque, since elements and ideas are borrowed and accumulated in a syncretic and not synthetic fashion. No choice is possible, no synthesis. The collection and addition of what individual member states consider as 'good practices' usually falls far short of a policy, and leaves ample room for contradictions. However, in this particular case, European policy has a certain amount of substance; it is identifiable since the 'liberal Anglo-Saxon model' is not considered as acceptable in its undiluted, unadulterated form. The pressure from the other cultures, be it the 'social democratic' one or the 'corporate' one is such that some kind of pluralism, (in the sense used by Hugh Clegg) is advocated. By pluralism, one must understand the sharing of costs and benefits by the two sides, employers and employees, and the method that goes with it, namely negotiation. Economic efficiency does not mean social regression, and there is no contradiction between productivity and high wages. Indeed, high wage countries can afford to be so because their productivity is high (European Commission, 1997b, p.10). The mantra is that a balance must be struck between security and flexibility (European Commission, 1997b, p.1) as far as individuals are concerned, and that flexibility is more complex than simply deregulating job markets (European Commission, 1997b, p.10). This is clearly seen as a deviation from real flexibility by the upholders of the liberal model. Here is a quote from the British House of Commons:

I pursued Mr Flynn on the question of flexibility. "We are talking not about flexibility, but about positive flexibility"...It emerged that positive flexibility can mean more, not less regulation: under its new flexibility policy, the Commission would as a matter of urgency be pressing to remove the current exemptions from the working time directive...It also means bringing forward the directive on part time work (Hansard, House of Commons, 3.12.1997, Mr Green, MP).

The arguments in favour of flexibility at Luxembourg are not terribly different from those one finds in the UK: the forward march of history and the pressure of competition make flexibility inevitable and necessary. What has changed is that the emphasis has somewhat moved away from the 'competitiveness' argument, and towards employment. This is contrasted with the current situation in Europe, which is somewhat disappointing as far as flexibility is concerned. One would have imagined, for example, that migration would have become much more common within the EU. This is clearly stated (European Commission, 1997d, p.3). The obstacles must therefore be removed.

The kind of flexibility which is advocated is obviously not the type that would be detrimental to employment, or at least to unemployment figures. Qualitative flexibility is an obvious candidate. The skills of the workforce must be enhanced and, more importantly, updated. 'We must bridge the skills gap' (European Commission, 1997d, p.2). A skilled workforce will more readily adjust to internal flexibility and will not be awe struck by external flexibility, since it will be highly employable, and will not have much difficulty finding a new job. This fits in neatly with unemployment policies, and the new notion of employability, dear to the heart of New Labour. Once again, this excludes reflationary, demand-led, Keynesian types of policies. A French proposal that the VAT rates be reduced in labour intensive industries was rejected at Luxembourg. A strategic shift in educational policies is also needed for this permanent updating of skills to be possible. Lifelong learning is regularly presented as the obvious solution but the financial and cultural implications of this are obviously left behind. The difficulty and cost of managing and improving current education systems are such that a strategic reorientation is unthinkable. In spite of limited efforts on the part of the Commission, lifelong learning remains a rather utopian slogan. It it nevertheless significant that one of Jacques Delors' contributions to French politics should have been the devising of legislation facilitating 'continuous education', in his capacity as special adviser to Gaullist Prime Minister Jacques Chaban Delmas in the early 1970s. It is difficult for intellectuals to find fault with a strategy based on education, but, quite apart from the political and financial obstacles, the strategy of 'employability' assumes that the whole population will be willing and capable of seeing its skills upgraded. Besides, the improvement of average skills has a negative consequence, in the sense that it makes employers more demanding and life particularly difficult for the unskilled or those whose competence has become obsolete. Large numbers of formerly unskilled jobs, such as clerical ones, now involve the use of sophisticated computers. An increasingly complex society, no longer based on the employment of vast numbers of workers, marginalizes the unskilled. The strategy of 'employability' therefore needs to be complemented by a policy of assistance, whose modern form is the 'struggle against exclusion', one of the most significant contributions of French social Policy to the EU. Employability and exclusion are two sides of the same coin.

The fact that flexibility is to be negotiated is stated quite clearly in Luxembourg documents, which certainly opens new opportunities for British trade unions. The real issue is at which level agreements should take place. Situations vary all over the European continent, and the neighbouring islands. In some cases, negotiation takes place at the national level, in each economic sector. This is quite typical of the corporatist model. In some rather extreme versions of this, local negotiations hardly take place at all. In the worst possible cases, such as that in France, national negotiations only take place when the political authorities, or a situation of crisis, make them absolutely necessary. This is very far removed indeed from the kind of pragmatic bargaining traditionally taking place in the UK at local level. This is the key to understanding the peculiar situation of France. The Luxembourg summit recommended local, pragmatic discussions, in a pluralistic framework, in the belief that flexibility implied in essence, concern for real, local problems, adaptability to real conditions, and not broad, theoretical or even politicized debates.[4] In this sense, the similarities with dilution, and the practice of the scientific organization of labour in the UK is also evident. Maybe the historical consequences of the localization of collective bargaining in the UK should also be kept in mind. One would have thought that the lessons should have been remembered. The proliferation of local negotiators, the 'dreaded' British shop stewards, and the demarcation disputes that went with them, eventually made the settlement of disputes more rather than less difficult in the 1960s and 1970s (Ravier, 1981, p. 218).[5] The French language does not even have a word for 'shop steward'. Because of the weakness of trade union organization in France, social regulation takes place through the medium of politics, or crises. The strategy adopted by the French government in order to facilitate the reopening of social negotiation on employment and 'internal flexibility' was therefore not that of local negotiation, but of national legislation on the 35 hour week. This is not necessarily understood outside France, and has even been criticized.

British Labour and French Socialists

For the British and French socialist governments of 1998, flexibility is also very central not just because of their commitment to European integration, but because of the extent to which the social fabric has been torn apart by unemployment and the shift in the economy. No government can openly admit the existence of a contradiction between the needs of the economy and those of its population. Throughout the 20th century, most left wing governments on both sides of the Channel, have had to choose between a head-on conflict with the property owning classes and the financial markets, leading to political defeat, or a dramatic scaling down of their ambitions. The challenge for the Blair and Jospin governments is to come up with a set of policies that will be at the same time compatible with the aspirations of their electorate, and acceptable for financial markets. The debate on flexibility is treated as an opportunity for influencing the course of events and putting forward a viable and more balanced social model.

In France, a significant body of informed opinion challenges the economic logic of flexibility. It is largely marginalized, and deprived of any real political influence other than negative and rhetorical. This naturally does not mean it is insignificant. It could easily provide a coherent radical discourse in case of a collapse of the system or a major crisis, an option which can never be entirely ruled out in France . In a political situation where the Marxist left and even the ecologists i.e. the two spiritual heirs of 1968, are associated to the management of the country, unorganized intellectuals and uncontrollable social movements have come to the fore. The symbolical leadership of people like Pierre Bourdieu, of film directors, actresses, famous doctors, has not been found lacking in two recent social movements, those of paperless immigrants, and of unemployed workers. This has not mobilized a significant section of the population, but has acted for the government as a reminder that changes were expected.

As usual in France, the government is expected to be the agent of change, a rather heavy burden in the circumstances, and one which set France apart from the EU, and places it in contradiction with the Luxembourg recommendations. This reliance on the State also highlights the cultural contradiction between France and the sheer concept of flexibility. Social settlements are negotiated and achieved nationally, sometimes under the pressure of demonstrations or strikes, somtimes through the medium of new political majorities. They are typically embodied by laws, statutes, regulations, documents codifying behaviour which can be implemented even in remote corners of industry. The deeply ingrained anti-liberalism of the French is due to the fact that left to its own, French industry does not negotiate nor adapt. Whenever flexibility is interpreted as the freedom to ignore the protective regulations obtained through hard struggle, it is fiercely opposed. The arch liberal supporters of the Thatcherite model who advocate external flexibility and labour market deregulation, only reinforce the worst fears of the 'world of labour', and society in general and its opposition to any kind of flexibility at all. Provocative moves, such as an attempt at abolishing the minimum wage for younger people have been not only politically disastrous for their supporters, but counterproductive in terms of flexibility. The term is largely negative, and even its milder European version, adaptability, is considered with much mistrust and cynicism. One might suggest that the French have adopted a clear cut division between employment and leisure, which leaves little room for voluntary intermediate situations. Common wisdom has it that part-time work is not helpful in terms of career and that it is not always voluntary. Indeed, female part-time work is much less frequent in France than it is in the UK. Large strikes took place in a number of sectors such as the railways in November 1995, in defence of a very generous provision concerning the age of retirement (at fifty).[6] The French trade union approach to the issue seems to be the reduction in working hours, whether on a weekly or life time basis, rather than a blurring of borders between work and non-work, which would offer employers countless opportunities for turning the clock back and clawing back whatever advantages had been won from them. That, at least, is the theory.

In practice, however, the Jospin government has been trying to give some substance to social negotiation, and encourage the adaptability and modernization of firms. The function of the law on the 35 hour week is precisely to restore some confidence among wage earners and trade unions, by proving their government was there to guarantee social advances. It is the mechanism through which a degree of flexibility can be instilled in the French economy, precisely because it makes local negotiation mandatory, within the legal framework of the new legislation. The organization of work must indeed be discussed and agreed by both sides before anything happens. Since economists are rather divided on the question whether the 35 hour week will create employment or not, one would suggest that the chief aim of the Jospin government is precisely the development of flexibility on a positive basis, and not job creation. The French way to flexibility also leads to local negotiations, via the Assemblée Nationale and a statutory reduction of the working week. Ad augusta per angusta for economists, but a political nightmare for liberals. The creation of new half way house jobs for the young unemployed, the 'emplois Aubry', the rewriting and adoption of a new law to combat social exclusion, although they are also functional in their own right, also play a part in this reassuring strategy.

One of Tony Blair's catch phrases is 'work for those who can, security for those who cannot'. This is the philosophy behind the March 1998 Green Paper (HMSO, 1998) and it is meant to be taken literally. People who are at work should expect no security, in the traditional sense of the word. 'The concept of security for workers has to be reformulated, focusing more on security based on employability in the labour market rather than security in a specific job'. (*Hansard*, House of Commons, 3.12.1997, Mr IanMcCartney)[7] The notion of employability is essential to this way of thinking. How much the distinction between employable and non-employable owes to the traditional one between able-bodied and non able-bodied, between deserving and undeserving is open for question. The obsession of the Green Paper with fraud does reinforce the impression that claimants are slightly dodgy people who require supervision if the 'taxpayers money is not to be squandered'. In this respect, Frank Field was closer to Chadwick than to Beveridge. It is naturally hard to tell who exactly was responsible for specific parts of the Green Paper, and why the July crisis came about, but the insistence on fraud and scrutiny strikes one as a distinct Victorian feature, designed to cow people into obedience, deference and subservience. Needless to say, there is little scope for policy transfers in this area, since France abhors deference. Indeed, that is what the 1789 Revolution was all about.

Strangely enough, the Blairite discourse on flexibility varies somewhat according to the arena in which it is held. In international forums, Blair goes out of his way to promote flexibility, sometimes in a rather undiplomatic way. Given the professionalism of New Labour PR men, or even the status of PR in the core philosophy of New Labour, this can only be deliberate, but one may wonder for whose benefits such quasi Thatcherite discourses are held. Within weeks of its election, the Blair government was making pronouncements whereby regulation in Europe could damage employment, and the promotion of flexibility would be a central concern of the British presidency. This lasted from June 1997 throughout the Stockholm meeting of European Socialist Parties, until the November 1997 Luxembourg meeting. The British public, and the financial markets needed to be reassured that the Conservative legacy would not be squandered on the altar of European Integration (see *Financial Times*,

1997). The political cost of this for New Labour was not negligible within the European left, and especially the French left. Commentators observed that, whereas Blair had been warmly welcomed by right wing MPs in the Assemblée Nationale, left wing députés sat on their hands.

Meanwhile, back home, the government was busy telling the House of Commons how limited the impact of European legislation would be in the UK. Directives adopted under article 100 of the EC Treaty on part-time work would be implemented, but would be practically useless, since part-time workers who are mostly women in the UK, are already protected against discrimination as women, under Equal Pay legislation. Besides, the proportion of part-timers is already quite significant, and its development on the continent is just bringing it into line with the UK (Select Committee on European Legislation 6th Report, *Hansard*, 27.11.1998). A rather defensive, somewhat self-statisfied stance.

Flexibility is, for New Labour as well as for Conservatives, a British speciality, part of British identity in Europe, something that should be cherished, defended and promoted.

Positive connotations abound whenever the term is referred to. The gender dimension, which was already present in a number of other government documents, is very much highlighted. Parental leave directives, the need for changes in the sharing of 'parenting', as well as the gender implications of new protective measures for flexible workers are put forward.

The difference between labour and its predecessors lies mostly in the stress on employability and on the idea that, if flexibility is to be enhanced, flexible workers should be offered more protection. This reflects European concerns for a sharing of the benefits as well as the costs.

The idea that partnership in industry is economically efficient became rather popular in industrial relations literature in the 1970s (more precisely between the 1973 crisis and Mrs Thatcher's victory on May 4th 1979). After this, the balance of power was tipped clearly towards employers, the seat of authority was clearly identified, and there was no need for an ideal model in which consensus would be sought, benefits would be shared, and intelligent contributions expected from the workforce. Whatever benefits accrued from firms would take the form of the trickle down effect and general economic prosperity. The 'unitary', organic model to which the EU refers, owes a lot to the culture of corporatism. This is the notion behind the development of works councils. In this respect, the negotiation of flexibility plays an important part in enhancing participative structures. The Labour government has welcomed this, at least in theory: 'It is equally important to foster a culture of partnership in the workplace itself. Employees who feel involved in their organization are much more likely to share its goals.' (*Hansard*, 3.12.1997, Mr Ian McCartney, MP). The gap between discourse and practices, however, is yawning.

Conclusion

A pervading sense of inevitability suffuses most of the discourses on flexibility, as was the case for Taylorism in the past. All governments seem to have adopted the idea that it is an essential element of competitiveness, and the basis for a new type of social organisation and life. However, the shape of things to come depends entirely on political factors, and, more precisely, on the balance of forces between the social agents. The state is as much involved in this evolution as the 'social partners' throughout the EU which seems to suggest a blurring of the classical distinctions between welfare regimes. We are told that the 'macdonaldization' of society, the coming into being of a purely liberal model can be avoided in favour of a more balanced, negotiated socially acceptable form of flexibility. Nevertheless, the generalization of flexibility itself, even in its most civilized version, raises serious issues in terms of exclusions.

Notes

1 Globalization, in the light of Paul Krugman's works, appears as a constituent element of neo liberal political discourse, not as an objective phenomenon. Krugman underlines, among other things, that the proportion of world GNP devoted to international exchanges has just barely caught up with its late 19th century levels (see Krugman, 1995).

2 For a good example of the kind of economic rhetoric deployed to convince the public of the economic advantages of the Single Market, see the Cecchini Report (The Costs of Non Europe) *Economie Européenne*, 1992: la nouvelle économie européenne: une évaluation des effects économiques potentiels de l'achèvement du marché intérieur de la communauté européenne.' mars 1988, No. 35.

3 All the documents related to Luxembourg can be consulted on DG5's web site. See in particular: *European Commission, Proposals for Guidelines* (1 Oct 1997) (European Commission 1997a); *Presidency Conclusions* (24 Nov 1997) (European Commission

1997b); *An Employment Agenda for the Year 2000: Issues and Policies* 24 Nov 1997) (European Commission 1997c); *Executive Summary* (24 Nov 1997) (European Commission 1997d).

4 An analysis of the French press at the time of the Luxembourg summit leads to the conclusion that the summit was given considerable prominence in France. See *La Monde* 21 November 1997, 4 columns, front page article 'Les quinze ébauchent une politique sociale'; *Libération* 20 November 1997, 3 columns, front page article 'Emploi, ce que l'Europe peut faire'.

5 See Jean-Paul Ravier, *Les Syndicats Britanniques sous les Gouvernements Travaillistes 1945-1970*. Lyon, PUL, 1981, p.124 et sec for a detailed analysis of the phenomenon (Ravier 1981).

6 French trade unions are divided on this. Force Ouvriére demands early retirement packages in return for job cuts, whereas the CFDT stresses a strict implementation of the 35 hour week. At the end of the day both organisations want to reduce time spent at work.

7 See also Select Committee on European Legislation Sixth Report. Part Time Work. *Hansard*, House of Commons, 27 November 1997.

References

Annales de l'Université de Savoie (1991), *L'Europe Sociale à Onze*, Annales de l'Université de Savoie, no. 14, Chambéry.

Annales de l'Université de Savoie (1994), *La Grande Bretagne de John Major : Changement ou Continuité?*, Annales de l'Université de Savoie, no. 17, Chambéry.

Boyer, R. (1986), *La Flexibilité du Travail en Europe*, La Découverte, Paris.

Brunhes, B. (1989), 'La Flexibilité du Travail. Réflexion sur les Modéles Européens', *Droit Social*, mars.

Cecchini (1988), '1992: la Nouvelle Economie Européene: Une Evaluation des Effets Economiques Potentiels de l'Achevement du Marché Intérieur de la Comununté Européene', (The Cecchini Report), *Economie Européene*, mars, no. 35.

Clegg, H. (1979), *The Changing System of Industrial Relations in Britain*, Blackwell, Oxford.

Coates, K. and Topham, T. (1977), *Industrial Democracy in Britain*, Spokesman, Nottingham.

Dahrendorf, R. (1996), 'Prosperity, Civility and Liberty : Can We Square the Circle?', *Proceedings of the British Academy*, vol. 90, pp. 223-235, The British Academy, London.

Esping-Anderson, G. (1990), *The Three Worlds of Welfare Capitalism*, Polity Press, Cambridge.

European Commission (1993), *Competitiveness and Employment*, (White Paper on Growth), 5th December, European Commission, Brussels.

European Commission (1997a), *Proposals for Guidelines*, 1st October, European Commission, Brussels.

European Commission (1997b), *Presidency Conclusions*, 24th November, European Commission, Brussels.

European Commission (1997c), *An Employment Agenda for the Year 2000: Issues and Policies*, 24th November, European Commission, Brussels.

European Commission (1997d), *Executive Summary*, 24th November, European Commission, Brussels.

Financial Times, 27th June 1997, 'UK Calls For More Labour Flexibility in Europe', *Financial Times*, London.

Gallacher, W. (1936), *Revolt on the Clyde,* Lawrence and Wishart, London.

Hansard (27th November 1997), *Select Committee on European Legislation: Sixth Report.*

Hansard, (3rd December 1997), Mr Ian McCartney, MP.

Hansard, (4th December 1997), Mr Streeter, MP.

Hansard, (15th January 1998), Mr Green, MP.

Hansard, (20th January 1998), Mr Green, MP.

Harris, J. (1993), *Private Lives, Public Spirit: Britain 1870-1914*, Oxford University Press, Oxford.

Her Majesty's Stationery Office (1998), *New Ambitions for Our Country: A New Contract for Welfare*, Her Majesty's Stationery Office, London.

Hinton, J. (1973), *The First Shop Stewards Movement,* George Allen and Unwin, London.

Johnson, C.V. (1991), *The Economy Under Mrs Thatcher*, Penguin, London.

Join-Lambert, M.T. (1997), *Politiques Sociales*, Presses de Sciences-po et Dalloz, Paris.

Krugman, P. (1995), *Development, Geography and Economic Theory*, MIT Press, Cambridge, Mass.

Le Monde (1997), 'Le quinze ébauchent une politique sociale', 21st November.

Liberation (1997), 'Emploi ce que l'Europe peut faire', 20th November.

Ravier, J-P. (1981), *Les Syndicats Britanniques Sous les Gouvernements Travaillistes 1945-1970*, PUL, Lyon.

Révauger, J-P. (1986), *L'Idée d'Autoqestion en Grande-Bretagne,* Thèse d'Etat, University de Grenoble III.

Ritzer, G. (1998), *The Macdonaldization Thesis,* Sage, London.

3 Flexibility and Policies in Employment: Reflections from Several European Countries

JEAN-LOUIS MEYER

Observers agree that reports on work and employment have entered a major transformation since the 80s. The practical institutional modalities of new work forces differ significantly in each of the countries recently observed. As seen from the historical, cultural, institutional and even the economical specificity of different member states, each one establishes a mode of adaptation according to economic restraints. From this point of view a line divides the Northern European States from the Mediterranean ones. This paper will try to show in what form and in which modalities this dividing line has arisen.

The involvement of companies in setting up flexible employment is fundamental. The jobs offered by companies obviously determines the general physiognomy (appearance) of the job market in the different countries. However the formation of the job market does not only come from companies. The powers-to-be in each country have also had their role in the transformation of the job market. Far from going along with the changes, their role has sometimes heavily anticipated the evolution that resulted from normal adjustments between offer and demand in the job market. I will develop this idea, using French and British public policies as a base, at the end of this paper.

Flexibility and Structure in Employment

All our problems are rooted in our archaic notions of society and of our place in society. We should stop complaining and adapt ourselves to the evolution of the world (Révauger, 1998).

This sums up, in a few words, all the problems and their solutions that can be thought of in trying to find *the* solution to finding the delicate balance that is the result of changes in the wage structures due to the economic crisis. Diagnosis and treatment depend on a certain idea of people, of their

33

place in society and the structural relationship between citizen and the system. Obviously the solutions in general are political. The art of governing is to make social inequalities due to the disparity of the job market acceptable. As concerns employment policies, each European state reserves the right to do as it considers fit; the European authorities are only there to give advice on the matter. Each state, according to its political colour, will emphasise certain factors more than others. In employment policy terms, homogeneity is a long way off; the care and caution used in applying the Luxembourg Summit's proposals is an example. However it would be wrong to under-estimate the power of politics to influence the structure of the job market not only in each member state but in the European Union in general. An assortment of different measures concerning flexibility in employment are an example of the political pressure on national employment structures. One must remember the illusion that this world of change was preceded by a stable world; that employment used to be something of a permanent character. The 'Glorious Thirties' belong more to the myth of Paradise Lost than to a period of stability and reliability in employment status (Fourcade, 1992). Flexibility in employment is not a recent phenomena; the evolution of certain situations in the job market is just a question of adapting to specific management needs created by companies and this is something constantly communicated in employment policies.

However this paper will not attempt to analyse the simultaneous evolution of different work structures; it will instead analyse the current measures concerning work structures in several different member states.

Employment as Social Structuring

The field of work can be defined as an exchange of services resulting in a form of payment. A salaried worker gives his or her skills and forfeits his or her liberty against financial payment. In France as in most European countries, employment rules determine the relationship between employer and employee. The rules that control these work relationships are rendered obsolete when one goes from an employer-employee relationship to a commercial one, as in the case of the self-employed. Self-employed status is therefore a guarantee of transactions working well as it places both parties outside the rules imposed by the work ethic/code. The United Kingdom is a unique case where the work code/ethic, and therefore work agreements, are essentially based on common law. Whatever the ultimate principle used in different countries, the act of work is placed within our societies by employment which provides a social status and a form of payment through a set of rules established in law or in usage. Employment as we know it today is being increasingly built on a network of complex social relationships; and this particular form of work recognition is a fluctuating social structure that never ceases to change. Under pressure of conventional and administrative logistics, employment takes on many different forms. In France, for example, it is customary to distinguish traditional employment from new forms of employment.

Traditional employment, defined as a full-time job for an unlimited period with the same employer, is still the standard form of employment in France and most European countries. Nearly 80 per cent of employment contracts in France are of a traditional nature, and it is therefore still the principal form of employment. A study carried out by CEPII shows that traditional employment is also the norm in the UK, despite recurrent speeches on flexibility in employment (Fouquin, 1998).

Nevertheless, whatever the country looked at, the number of jobs that do not fit the norm has increased steadily for the last twenty years. New job definitions have made employment more heterogeneous and more complex. What importance can be accorded to employment figures today that include part-time jobs (sometimes just a few hours a week) over a much more limited period of time (sometimes less than a month)? Employment status has become crucial in distinguishing between those who are totally integrated into the work system and those who live on the edge - either in employment considered as a secondary status (the majority of atypical jobs), or out of employment as a registered unemployed person, or as a 'discouraged' out of work person. Jobs that qualify as atypical corrode the idea of ordinary employment, whether from a question of hours, the nature of payment or even the status of the employer. These are not the same people who do the 'dirty jobs'. Furthermore, the division between the active members of the community and the unemployed ones varies considerably according to different European countries. This difference in the unequal division between active members and the unemployed ones or between salaried part-time workers and short-term contract workers gives us one explanation of changing employment structures.

Employment Structures

Whatever country one looks at, the disorganisation of employment is attributable to the effects of job restructuring and the new ways they are distributed in the different work markets. In fact a historical perspective shows that the evolution of the active population is accompanied by an increase in available jobs, but the outstanding fact is above all the evolution in employment structures. Over the last 30 years we have gone at a fairly steady rate from an agricultural or industrial society to a society of service industries.

Table 3.1 Evolution of the service industries in various European countries

	Percentage of workforce in service industries			
	1975	1985	1996	% change
UK	56.8	63.0	70.6	+24%
France	51.1	59.4	68.6	+25%
Italy	45.7	55.5	61.1	+33%
Spain	39.7	52.0	62.0	+56%
Germany	47.8	53.8	61.8	+29%

Source: Eurostat 1998

The table shows that over 60 per cent of the workforce today works in the service sector, and that Italy and above all Spain have seen particularly important increases. These divisions in employment according to sector and the different countries observed are fundamental to the subject we are concerned with. Indeed, the use of flexibility in employment will depend on the economic sectors and the constraints that a particular member state is facing.

Before embarking on the central question of flexibility it must be said that this evolution in employment in the countries studied is most certainly produced by the re-orientation of economic activity but also (and above all), by distinct social differences. The societal approach underlines how much the structures and specific social relations are combined where salaries are concerned. The populations who are mobilised to assume economic activities are not the same. The recourse to standard categories varies greatly from country to country. Each member state mobilises specific categories of the population according to its particular socio-economic situation.

The percentage of activity (comparing the active working population and the population of working age) already underlines the differences between the countries. Great Britain, Germany and France have the highest percentage for an active working population with 76 per cent, 68.9 per cent and 68.8 per cent respectively. This compares with 58.4 per cent for Italy and 60.6 per cent for Spain. These unequal percentages are determined by distinct social differences which is why the active population in the over 55 age bracket goes from 43.7 per cent in France, to 54.5 per cent in Germany and more than 60 per cent in the united Kingdom. The percentage of under-twenties in active employment also varies between less than 10 per cent in France and nearly 60 per cent in Great Britain (with 20 per cent in Italy, nearly 30 per cent in Spain and 35 per cent in Germany). Employment amongst the working age population is more evenly distributed in the northern countries (here Great Britain and Germany) whereas it is concentrated on the adult generation only in the Mediterranean countries. From this point of view France is part of the Mediterranean group of countries, but this distinction is not valid in other areas. The specificity of its training courses and in particular its adult training courses, explains the basis of this exception. This regrouping around one generation is obtained because teenagers leave school at a later date (the number of teenage pupils is greater in France than in other countries) and also because of the high unemployment rate amongst the same young generation. To this 'neglect' of the young generation must be added the forced movement of older generations towards a sheltered position in society (early retirement in particular).

Another interesting division concerns the unequal distribution of employment between men and women. Important differences can be seen of we compare the percentage of working women in Italy at 43.7 per cent to 46.3 per cent in Spain, 53.8 per cent in Germany, 61.8 per cent in France and to 67.5 per cent in the United Kingdom. The female workforce, with the advantages and disadvantages that it entails, its distribution in different jobs and taken within a precise economic context, differs according to the workforces available in the various member states. One recent characteristic of these European countries is to present very different salary rates from one country to another. Once again it is necessary, when analysing these data to make the distinction between the Mediterranean European countries and the Northern European ones. Salaried workers are in a strong majority in the Northern European countries. Over three-quarters of the active working population belong to the salaried classes in these countries (77 per cent in Germany, 79 per cent in Great Britain and 76 per cent in France). On the other hand the Mediterranean countries stand out with a much lower than average percentage (66 per cent in Italy, 58 per cent in Spain).

These distinct divisions within the active working population encompass different work features which correspond to different modes of flexibility in different jobs in relation to the job market. Let us now define the notion of flexibility as it is used in the different countries.

Understanding the Notions of Flexibility

Before trying to define these notions, it is well worth noting what Boyer has had to say about flexibility being characterised by its particularly ambiguous general meaning/form. Inspired by a homeostatic model, the concept of flexibility is similar to, in the widest sense, the ability which a system develops to thwart the disorganisation of which it is the object. Flexibility therefore becomes the essential capacity of a system to regularise its own functioning (Boyer, 1986). From this point of view, flexibility and adaptability are synonymous. Flexible working hours should be understood as 'the possibility to adapt the workforce to production needs' (Brunhes, 1989). This means that a firm can reduce cost and delays in adapting to new economic situations by using various different adjustments. Traditionally the relative approaches break down into two distinct forms which can be used together or separately: external flexibility and internal flexibility.

External Flexibility

External flexibility helps the system to adjust by using external markets; that is to say, by drawing on reserves in the available working population. Several strategies are used in this mode of flexibility.

The necessary workforce can be mobilised in handing out part of the work to a sub-contractor. The operation consists in employing the help of a third party to undertake part of the work through means of a business contract. This resort to external solutions is frequently used by large industries in the majority of the countries studied. Italy is a typical example of this resort to an external market. Most of Italy's economy is centred in small business units (more than 66 per cent of the workforce is to be found in companies with less than 50 employees against 54 per cent in France; there are 68 companies for each thousand inhabitants in Italy as compared to 35 in France and 46 per thousand in Great Britain). One example of this type of production line is the Benetton company which sub-contracts out work to 30,000 workers in 250 small to medium sized companies (Cazal and Peritti, 1992).

Another kind of employment on the increase must be added to the phenomena of sub-contracting, and that is self-employment. Twenty-four point eight per cent of people working in the Transalpine Peninsular are self-employed. These extremely small companies are often created by former employees of larger, more powerful companies. They often employ the aid of a member of the family or a close friend. Similar employment patterns are to be found in other Mediterranean countries. This form of flexible employment can be considered seasonal in these countries in so far as it is largely used in the agricultural sector and in areas such as tourism. Non-salaried work represents 21 per cent of employment in Spain, and 26.8 per cent in Portugal. In comparison, Great Britain only has 12.6 per cent of its workforce in non-salaried employment, of which 9 per cent are self-employed, despite its image in France as a country of external flexibility. In France 11.3 per cent are self-employed and in Germany, 9.6 per cent. Italy, Spain and Portugal have delayed some of the hazards of the present economic crisis posed by these forms of externalisation and autonomy (temporary work is not allowed in Italy or at least it is very strictly run, and there is very little call for part-time work).

The call for temporary work also represents another level which external flexibility can use. It is either applied by limiting the length of the contract, which enables the company to adapt the number of salaried workers to production needs, or by using interim workers. There are important differences between member states here as well. The distinction between the Northern European countries and the Mediterranean ones is once more in evidence. Italy is the only Mediterranean country not to use interim workers, but it has limited its short-term contracts to 7.5 per cent which is clearly below the level of its European neighbours. Portugal however, with 11.1 per cent of its workforce in short-term contracts, relies heavily on external flexibility, as does Spain, with more than a third (33.6 per cent) of its workforce on short-term contracts.

Apart from the unique case of Spain which can be explained on the whole by the passing of an Act in 1984 giving large autonomy to temporary employment, and by the creation of employment training courses, the use of external flexibility is proportionally comparable in the majority of European countries. Short-term contracts make up 7.1 per cent of the workforce in the United Kingdom, 12.6 per cent in France and 11.1 per cent in Germany.

The majority of European countries therefore use this kind of external flexibility; however different grades of precariousness exist. In Germany, short-term contract employment is relatively well protected through workers' representatives, whereas Great Britain has contracts which rely on a 'reserve' workforce where there is no legal requirement on the part of the employer to supply regular work or even to pay National Insurance contributions (zero hour contracts).

Interim work presents another aspect of the kinds of external flexibility that have been studied here. There is an important difference between the Mediterranean countries and the other European countries as has already been shown. Strictly speaking, interim work does not exist in the Mediterranean countries. In Italy it is on the point of being legalised, whilst in Spain it is still illegal even if in reality it exists. As concerns other EU countries, interim work is characterised by the particular needs of the member states in question. In Germany, unlike France, interim workers are usually qualified industrial workers. The explanation for German industrial workers preferring this system is most certainly due to the way that employment in this sector is organised. For several years there has been an increasing number of lesser skilled workers in the interim sector. From being a choice of how to work, interim work has become a necessity for these workers. However, while this tendency is true in the Upper Rhine region, in the UK it is the skilled workforce that has become the interim workers. This British workforce is concentrated in the service industries but it is difficult to analyse the details as there appear to be no official statistics. (The only reliable information comes from interim work agency statistics and not from the workforce). Finally, in France, interim work has been through periods of restrictions followed by periods of development depending on the political climate. The industrial sector is the biggest user of this kind of flexible employment; employees employed as interim workers are usually young men in unskilled manual work.

Having several jobs at the same time, where some of them (or all of them) are done 'on the side', is part of the flexible employment system, even though this is often illegal. This is widespread in the Mediterranean countries (in Italy for example the Banca d'Italia estimates that 10 per cent of its workforce in the economic sector has a second job, and that 7 per cent have a job 'on the side'; in Spain the problem of irregular work is also considerable - more than 3 million people are employed thus). Multiple activity is also found in other European countries where illegal work plays an undeniable role in flexible employment especially in sectors sensitive to fluctuations in the market such as the building and confection industries.

Finally, one must remember that the majority of countries have made their redundancy procedures more supple, allowing companies to adapt the number of salaried workers to the changes in the market. Due to these changes in redundancy procedures, employees now receive more protection but this protection varies according to the country. In Great Britain, according to Cazal and Peretti (1992) the absence of employment laws is particularly noticeable. Certain jobs, such as those concerning interim workers, the newly employed, part-timers and intermittent workers are excluded from the work code. In other countries, notably Italy and France laws on redundancy, and in particular laws on group redundancies, are much stricter and adjustments are made by leaning on public services (social aid and training course allowances in France and the Case Integrazione in Italy).

Internal Flexibility

This kind of adjustment relies in the main on the managing of human resources within the company. Several dimensions, often complementary, are used and one kind of flexibility rests on the quantitative management of employees. This is organised through varying the length of contracts and through the adjustment of payments.

Internal quantitative flexibility uses a permanent workforce and adapts the number of hours worked. This flexibility is obtained, says Brunhes, by using the salaried workers differently (Brunhes, 1989). Two kinds of adjustment have been noticed: on the one hand, the establishment of a yearly number of hours, and on the other, the use of overtime. The changing demands of production are therefore met through supplying the company with the necessary workforce, the workforce being modulated by prolonging the number of hours worked. An average working week differs according to the member state; the United Kingdom comes top of the list with 43.4 hours a week, followed by 39.8 hours a week in France and 38 hours in Belgium. However, if this is calculated on an average yearly basis over the entire workforce, the Mediterranean countries have a higher weekly average, due to the low number of part-time workers. Briefly, this internal flexibility allows a balance in work between countries with a shorter working week but a higher percentage of working people and countries with a lower percentage of workers but a longer working week. The exception to this rule is the United Kingdom, which not only has a high percentage of people working but also a long working week.

To these various possibilities of a working week must be added the increasing use of part-time workers; this shows the reasoning behind only using the services of certain employees at certain times. Extra workloads are assumed by staff working overtime. Again the difference between the Mediterranean countries and the northern ones is noticed when one looks at statistics in part-time work. The number of part-time workers in Spain, Italy and Portugal is less than half of that in the Northern countries. Part-time work is typical of Northern countries: in Sweden the percentage reaches 24.5 per cent and 38.1 per cent in the Netherlands. However, whatever the country, this percentage concerns women much more than men and this is true right across the board. In the fifteen countries that make up the European Union, part-time work accounts for 5.5 per cent of employment amongst men and 31.6 per cent amongst women. The European Community's report on employment for 1997 points out that in the majority of countries where there is a high percentage of people in employment, a large part of that percentage is of people in part-time employment. In a country like the United Kingdom, the percentage increase in employment is reduced by half if one takes into consideration the jobs considered 'full-time equivalents'. If employment can be considered as an adjustable variable, we are forced to admit that this variable changes according to distinct modalities and according to the country. The table below summarises the information concerning the ways quantitative flexibility is used in the countries studied.

Table 3.2 Quantitative flexibility: summary data

	Total pop. ('000)	% in employment	Non-Salaried workers (% of total employment)	Part-time workers (women in brackets)	Short term contracts
Spain	39270	45.1	21.5	8.0 (17.0)	33.6 (36.7)
Italy	57399	50.0	24.8	6.6 (12.7)	7.5 (8.9)
France	58375	60.3	11.3	16.0 (29.5)	12.6 (13.9
Germany	81923	62.6	9.6	16.5 (33.6)	11.1 (11.2)
Portugal	9928	63.8	26.8	8.7 (13.1)	10.6 (11.1)
UK	58784	59.3	12.6	24.6 (44.8)	7.1 (8.2)

Source: Eurostat 1997

The other question of internal quantitative flexibility concerns cost management. Some member states have imposed legal limits concerning a minimum wage, whereas others, arguing the sacrosanct workings of the free market and its effect on prices, are firmly against it. The United Kingdom has been one of the few European countries until very recently not to fix a minimum wage (the minimum wage agreement disappeared during the Thatcher era as did the Wage Councils). It was only in April 1999 that the UK introduced a minimum wage at £3.90 per hour. On the other hand, company court cases have often pinpointed the French exception where the rigidity of salary scales, of which the SMIC (Salaire Minimum Interprofesionnel de Croissance: the minimum Wage Agreement) is the symbol, has played against employment. Despite these extreme positions, all member states have found themselves following the same downward logic concerning employment costs, in using government policies that offer various employment training courses or exoneration from various compulsory employers' contributions such as National Insurance. Plus the fact that non-qualified employment (and here France is the typical example), is increasingly subsidised by the state through concessions to employers, while job losses are concentrated in the least qualified professions. These different measures contribute undeniably towards reducing salary costs and giving more flexibility in the mediations between capital and work.

One last element of quantitative flexibility is that of salaries. The majority of salary policies in the different states re-orientate direct work revenue by personalising requirements but also through developing salary associated elements such as profit-sharing schemes, share schemes and saving schemes. To take the example of the United Kingdom again, salaries are firmly based on performance related activities such as individual performance related pay and profit related pay schemes. These payment reorientation policies help to widen the gap between permanent and temporary staff in a company; the latter do not receive the same advantages as the former. From the point of view of staff shareholders and staff profit sharing, there is a similarity between France and the United Kingdom and in this they are both at the forefront in Europe.

One final point in internal flexibility is qualitative or functions flexibility, which I will not deal with in this paper. Qualitative flexibility is essentially based on the reorganisation of salaries in terms of skills and responsibilities. Investing in training courses is of course central to a successful modification of the workforce.

Employment Policies and Using Flexibility as a Solution

Bearing in mind the importance and the complexity of the systems which make up employment policies in the different European states, present coverage will be limited to an analysis of employment policies in France and in Great Britain and in particular their ability to apply flexible forms of employment.

Unemployment as a general justification for employment policies

The use of different flexible employment measures in the various member states has been legitimised as being an answer to economic difficulties and above all being an answer to the rise in unemployment - which all member states have experienced at one time or another (Gautie, 1993). The struggle for employment has become an alibi justifying all flexible applications to work market regulations; this interpretation was behind John Major's statement, after the signing of the Maastricht Treaty, that 'you keep Europe Socialist and we'll keep the jobs...'

Unemployment, presented as a real social cancer, has hit the European countries hard, as the table below shows.

Table 3.3 Unemployment figures for the various European countries studied in 1996

	% of active population	Unemployment %	Youth unemployment	Long term unemployment	Male long term unemployment (Women)
UK	76.0	8.2	15.5	39.8	45.9 (28.1)
France	68.8	12.4	28.9	38.3	26.4 (39.8)
Italy	58.4	12.0	33.5	65.6	64.1 (67.1)
Spain	60.6	22.1	41.9	52.9	45.9 (59.6)
Germany	68.9	8.9	9.6	47.8	44.5 (51.7)

Source: Eurostat, 1996

It is certain that unemployment figures are only a rough indication of what workers really face in the different European countries. It is extremely difficult to compare living standards among the employed with those amongst the unemployed. However, between a person who works just a few hours a week (not forgetting that these people are counted amongst the active working population), and a person who is entitled to full unemployment benefit (or job seekers' allowance), the difference is very slight. It is therefore prudent to restrict the comparison of unemployment figures, as public opinion on this can vary. However, identifying the people who should receive priority on government employment schemes relies on analysing the unemployment risk factor that these people run, whatever the country and although these figures can be criticised, it must be noted that they are uniformly used to identify the target publics in the member states.

Flexibility and Employment Policies: France and the United Kingdom

In France and the United Kingdom national culture has shaped the distinct logical plans of action which aim to improve job and employment situations in both countries.

On the British side of the Channel free market choice tries to resolve employment and unemployment problems by using the homo economicus model. This model is geared towards maximising profits in the job market in a rational way. The state's role in this context, is essentially to remove potential obstacles from the smooth workings of the free market as well as to encourage the active population to seek work. In this optic the constant worry of Conservative governments was to remove all possible brakes which might have upset the balance of the free market. A major obstacle to the 'natural' workings of the market is of course voluntary withdrawal amongst the people who make up these workforces. In this context (and the Blair government does not seem to have changed its opinions much from its predecessor) it is a question of encouraging people actively to seek a job either through checking out fraudulent claims (for unemployment or sickness benefit) or through limiting the period of time that allowance is paid (since 1996 the Job Seeker's Allowance has been reduced to six months, after which supplementary benefit takes over). In order to change the flux within the job market the British government has tried to re-orientate job seeking and to adapt it to market needs. It is worth noting here the 'thirteenth week review' where job seekers are interviewed by Job Centre staff to ensure that a job is being actively sought; only after this interview is the Job Seeker's Allowance extended. This in addition to the in-depth interviews conducted every six months (Restart Interviews) where Job Centre staff check on how work has been sought and then re-motivate the job seeker. It can be supposed that indirectly the aim of these procedures is to control the ways in which work is sought in order to minimise fraudulent claims and to encourage an active attitude towards re-joining the work population.

From this point of view there is a major difference between France and Great Britain. French state benefit in the form of an unemployment allowance can be paid for a maximum of 27 months, with a further 33 months at a progressively reduced rate. As concerns methods for encouraging job seeking, French public state employment staff are most surely less demanding than those in the United Kingdom. Public employment services in France have noticeably smaller budgets than the majority of Northern countries, and have suffered from a non-stop rise in job seekers; this has led them to contacting companies with a view to developing job offers rather than to controlling the unemployment system.

In France the importance of employment figures is represented by two statistics: in 20 years 30 million people have passed through 76 different job employment schemes. The evolution of public policies has been delicate. It has gone from categorical, targeted policies to more generalised policies where the first priority is to look for ways of creating employment rather than to find answers to specific difficulties encountered by certain categories of salaried workers. This creation of employment is achieved by using all the different forms of flexibility that have been mentioned above.

The objective in employment as recommended by government institutions, is to increase the number of jobs, or job-sharing, by creating part-time jobs. Employers therefore seek to decrease job costs through the quality incentives offered if they follow certain recruitment plans. The strategy for activating the job market in France is quite different from that adopted by the United Kingdom, despite the fact that they have the same objectives: to make the market more adaptable and more flexible. In France the emphasis is on the employers, and schemes are based on the jobs that companies offer. Over a million people a year have profited from employment incentives in the commercial sector. They take the form of direct financial incentives in recruitment (employers' exemption from National Insurance contributions, or a cash sum), financial aid in setting-up one's own company, financial support with in-company training schemes and re-training courses or redevelopment projects in industrial areas. The importance of schemes that cut employment costs in the French employment system can be seen in the amount spent each year: more than 40 billion francs in 1997.

These schemes favour external flexibility as most of them are either temporary work contracts or short-term contracts. These measures apply just as much as the commercial sector as to the non-commercial sector. Of these schemes, two stand out as being examples of re-activating the job market, French style, by offering attractive recruitment incentives and encouraging flexible employment. The Employment Incentive Contract (CIE) and the Encouraging Employment Contract (CES) (see Meyer, 1996). Both these schemes are made for a particular public - long-term unemployed people, and people who have been on state benefit for a long time. The CIE offers a cash incentive plus exemption from employer National Insurance contributions, and covers all forms of flexible employment. This kind of contract justifies its bad name in large areas of employment because it is aimed at people 'excluded' from the job market. Employing salaried workers who are not really employable is encouraged through an idea of 'positive communication', which leads on indirectly from the windfall effects appreciated by these employers (choosing a salaried worker who might be less efficient, but who is much more profitable for the company). To give an idea of how important this phenomena is, over 400 thousand people benefited from a CIE in 1997.

The same idea for creating jobs is also to be found in the non-commercial sector. Public institutions, community organisations and non-profit making groups can employ part-time staff in jobs which are 'socially useful', whilst their salary is paid by the State. About 400 thousand people are employed under such contracts (Contract Emploi Solidarite and its derivations). Essentially they allow services to be created that did not exist before, but above all they are there to get around the rigid employment regulations. Nearly 300 thousand people work under CES contracts within the state sector. This is the first example of flexible employment used by government departments to resolve their own employment problems.

Finally, one must mention the tendency towards job-sharing through encouraging part-time work. The Conseil Superieur de l'Emploi, des Revenues et des Coûts (National Council for Employment, Revenues and Costs) in its annual report has remarked that the employment surplus of the 1990s follows on from a long period of decline and that this is due to the development of part-time jobs (created) through reduced employers contributions (30 per cent reduction in NI contributions).

If the two countries differ in the strategies used to ensure a better moving job market, they undeniably meet up in their efforts to improve the quality of the available workforces. In particular the efforts to improve the quality of the available workforces is a favourable answer to the employability problems concerning certain parts of the population. Favourable attention is paid to young unqualified, or little-qualified people to long term unemployed people. The Youth Training Scheme in Britain is very similar to training courses for young French people; the Training for Work is very like the back-to-work training courses for adults in France. This dimension of employment policies contributes towards company preferences for flexible employment by supplying the job market with people perfectly trained for the skills needed by the productive structures. Not only is the qualitative dimension which aims for a greater adaptability in the possible uses of the workforce potential reached through these training courses but the quantitative dimension is reached particularly in the reduction of production costs through in-company training courses. The trainee works for the company, very often for nothing, and does not cost the company anything.

Conclusion

In this paper I have tried to show how the reading of the idea of flexibility can be interpreted differently according to the country concerned. Far from corresponding to an image of common sense which sees flexibility north of the Channel and rigidity south of it, the various examples demonstrated here show that each country, in accordance with its societal logic, shapes and re-shapes its uses of flexibility.

Drawing a comparison between France and the United Kingdom underlines the differing conceptions that are at the base of these various societal logistics. The British tradition organises flexible employment under various individual behaviour patterns that have to be controlled in order to allow the market to fulfil its function of stabilising the social structure. On the other hand the French argument, in the Colbert tradition, rests on the primacy of jobs offered by companies and that the State must direct itself towards public schemes.

Each of these strategies in employment shows a series of plans set up to obtain precise goals: to bring the working population to the job market, or to convince companies to recruit. There is a similarity between the British 'get on your bikes' attitude and the development of job offers balanced against demand in the French tradition of the state as supplier. In this context one can assume that the recommendations for flexible employment as made by the Luxembourg Summit will be interpreted by the different member states according to their needs. The homogenisation of the different forms of flexible employment is far from being complete.

References

Barbier, J.C. (1997), 'Les politiques de l'emploi en Europe', *Flamarion*, Dominos.
Benoit-Guilbot, O. (1989), 'Quelques reflexions sur l'analyse societale : l'exemple des regulations des marches du travail en France et en Grande Bretagne', *Sociologie du Travail* No. 2, pp. 217-225.
Boyer, R. (1986), 'Modernisation et flexibilité', *Travail*, No. 11, avril, pp. 54-60.
Boyer, R. (1987), 'La flexibilite du travail en Europe', *Editions La Decouverte*, p. 331.
Brunhes, B. (1989), 'La flexibilité du travail. Reflexion sur les modeles europeens', *Droit Social* No. 3, pp. 251-255.
Cazal, D. and Peritti, J.M. (1992),'L'Europe des resources humaines', *Editions Liaisons*, p.257.
Chassard, Y. (1998), 'Assistance sociale et emploi : les lecons de l'experience britannique', *Droit Social* No. 3, mars, pp. 269-272.

Fouquin, M. et al (1998), 'Le marche du travail britannique vu de France', *La lettre du CEPII*, No. 167, avril.

Gautie, J. (1993), 'Les politiques de l'emploi. Les marges etroites de la lutte contre le chomage', *Vuibert Eco*, p. 208.

Join-Lambert, M.T. (1997), 'Politiques Sociales', Presses de sciences Po-Dalloz.

Kaisergruger, D. (1997), 'Negocier la Flexibilité', *Editions d'Organisation*, p. 237.

Meyer, J. L. (1996), 'L'Etat et les emplois intermediaries : l'example des CIE et des CES', in *La construction sociale de l'emploi en France*, A. Friot and S. Rose, L'Harmattan, Paris, pp. 87-101.

Meyer, J.L. (1998), 'Intermediaries de l'emploi et marche du travail', *Revue Française de Sociologie* no. 3, pp. 345-364.

Révauger, J.P. (1998), 'Les concepts structurants de la protection sociale en Grande-Bretagne et en France : divergences et convergences', *Revue Française de Civilisation Britannique*, Université de Provence Aix-Marseille I, Aix en Provence.

4 The New Employment Flexibility: the Perversion of an Ideal?

ANTOINE CAPET

It is tempting to begin with an anecdote. I wanted to know when the expressions 'job flexibility' or 'work flexibility' first appeared, and I therefore looked up the word 'flexibility' in the latest edition of the *Oxford English Dictionary* (1989): the first occurrence in the English language, in 1783, is attributed to Hugh Blair in his *Lectures on Rhetoric and Belles-Lettres*. Interestingly enough, the 1989 *Oxford English Dictionary* does not give examples of 'job flexibility' or 'work flexibility', which tends to indicate that these are fairly recent additions to the language.

Indeed, it seems evident that we have here more than an evolution in the English language: we have an evolution in attitudes, and I propose to look at the subject with a historical perspective. Is not 'The New Employment Flexibility' a total about-turn in the Labour approach? Is it not the perversion of the old 'popular' ideal of 'a fair day's wage for a fair day's work', embodied in the Labour creed in the form of 'decent hours', 'decent wages'[1] and 'jobs for all'? In fact, it can be pointed out that this 'flexibility' is nothing new – what is new being its adoption by The Party of the Working Man, as Labour used to like to call itself.

The seminal idea of the 'Founding Father of Capitalism', Adam Smith, was that labour is only a commodity, like any other, and should be treated as such. It is perhaps in order here to recall his vigorous plea in favour of what we would now call 'flexibility' in the labour market:

The property which every man has in his own labour, as it is the original foundation of all other property, so it is the most sacred and inviolable. The patrimony of the poor man lies in the strength and dexterity of his hands; and to hinder him from employing this strength and dexterity in what manner he thinks proper without injury to his neighbour is a plain violation of this most sacred property. It is a manifest encroachment upon the just liberty both of the workman and of those who might be disposed to employ him (Smith, 1776).

We should note that Adam Smith sees flexibility as reconciling the interests of the three interested parties of the national economy: employers and employees, of course, with the customer benefiting from this mutually-advantageous arrangement between 'master and servant'. The case for non-intervention by the Government is also made out by one of his greatest admirers, Malthus, who writes about 'the absurdity of supposing that it is in the power of a government to find employment for all its subjects, however fast they may increase' (Malthus, 1798). Yet, actions 'in restraint of trade', i.e. hampering the full operation of the 'free market' of labour were increasingly successful in Malthus' lifetime. It is interesting to note that in the 1825, revised, edition of his *Essay*, Malthus remarks that 'combinations' are no longer illegal (as they were when the original version was published in 1798) and play *against* full employment:

> The workmen are beginning to find that, if they could raise their wages above what the state of the demand and the prices of goods will warrant, it is absolutely impossible that all, or nearly all, should be employed. The masters could not employ the same number as before without inevitable ruin (Malthus, 1798).

Now, by the end of the 19th century, the principle that 'restrictive practices', 'protection', etc. were ultimately 'bad for the working man' was vigorously fought by the emerging Labour movement. Indeed the early-20th century apocryphal slogan of the trade unions supported by the Labour Party, 'More Protection!', was the exact antithesis of the current talk of 'flexibility', and even though the Labour Party, too, was a 'Broad Church', it is impossible to think of a Labour personality who did not subscribe to this uniting agenda at the time of 'Old Labour'. On the contrary, countless speeches and mountains of books and pamphlets were devoted to a refutation of the 'free market' arguments of the 'capitalists' largely founded on the 'orthodox' interpretation of the canons laid down by Adam Smith, Malthus and Ricardo. In the British Press, there was a ritualistic denunciation of 'restrictive practices' – foremost among them 'the closed shop' or 'jobs-for-life' in the 'feather-bedded' nationalised industries[2].

But no prominent Labour politician or supporter, even on the 'right' of the party, would have entered the fray. To do so was 'passing to the enemy', and the penalty was leaving the party. This should not be seen as inordinate party discipline or even narrow-mindedness : it must be borne in mind that the Labour Representation Committee was formed in 1900 with the object of 'promoting legislation in the direct interest of labour'[3]. Now, if you equate 'the direct interest of labour' with the refusal of 'flexibility', as many Britons still do[4], there is only logic in the idea that if you are a 'Labour man', you should not adopt the arguments of the other side against 'restrictive practices'.

The General Election of 1945 was archetypal of this 'bipartisan dissensus' as exemplified by the manifestos of the two major parties on the subject of full employment. The Conservative manifesto, *Declaration of Policy to the Electors*, took up almost verbatim the opening sentence of the White Paper, *Employment Policy*, published in May 1944 – a sentence which pointedly omitted the word *full* and made employment policy only 'one' of the post-war priorities:

The Government accept as one of their primary aims and responsibilities the maintenance of a high and stable level of employment after the war (White Paper, HMSO, 1944).

The Government accepts as one of its primary aims and responsibilities the maintenance of a high and stable level of employment (Conservative manifesto, Craig, 1975).

Samuel H. Beer shows in *Modern British Politics* (Beer, 1965) how Conservative policy was adapted between 1945 and 1950, with the corresponding phrase in the 1950 manifesto becoming:

We regard the maintenance of full employment as the first aim of a Conservative Government (Craig, 1975).

This, of course, is an alignment on the blunt commitment of the 1945 Labour manifesto, with a chapter unambiguously entitled 'Jobs for all'. The opening paragraphs of the chapter are worth reproducing here because they clearly state the 'interventionist' case as it was to dominate Labour thought until the 1980s – and as it no doubt remains ingrained in the minds of many Labour supporters and militants (if such there still be):

All parties pay lip service to the idea of jobs for all. All parties are ready to promise to achieve that end by keeping up the national purchasing power and controlling changes in the national expenditure through Government action. Where agreement ceases is in the degree of control of private industry that is necessary to achieve the desired end.

and

Our opponents [...] say, "Full employment. Yes! If we can get it without interfering too much with private industry". We say, "Full employment in any case, and if we need to keep a firm public hand on industry in order to get jobs for all, very well. No more dole queues, in order to let the Czars of Big Business remain kings in their own castles. The price of so-called 'economic freedom' for the few is too high if it is bought at the cost of idleness and misery for millions" (Craig, 1975)[5].

This part of the manifesto, in its *'Daily Mirror'* style, is a nice blend of Keynes (Keynes 1936) and Beveridge, (the Beveridge of *Full Employment in a Free Society*), and indeed the attack on 'economic freedom' seems to be taken from Beveridge's 'Second Report' as he liked to call it, because after writing that 'the proposals in this Report preserve absolutely all the essential liberties which are more precious than full employment itself' (Beveridge, 1944) he goes on to suggest that economic freedom is not among these 'essential' liberties.

In 1950, the vocabulary of the Labour manifesto is a little less 'popular' since the title of the chapter on full employment becomes 'Work for all'. But the commitment remains equally unambiguous:

The supreme aim that we set before the nation is the maintenance of full employment. Here is Labour's policy (Craig, 1975).

In 1955, unemployment clearly belongs to a distant, pre-war past : it no longer deserves a chapter and it is no immediate danger unless the abolition of state controls by the Tories is allowed to go unchecked :

The Tory Government have scrapped many of the essential controls, and now, once again, some areas face the danger of unemployment (Craig, 1975).

The same argument is more or less taken up in 1959 with the title 'The danger of complacency':

Full employment has *not* been maintained (Craig, 1975).

The ghosts of Adam Smith and Malthus reappear in the manifesto of 1964 in the chapter 'A philosophy of the past':

At the root of the Tories' failure lies an outdated philosophy – their nostalgic belief that it is possible in the second half of the 20th century to hark back to a 19th century free enterprise economy and a 19th century unplanned society (Craig, 1975).

All the Opposition manifestos were largely negative, more an attack on the Conservatives than a bold statement of objectives. Characteristically, the 1966 Labour manifesto includes among 'the four central objectives of policy':

To maintain full employment and a high level of investment in productive industry (Craig, 1975).

Clearly, this ideal had failed by 1970, since the manifesto of that year no longer spoke of full employment. The chapter on 'People and Jobs' alludes to 're-equipping our employment services, moving in swiftly to deal with redundancies, placing workers more quickly in employment with modern techniques' (Craig, 1975), a clear indication that full employment had not been attained. Still, planning for full employment remained a central preoccupation:

Without planning, with a return to the Tory free-for-all, people become the victims of economic forces they cannot control (Craig, 1975).

Both manifestos of 1974 have a chapter devoted to 'Employment and Expansion', with a virtually identical passage on redundancies :

Redundant workers must have an automatic right to retraining; redundancy should then lead not to unemployment, but to retraining and job changing (February) (Craig, 1975).

Redundant workers must have an automatic right to retraining, with redundancy leading not to unemployment, but to retraining and job changing (October) (Craig, 1975).

The 1979 manifesto, though not going as far as that of 1945, still gives pride of place to full employment in its chapter on 'Jobs and Prosperity':

The Labour Government will pursue policies which give a high priority to the return to full employment (Craig, 1975).

Now, at a time when the CBI was adopting 'a very neo-classical' attitude[6], Michael Foot's 'left-wing' leadership led to a return to the 'top priority' commitment in the chapter of the 1983 manifesto significantly entitled 'Ending mass unemployment'. The fight against unemployment 'remains the central objective of our economic policy', and the chapter ends with a tone decidedly reminiscent of 1930s Labour:

Economic expansion will make it possible to end the waste of mass unemployment. But it will also reduce the *human* costs of unemployment – the poverty, the broken homes, the increase in illness and suicides (Craig, 1975).

Under Kinnock, the reduction of unemployment, the 'Jobs Programme', figures under the general heading 'The Priority Programme' along with 'The Anti-Poverty Programme' and 'The Anti-Crime Campaign' in the 1987 manifesto (Craig, 1975), and in itself the title of the 1992 manifesto indicates Labour's priorities: *It's Time to get Britain Working Again*. The tone is reminiscent of the last months of war, when everybody was thinking of reconstruction, when victory was certain, but not yet obtained:

Britain faces a huge task of national reconstruction. From day one, the new government must start to get Britain working again. It must get the economy out of recession, it must lay the foundations for the future. Recovery must be based on investment, for only investment will create lasting prosperity (Labour Party, 1992).

In his Foreword, Neil Kinnock goes back to the central theme of *Full Employment in a Free Society*: 'Political freedom needs the sure foundation of economic security', and the (short) section on 'Action for jobs' takes up a long-standing theme of Labour oratory:

Our aim is to prevent long-term unemployment, rather than just trying to cope with it after it has occurred (Labour Party, 1992).

With Tony Blair in 1997, as I have noted elsewhere (Capet, 1998), we have an astonishing reversion to the vocabulary of the 1945 Conservative manifesto:

Our long-term objective is high and stable levels of employment (Labour, 1997).

Nicholas Parsons concludes an article on labour market reform with the opinion that:

There has certainly been change over the period from 1979-97, but there has been no Thatcherite revolution. Rather, what has happened has been the difficult adaptation of the British economy and labour market to changing world conditions (Parsons, 1998, p.116).

But then he somewhat optimistically argues that:

The election of Tony Blair as the first Labour Prime Minister for eighteen years translates the feeling that some measure of positive action on the part of the state is required to attenuate the undesirable effects of the uncontrolled workings of market forces on social inequality and poverty levels in the country (Parsons, 1998, p. 116).

This is because the general tenor of the manifesto in no way substantiates the idea that this kind of 'Old Labour' disparagement of 'market forces' will continue under Tony Blair. The Conservative, Brendon Sewill, in his 'Reflections on the Demise of Full Employment', seems to have a far more 'realistic' approach, in that he has understood that 'New Labour', even though it is unable to convince the die-hards of 'Old Labour', agrees that flexibility is now inevitable:

The Labour leadership has accepted this situation, and realises that it cannot promise to restore full employment. Yet, because over the past 20 years the political debate has never clearly identified the reasons for the demise of the Keynesian system, many of their supporters find the lack of a commitment to full employment hard to comprehend (Sewill, 1995).

This 'realistic' approach to Labour policy consists therefore in acknowledging that 'New Labour', too, has adopted a 'realistic' – some would say a 'fatalistic' – approach to the feasibility of full employment and concluded that it is now probably an unattainable objective. In 1984, Jean-Pierre Ravier, though writing from the 'progressive' point of view, reluctantly ended an article on the rise of unemployment since 1967 with the pessimistic opinion that unemployment had a bright future in Britain (Ravier, 1985). This kind of analysis was anathema to the 'voluntarist'

Left, who warned the Labour leadership against fatalism even before the political turning-point of 1979. In a remarkable *Full Employment Appeal* released as early as 1977 – twenty years before the electoral triumph of 'New Labour' – a number of Labour MPs (among them Robin Cook and Neil Kinnock) and left-wing activists and academics like E.P. Thompson denounced 'the sinister fact that the very idea of full employment has been officially abandoned as a practical option for the entire foreseeable future' and, quoting 'pessimistic predictions... which anticipate levels [of unemployment] reaching two million', they openly attacked the Callaghan Government:

> The Government has clearly based its current policy on the notion that this is now "acceptable", and has taken a whole series of measures which, unless they are reversed, will ensure that it becomes unavoidable (see Brown, Coates, Fleet and Hughes, (eds), 1978).

Obviously, this 'idealism' had strong roots in the party, and it regained prominence with a vengeance under Michael Foot but, for the dispassionate observer, it now seems tempting to assimilate the 'old' commitment of 1945 to 'jobs for all' to one of those old nostrums which tended to associate Labour with 'the cloth-cap image' and the 'loony left' and seemed to make it a perpetual election loser. On the (relatively) old theme of 'Must Labour Lose?', David Childs, in his section on 'Why did Labour Lose?' (in 1992), explains that 'Labour had not been able to re-define democratic socialism in terms attractive to the majority of voters' (Childs, 1995, p. 242).

The proof of the pudding being in the eating, and 'New Labour' having won in 1997, the 'redefinition of democratic socialism' has been electorally successful. But in what way is flexibility 'attractive to the majority of voters'? Can we not reverse Will Hutton's proposition that 'Blair is trying to convey the idea that the Labour party is travelling in an individualist direction while espousing collective values'? (Hutton, 1996).

Is not the abandonment of the commitment to full employment the signal that 'New Labour' has also abandoned the 'collective values' which made it a party with an ideal, an ideal which seemed close to achievement during what Pauline Gregg has called the Age of the Working Classes? (Gregg, 1967). There was a coherence, an 'idealistic' coherence perhaps, in the 'Welfare State' glowingly described by Pauline Gregg : after all, in 1942, Beveridge himself had made full employment one of his three 'assumptions' for the success of his Plan. A row of dominoes is not 'flexible' – or, rather, it is in a way: if you topple one, the rest will smoothly follow. 'Old Labour' firmly believed that touching one aspect of the 'Welfare State' would affect the whole structure: is not Tony Blair's 'New Labour' playing the Sorcerer's Apprentice by denying that its acceptance of 'flexibility' has far wider practical and ideological implications than it is prepared to admit?

Notes

1   I will not here discuss 'decent wages'. The interested reader will find such discussion, with substantial bibliographies in *The National Minimum Wage : Pride or Prejudice ?* (Whitton 1997a) and *Labour's National Minimum Wage* (Whitton, 1997b). However, though it would seem that the current introduction of a minimum wage by the Labour Government contradicts the argument that it is opting for all-out fllexibility, wage flexibility is allowed to creep in by devious means, as the Vauxhall 'deal' would tend to indicate : 'Vauxhall, in a deal which saved its Luton plant from closure, announced it would pay its workers a 3.5% rise this year, 3% next and, in 2000-01, an increase in line with inflation, plus 0.5% if the pound falls below a certain level, DM2.70 (it is currently DM3.00), for two consecutive months against the German mark. Since the mark will no longer exist as a separate currency after January 1 next year, the deal effectively links British workers' pay to the pound's euro value'. (Smith, 1998).

2   It is also worth noting the success of Penguin Specials like *The Stagnant Society* by Michael Shanks (Shanks, 1961) or *What's Wrong with the Unions ?* by Eric Wigham (Wigham, 1963).

3   Resolution put forward by Keir Hardie and carried by the Conference. (See Beer, 1920).

4   Like John Edmonds, the TUC spokesman who, during a debate on Radio Four (10 September 1997), replied to Ted Turner of the CBI who was promoting 'numerical flexibility' : 'for us, this "flexibility" only means making it easier for the boss to sack you'. A far more 'positive' definition is provided by Christopher M. Law : 'A key word today is flexibility, which means that there is no monolithic pattern but rather a great variety of work practices. There is more part-time work, more seasonal or occasional work, more shift work, more multi-skilling on the factory floor, and less stereotyping of jobs between men and women'. (See Obelkevitch and Catterall, 1994)

5   According to figures by Cook and Stevenson, the numbers of unemployed at relevant dates from 1945 were : 1945 : 137,000 ; 1950 : 314,000 ; 1955 : 232,000 ; 1959 : 475,000 ; 1964 : 380,000 ; 1966 : 353,000 ; 1970 : 579,000 ; 1974 : 542,000 ; 1978 : 1,381,000 (Cook and Stevenson, 1996).

6   'Dans un document de janvier 1980 [*Jobs : Facing the Future.* London : CBI, January 1980] le marché du travail est présenté dans une optique très néo-classique. Comme tout autre marché, il obéit aux lois de l'offre et de la demande'. Esposito, 'Le patronat et le chômage'. *Emploi et Chômage en Grande-Bretagne, 1979-1983.* Revue française de civilisation britannique 2-4 (1984) : 33-48, p. 34. (See Esposito, 1984).

References

Beer, S.M. (1920), *A History of British Socialism*, vol II, Bell, London.

Beer, S.M. (1965), *Modern British Politics ; A Study of Parties and Pressure Groups*, Faber, London.

Beveridge, W. (1944), *Full Employment in a Free Society*, Allen and Unwin, London.

Brown, M.B., Coates, K., Fleet, K. and Hughes, J. (eds) (1978), *Full Employment*, Spokesman, Nottingham.

Capet, A. (1998), 'L'Ideal Travailliste de Attlee à Blair dans les Manifestes Electoraux', *Annales de l'Université de Savoie*, Grenoble.

Childs, D. (1995), *Britain Since 1939 : Progress and Decline*, Macmillan, London.

Cook, C. and Stevenson, J. (1996), *The Longman Companion to Britain Since 1945*, Longman, London.

Craig, F.W.S. (ed.) (1975), *British General Election Manifestos 1900-1974*, Macmillan, London.

Esposito, M-C. (1984), 'Le Patronat et le Chomage: Emploi et Chomage en Grande-Bretagne 1979-1983', *Revue Française de Civilisation Britannique*, no's. 2-4, pp.33-48, Université de Provence, Aix-Marseille 1, Aix en Provence.

Gregg, P. (1967), *The Welfare State*, Harrap, London.

Her Majesty's Stationery Office (1944), *Employment Policy*, Cmnd 6527, Her Majesty's Stationery Office, London.

Hutton, W. (1996), 'The Stakeholder Society', in D. Marquand and A. Seldon, (eds), *The Ideas That Shaped Post-War Britain*, Fontana, London.

Keynes, J.M. (1936), *The General Theory of Employment, Interest and Money*, Macmillan, London.

Labour Party (1992), *It's Time to Get Britain Working Again*, Labour Party, London.

Labour Party (1997), *New Labour : Because Britain Deserves Better*, Labour Party, London.

Malthus, T. (1798), *An Essay on Population*, Dent 1914, London.

Obelkevitch, J. and Catterall, J. (1994), *Understanding Post-War British Society*, Routledge, London.

Parsons, N. (1998), 'The Welfare State and Labour Market Reform 1979-1997: L'Etàt-Providence : Bilan de Dix-Huit Annèes de Pouvoir Conservateur (1979-1997)', *Revue Française de Civilisation Britannnique* no's 6-4, Université de Provence, Aix-Marseille 1, Aix en Provence.

Ravier, J-P. (1985), 'La Montée du Chômage Depuis 1967 : Quelques Explications', *Chômage et Emploi en Grande-Bretagne : Actes du Colloque de Chambéry*, 12-13 octobre 1984. Annales de l'Université de Savoie No. 6/7, Chambéry.

Sewill, B. (1995), 'Reflections on the Demise of Full Employment', *Contemporary Record*, vol. 9, no.3, pp. 651-656.

Shanks, M. (1961), *The Stagnant Society*, Penguin, Harmondsworth.

Smith, A. (1776), *The Wealth of Nations*, Dent 1910, London.

Smith, D. (1998), 'Don't look now but the big bad euro is coming up behind you', *The Sunday Times*, 26 April.

Whitton, T. (1997a), 'The national minimum wage : Pride or prejudice?', in J. Edwards and J-P. Révauger, (eds), *Discourse on Inequality in France and Britain*, Ashgate, Aldershot.

Whitton, T. (1997b), 'Labour's national minimum wage', *Revue Française de Civilisation Britannique*, 9-3, pp. 115-117, Université de Provence, Aix-Marseille 1, Aix en Provence.
Wigham, E. (1963), *What's Wrong With the Unions?*, Penguin, Harmondsworth.

5 Part-time Employment, the 'Social Movement' and Citizenship: Work in the Arts

LAURENCE DREYFUSS AND ALAIN MARCHAND

Two major aspects can be pinpointed behind the new internal and external flexibility's quantitative and qualitative performance dimensions - the individualism of producers and their over-involvement in the production process. Be they self-employed or subordinate wage-earners, part-time or permanent, workers become, in a way, the entrepreneurs of their labour power. They are not merely the carriers of this force into the labour market but also managers in the act of production. Our hypothesis is that these new postures, based on the individualisation of work processes, produce suffering which reshapes the classic notion of work alienation or as Marx said, in the market, human beings, as the carriers of commodities, move about wearing a mask. An apparent paradox ensues concerning the collective expression of these new 'postures', a paradox of the emergence of 'new social movements' based on the affirmation of professional identities and a re-establishment of politics in the public sphere.

These two 'novelties' are our concern and we will study them in a sector which appears, in many regards, as a genuine 'dark box', a laboratory of the mutations of contemporary capitalism – 'the cultural sector'. Both work and conditions in the arts world, indeed, reveal in a clearer way than others, both the mutations taking place in the world of work and the new configurations of the 'social movement'.

'Arts', which is characterised by its 'here and nowness', its authenticity, was apparently marginalised by the accumulation and reproduction processes of capital, and by the standardisation of response-commodities which are characteristics of fordism. In fact, culture as communication is massively affected by the colonisation of the lived world. Artistic and cultural goods, art in the making, and 'time' have themselves become true commodities, albeit often 'immaterial' as in live shows or in the communication field, but produced and consumed as common-

-place merchandise. Reproducible, these goods become objects of mass-consumption. The cultural production and diffusion - as well as entertainment or personal services, - are the objects of productive investment by large finance groups as well by firms of a new type from the 'third sector'. These can take the form of individual firms - self-employment - or of co-operation between several actors, and even of co-production. But contrary to the Anglo-Saxon vision of volunteer or non-profit sector, defined in a doubly negative way (neither market nor public sector), the interventions of these new actors from the cultural sector are involved in the money-economy and are regulated by the market. They participate in the French conception of 'social economy', defined not by the object of its production (social services and fabric) and its finalities (social reform) but by the institutional singular forms of its firms (such as collective ownership and non-shared profits, and modes of executives' appointments).

Cultural industries become thus one of the 'chambres noires' ('dark rooms') of contemporary investigations into the performances of entrepreneurial and innovative organisation, in the relationships between work and activity, flexibility and involvement, the individual and co-operation, diffuse intellectuality, and mobilising subjectivity.

Besides the mutations of cultural work itself (a greater creative-technological combination), it is the very aspect of the political and social movement which appears interesting. In the 1930s, Walter Benjamin already saw in the 'mechanised reproduction' of works of art, a mutation of the social function of art: 'A foundation made up by a different practice; politics must be substituted to its ritualistic foundation' (Benjamin, 1991).

It is the hypothesis of a 'travail de l'art' ('work in the arts world') experimenting with and anticipating the ongoing mutations in our societies characterised by a type of neo-liberalism mixed with a 'social' element which we defend here through a comparative approach of artistic work in the United Kingdom and France.

Work in the Art's World

Art, incorporated in the work of art, symbolically defined itself through its gratuitousness. It becomes the object of a fully-fledged type of work, artistic work reified into a commodity, participating in the passage from 'culture discussed' to 'culture consumed' (Habermas, 1978). Thus, as a vector of communication, art works *on* society, and reshapes the public sphere.

By essence, artistic creation is close to this 'activity', which might be sought behind the proclamation of the 'end of work' dear to Jeremy Rifkin; it refers to the founding ambivalence of work between freedom and necessity, between emancipation and constraint. Nevertheless, it happens that it *is* in the market, (in particular the artist's one) where the relevance of creative choices are tested, whether they originate from a wage-earning collective operating within cultural entrepreneurship or from co-operation produced by a group of fledging artists, or of the particular involvement of self-employment. Creation *is* therefore merchandise in a sense and the development of immaterial work, a characteristic of post-fordism, finds a favourable breeding-ground in this reproducible and speculative cultural merchandise.

Fordism had already negated crafts to the advantage of qualifications

> Another of our principles is that with us, no man is allowed to consider himself as belonging to a particular trade preventing himself from being employed in a different work position (Ford, 1926).

Today, the production process mobilises, in adding the singular convocation to the former prescriptive injunction, a collection of crafts and necessarily individual competences. This productive tension between the prescription of the organisation (the productive imperative) and the individualised involvement (the 'singular colloquium' - i.e. a relation which evokes the psychoanalyst - psychoanalysed relation - as a management mode which individualises humans from the hierarchical relationship), produces this 'suffering at work' which sociologists of work have rediscovered. Technological mutations allow an 'active subordination' (Vincent, 1996), and the productive mobilisation of the wage-earner's subjectivity. Action 'has no other source but that of the agent who implements it and who is solely to be held responsible for it. Individual initiatives move into the foreground of the criteria which test people's worth' (Ehrenberg, 1998). Robotised direct production and assembly-line automation reduce work behaviour to survellience-maintenance and thus open the field of 'human error' for any production incident. It is not the wage-earner's productive body, broken down into parts and remodeled by machines' discipline which is called forth into the production act but his feelings and his mental capacities according to Ehrenberg for whom 'the firm is the ante-room to nervous breakdowns'. The worker's imagination is no longer an escapist outlet through which the mind could wander and escape the constrained body, founding thus a double life at work and making productive time bearable, it is itself confiscated. Even if some 'co-operative' forms based on deliberation can emerge in some isolated islands of immaterial work where workers 'have their tools in their heads', in the end, this re-emergence of the individual into the process of work takes place with urgency and feelings of guilt.

In many regards, artistic work which uses urgency as a constitutive dimension of its specificity, (one of the conditions of the production of art), has anticipated these mutations taking place within productive art. Whether salaried, temporary or free-lance, the artist was already summoned to over-involve himself in a permanent back and forth movement between the professional sphere and off-work fields. Creativity implies this subjectivity which is today required from the 'ordinary' wage-earner. For a long time, diffuse intellectuality (personal competences beyond the know-how linked to trades and qualifications) which is called up today in the production process, has been constitutive of artistic work. Several interviews, conducted during fieldwork in London and Montpellier[1] show that 'art workers' whether they operate within the wage earner's standards of the schemes of cultural politics or they directly valorise their independent cultural production on the market, state this 'appertenance'[2] (sense of belonging and membership), or suffering, often in the same terms used in other sectors or by bringing back the figure of the 'artiste maudit' (the doomed artist starving in the garret)[3].

Individualisation and flexibility are at work within and outside work collectives. Flexibility should not be reduced neither to the sole legal dimension (fixed-term contracts, particular forms of employment, atypical positions) nor to the sole management of time which is moving and not simply stop-watched (part-time, sequential activities, annual pay system etc.).

Within the firm, in the new procedures, the organisation must be 'qualifying' but always efficient. Flexibility becomes the management mode of production (direct production flux, in-timing) and of human resources, as well; it also allows the valorisation of individualisable products ('zero stock' option).

Flexibility means the externalisation (i.e. contracting out) of numerous functions of the firm: recruiting, communication, etc. Network management and partnership become the market's substitutes and allow the construction of rational *ex ante* choices which replace *ex post* adaptation-responses, to the market's indications. Individualised employment forms (self employment, temporary work, part-time work, placements, etc) and even informal work do not constitute a second sealed off world separated from the formal economy but are transversally called up by productive modernisation.

Thus, the productive mobilisation of work *does* have as pre-requisites, at a pre-work stage, the freedom of the individual, as a carrier of autonomous labour which is only 'virtual' on the labour market and in the mobility of the labour force (and thus its flexibility and volatility). Between mobility and mobilisation, between virtuality and the effectiveness of its realisation, this discrepancy grows, this gap which Rhenish capitalism had solved by the conventional complexity, by establishing the forms of mobilization and by turning the work market into something which is instituted and institutional. The qualities of the workforce (knowledge and skills) were attested by qualifications and diplomas, were certified by the public training bodies and know-how within firms was codified by the firm's inner sets of regulations. The passage from the trade agreements to contractual individualisation, gives a role to a third party, to a 'smuggling go-between', to mediation practices. One can witness the progressive establishment of a 'triangulation' of the labour market and of access to working positions where meditation is mobilized, on the one hand, to 'attest' to the qualities of the labour force (certification systems of the labour force such as youth employment schemes and placements, intermediary firms and associations, part-time agencies, job centres, etc.), and on the other hand, to accompany it in its productive implementation (procedures, referencing and 'resource-persons'). One only needs to go back to the role of the French 'Bourses du Travail' (i.e. Labour Exchanges), XIXth century labour firms, to attest to the services of employees (wages, good behaviour certificates, workers' logbooks in France) which existed in risk professions. Trade-unions can moreover find in this new triangulation, the rehabilitation of one of their historic roles, that of collective attestation to qualifications and salaried attributes; employers (the BBC, for example) often remain keen on maintaining one-sided practices, as for example, where the Actors' Equity trade-union and the Musicians' Union still play the role of 'go-betweens', of privileged partners for productions.

The new productive modalities, founded on individualism, require the overhaul of the traditional forms of the division of labour, of the productive units and of the organisation, be it through Toyotism or other ways of involving wage-earners. The efficiency of the managerial organization/ command combination is questioned and leads to new thinking about forms of co-operation, of autonomy, of procedure management and of decision-taking within collectives. Besides, the particular forms of the mobilisation of immaterial work are not applicable to that of the entire work process since some unqualified and devalorized, subjugated work is assigned within the working collective themselves or externalized via the use of subcontractors. Moreover, these autonomy and co-operation modes are confiscated by the new managerial techniques (quality circles, competence assessment tests, etc.) and go beyond the actors' reach. The subjective expression of these new collectives is at stake and opens the field to new potential conflicts on and off work which the classical forms of trade-union action cannot alays detect.

Art, more than any domain, values the individual - via his 'work' - and at the same time, it constitutes a social fact as defined by Marcel Mauss. George Simmel also reminds us that 'art as totality and the work of art in its singularity form a typical relationship which can be designated as a phenomenon originating from the world of the mind. That is to say: a member, an element or a fragment of a unitary whole which is itself or claims to be itself, a unified, self-enclosed whole' (Simmel, 1914). Art founds this alchemy of the individual and the collective, both in its productive dynamics (shows, but also movements, and 'schools', recognition by peers, etc.) and in its social expression: 'the show feeds itself from a two-fold well of creativity, creativity proper to the freedom of individual expression and the one proper to the power of co-operation' (Nicolas-Le-Strat, 1995).

The cultural domain thus constitutes a true laboratory of new forms of work mobilisation.

The cultural enterprise may exist, whatever its commercial, associative or individual form, as a project instance or as an enterprise product. Part-time work, 'fixed-objective contracts' are particularly welcomed for a production based on short-living projects. The cultural entrepreneur, an individual as in self-employment, a carrier of a collective project, or even negotiating with public officials, brings back the Schumpeterian spirit of the entrepreneurial function - innovation. Doomed to 'let his difference be heard' he will value and implement (in the economic sense of the term) his creation via the market, whether it be public or private (the private market of art, the search for subsidies from sponsors or public agencies).

In his domain, the role of the 'mediating third party' is fundamental: the certification of the artist through his work or of his performances is achieved by traditional sponsors (art gallery owners, agents, patrons, producers, etc.) but innovation can favour the emergence of managed or self-organised collective mediation forms : welfare rehabilitation associations of artists, persons receiving the 'Revenue Minimum d'Insertion' in France, (i.e. 'living off welfare'), cultural movements, fledgling artists' groups and so on. Often, the performance of such networks is not limited to the certification of the virtual 'value' of artists; they can create true co-operative endeavours and even co-productions with consumers. The same thing takes place within the cultural rehabilitation of industrial rust-belt zones, of 'ephemeral shop-windows' during urban renovation operations, of 'cultural routes', co-operative workshops which 'give something to be seen' and at the same time they attest to the 'merchant' value of the creator. In this regard, formal and informal economies interweave, generating maximal flexibility of work. In London, for example, some people benefiting from the safety net of welfare help create associations, endowed with public funding (such as City Challenge), and sell on the competitive market.

Temporary Work, Self-Employment and the Social Movement

The sedimentation of social relations and work is different in the United Kingdom and in France but some comparative data on flexibility, subjectivity and collective expression in the domain of artisic work are neverthless revealing.

From a global point of view, the growth of cultural occupations is very important and particularly in the form of temporary and precarious work for both technicians and artists. The vitality of this sector is particularly apparent in the emergence of the economy of new services.

The artistic sector creates jobs or is at least seen as being able to do so. Thus, in France, from 1982 to 1990, the growth of cultural professions was ten times higher than that of total employment (37 per cent as compared to 3.7 per cent). Nearly 400,000 people work in the sector of cultural industries and communication. In Great Britain, cultural professions went up by 34 per cent from 1981 to 1991. The Languedoc-Roussillon region, the second in France for the density of artistic occupations, witnessed a 57.7 per cent progression from 1982 to 1990. Another possible indicator is enrolment for universities' 'arts' curricula (up 31 per cent from 1997 to 1998, 30 per cent in plastic arts, 34 per cent in show-business arts, 8 per cent in cultural mediation, in the Montpelier regional academic authority, at a time when students' enrolment went down by 1.5 per cent).

Women's access (70 per cent in Great Britain from 1981 to 1991) into these occupations explains the greatest part of this growth. The female rate went up from 30 to 38 per cent in Great Britain in this period and this rate is at 39.2 per cent in France. Moreover, the particular typology of women's work (part-time and sequential work, etc.) partly accounts for this new flexibility.

This rising number of occupations has been fed by an explosive growth in precarious, insecure work. In France, from 1980 to 1992, the number of permanent jobs in the cultural sector rose by 25 per cent and that of part-time jobs by 97 per cent (34 per cent for artists), 296 per cent for technicians (that is to say 100,000 jobs of which 54,000 were artists and 46,000 technicians). In Great Britain, from 1981 to 1991, full-time employment in the cultural sector went down from 64 per cent to 51 per cent of all jobs in the sector for men and from 54 per cent to 48 per cent for women, whereas at the same time, self-employment rose from 32 per cent to 45 per cent for men and from 30 per cent to 40 per cent for women, and whilst the number of employees rose by 12 per cent that of self-employment rose by 81 per cent,

Generally, in France, one witnesses stiffer competition, the fragmentation of activity and a shortening of contracts (Menger, 1997). A survey conducted by O'Brien and Feist demonstrates that flexibility of artistic work in Great Britain compared to that of other activities shows greater variations in the length of the working week, a multi-activity which is higher than in other sectors and a smaller use of overtime work (O'Brien and Feist, 1997). Their analysis of the 1981-1991 period also shows a very high turnover with 46 per cent of the people working in the cultural sector in 1981 having another activity 10 years later, as well as a tendency to move into self-employment (38 per cent of musicians and 23 per cent of actors). This phenomenon is confirmed in the Languedoc region with a turnover which nearly reached 40 per cent between 1995 and 1996 for job-seekers in live arts' shows. This is explained by the fact that 'live show artists and technicians do not stay in the branch if they do not receive any compensation or do not hope to do so' (Giorgio and Guerre, 1996). This turnover is also related to age ; interviews in London demonstrate that if an actor does not succeed before the age of 30, he moves into another activity

69

sector. In the Languedoc-Roussillon region, cultural occupations are younger than higher intellectual professions. This region has a very high geographic mobility particularly in the domain of cultural employment when one still 'goes up to Paris'! If heliotropism (i.e. attractiveness of the sun) makes the South particularly attractive, the concentration of artistic professions in the capital zones plays the role of a pump : 47 per cent of cultural jobs are concentrated in the Ile de France region, (34 per cent in London), and 21 per cent in the South-West of France. There is another element to flexibility: unemployment rates are higher in the cultural sector than elsewhere (8 per cent in Great Britain in 1991, 13.2 per cent in the Languedoc-Roussillon region against 5.2 per cent for all the higher intellectual categories).

One can nevertheless note a difference : it seems that in Great Britain the initial level of training and qualification of the intellectual working population is higher than in France, which bears upon the 'diffuse intellectuality' which has already been mentioned.

Today, artistic activity transcends the boundaries of creation, of the work of art towards 'diffuse creativity', incorporated into the very process of production. The best proof of this is the popularity of the trades of design,[4] and photography which favour liberal and informal types of professional work – multi-activity. Far from becoming autonomous, cultural industries spread their branches and their growth is linked to that of other sectors. The current indicator of artistic activity is its 'network-constitution' (Nicolas-Le-Strat, 1998) as evidenced by the co-operatives, employers' associations, socio-organisational and socio-political arrangements which rule it.

The emergence of new social movements feeds on this particular organisational mode. The procedures of co-ordination (usually of independent strike-committees or of autonomous organisations set up for particular objectives), of manifestos, the circulation of information on the 'net', forms of mobilisation, and the quest for visibility are their socio-political expression (Dreyfuss, 1998).

One of the differences between France and Great Britain stems from forms of organisation of cultural workers. Trade-unionisation remains strong in the United Kingdom among 'traditional' artists (56 per cent among musicians, 39 per cent among actors), but it is weak in the new trades (15 per cent among designers and commercial artists, 12 per cent in the audio-visual sector, with 32 per cent being the average rate) (O'Brien and Feist, 1997). In France, trade-unionisation in general is weak, but the social movements of live show temporary workers, the forerunners of the December 1992 movements of the unemployed, the creators and actors against the Debre-Pasqua laws were an exception.

The subjectivity of work collectives has been negated through suppression from corporations, by the decay of trades, by the confiscation of its autonomous expressions by paternalism, consumption, and corporate culture. Workers' negativity become bogged down in trade-union bureaucratisation. This 'singular colloquium', internally present within firms and in the market, between the supplier and the demander, finds its extension today within local government with what we have called 'singular democracy' (Dreyfuss and Marchand, 1995) where, using bonapartist practices, mayoral power individually questions the 'citizen' (by consultations, referenda, etc.) distinguishing the citizen from his social environment and his solidarity practices. This new individual/collective space is thus criss-crossed with major stakes: it will either seal the ideological pact of neo-liberal individualism, negating social solidarities and collective actors according to the Thatcherite model, or it will renew the forms of deliberative democracy by procedures which are prefigured by the setting up of co-ordinated strike-committees (such as nurses etc.), new social movements (the unemployed, undocumented aliens, live show temporary workers) thus mixing workers and undocumented aliens, wage-earners and 'freelance professionals' who intervene and 'speak' on the public scene. For example, temporary work is, first, a particular status (with unemployment compensation), and it is this very unemployed status that artists and technicians claim as their 'identity'. In fact, the protest forms which have been characterised as neo-coporatist and neo-localist, mix professional visibility with a political dimension.

Thus if art, when politcally committed, has always involved social movement, artists appear today as if they are refounding politics through new protest modes. This way, they perfectly illustrate the logical movement which goes from the 'particular to the general' (Aguiton and Bensaïd, 1997) which has forged the peculiarity of the social movement in France since 1995, opening the so-called period of 'proxy' strikes and movements. Combined with this external action mode – demonstrations – an 'internal action mode' comes into existence which evokes the idea that people who mobilise themselves make up a community. In this positioning of cultural actors, new configurations of social movement come to the foreground which combine professional posturing with an ethical stand.

One can see, in fact, that political protest and commitment which used to be the domain of intellectuals are now that of cultural actors. Cultural actors do not position themselves as fellow-travellers, party-members or as the 'organic intellectual' of a social class as analysed by Gramsci. In their works,[5] their protect manifestoes, their involvement in minority movements (in support of undocumented aliens and socially excluded groups and anti-racist, anti-fascist and gay movements) in provocative acts during official events, cultural actors help new protest forms to emerge. Public space then reformulates the relationship between the individual and the collective, a fusion of private and public roles. These cultural movements are characteristic of the emergence of a third level between the state (the political system) and the market which constitutes those institutions which provide collective action.

These new social movements bring an ethical dimension to politics and rehabilitate the fundamental idea of the existence of moral and ethical determining factors. Actors produce collective goods not as a result of their rational capacity to maximise what is useful to them or to avoid being punished, but due to their normative disposition to do so, or from the existence of the relationships of trust, reciprocity, sympathy or equity which they have experienced in their relationships with their peers (Offe, 1997).

Another major aspect of the social movement is the 're-territorialisation of politics'. The occupation of public premises and of streets by live show temporary workers, unemployed people, undocumented aliens, the homeless, etc., give them an open social 'visibility'. In the eighties, Alain Touraine had underlined that what he called 'new social movements' was a 'reappropriation of time and space'. Cultural creation tends to the universal and the artists' mobilisation allows for the recomposition of urban space within its social and political dimension.

Artists and creators, through the 'spectacular' forms they give to their professional and political protests, invent a new citizenship which transcends the divide between the concrete man (driven by his interests and passions) and the abstract citizen (holder of civic rights). In total, even beyond cultural politics, culture re-establishes politics as a citizen's requirement, in its relations to the city's territory, in the conjugation of cultural rights. As a building block of urban management, artists spell out their social rights by being involved in the city and take sides, and at the same time, then bring the issue of fundamental cultural rights into life, reviving notions of citizenship which had been badly damaged by the devaluing of the nation-state. We are here at the heart of the construction of new degrees of citizenship based on the recognition of new rights, shaping a new social contract. This is a utopian vision of the complexity of artistic work, of its entrenchment in the individual and the collective, of its reappropriation of forms of co-operation, and of the social commitment which it generates among its agents. It opens the door of the citizenship which Jean Leca defines as 'the degree where a person can control his/her fate by acting within his/her group' of reference (Leca, 1991). But another and more realistic vision could claim that the logic of the market, present in every production, circulation and consumption of cultural goods, corrupts the public sphere of discussion, the 'commerce' of society. Therefore the 'common-place' culture, far from being a particular commodity, will be firmly in the new market society. In any case, it will remain a power issue.

Notes

1   This analysis originates from the research undertaken by a team of the ARPES laboratory (See Bernié-Boissard, Dreyfuss and Nicholas-Le-Strat, 1998, and Dreyfuss and Marchand, 1998) for the 'Plan Urbain' ('Ville et emploi culturel – le travail créatif culturel dans les agglomérations de Nîmes et Montpellier', May 1998) and from interviews made in London (Dreyfuss and Marchand, April 1998).
2   'When you work for X (Mayor of a big French town) you belong to him', as one theatre director said.
3   The actor must 'have a rough time of it' to become successful, as we were told by the young trainee-director of one London theatre.
4   In Great Britain self-employment in the clothes designing sector had the highest increase (+226%). In France the number of part-time technical personnel rose more than fourfold whereas that of artists went up by 30%.
5   A peculiar phenomenon is occurring in the world of music, that of musicians' and groups' commitment to and involvement in, 'causes', either by publicly taking a stand (festivals, campaigns, etc.) or within the form and content of work itself (Rap, so-called 'urban' rap, alternative rock, rock against fascism and racism, etc). Cinema also demonstrates a new social commitment with films such as Full Monty and Brassed Off in Great Britain and Guediguian and many others in France.

References

Aguiton, C. and Bensaïd, D. (1997), *Le Retour de la Question Sociale*, Cahiers Libres, Lausanne.
Benjamin, W. (1991), *Ecrits Français, l'Oeuvre d'Art*, Payet, Paris.

73

Bernié-Boissard, C., Dreyfuss, L. and Nicolas-Le-Strat, P. (1998), *Ville et Emploi Culturel – le Travail Créatif Culturel dans les Agglomerations de Nîmes et Montpellier*, ARPES, Université de Montpellier III, Montpellier.

Dreyfuss, L. (1998), *Réseaux Culturels et Space Politique*, ARPES, Université de Montpellier III, Montpellier.

Dreyfuss, L. and Marchand, A. (1995), 'Gouvernement Local et Legitimation vers des Républiques Urbaines ?', *Future Antérieur*, no. 29, L'Harmattan, Paris.

Ehrenberg, A. (1998), *La Fatigue d'Etre Soi*, Odile Jacob, Paris.

Ford, H. (1926), *Aujourd-hui et Demain*, Payot, Paris.

Giorgio, R. and Guerre, C. (1996), *Le Spectacle Vivant en Languedoc-Rousillon*, Observatoire Regional de l'Emploi Culteral, Montpellier.

Habermas, J. (1978), *L'Espace Public*, Payot, Paris.

Leca, J. (1991), *Sur Individualism*, Presses de la FNSP, Paris.

Menger, P-M. (1997), 'Les Intermittents du Spectacle', *INSEE Premiere*, no. 510 : fevrier.

Nicolas-Le-Strat, P. (1998), 'Multiplicité Artistique et Reseaux' in C. Bernié-Boissard, L. Dreyfuss, and P. Nicolas-Le-Strat, (eds), *Ville et Emploi Culturel – le Travail Créatif Culturel dans les Agglomerations de Nimes et Montpellier*, ARPES, Université de Montpellier III, Montpellier.

O'Brien, J. and Feist, A. (1997), *Employment in the Arts and Culture Industries : An Analysis of the 'Labour Force Survey' and Other Sources*, ACE Research Reports no. 9, The Arts Council of Great Britain, London.

Offe, C. (1997), *Les Démocraties Modernes à l'Epreuve*, L'Harmattan, Paris.

Simmel, G. (1914), *L'Art Pour l'Art*, Editions Rivages, Paris.

Vincent, J-M. (1996), 'La Déstabilisation du Travail', *Futur Antérieur*, no 35-36, L'Harmattan, Paris.

6 'Modernisation' or Insecurity: Labour Market Deregulation and State Retrenchment: the British Case

TONY CUTLER, PHILLIP JAMES, SUSANNE MACGREGOR AND
BARBARA WAINE

The object of this paper is to discuss the relationship between two central features of contemporary economic and social policy: the development of 'flexible' labour markets and of policies of labour market deregulation; and welfare state retrenchment. With respect to the former, 'flexible' labour markets are characterised by increased variations in employment relation patterns, e.g. a move away from the dominance of continuous full-time employment to the coexistence of this form with part-time, self employment and fixed term contracts and, although this claim has been disputed, that job tenures have become shorter and job changing is more frequent. This has been accompanied at the policy level by support for labour market deregulation - the reduction in the extent of employment protection regulation. Welfare state retrenchment refers to the process of reducing the role of the state in the finance and provision of social services and is thus associated with a policy of seeking to limit or reduce the share of state expenditure in national income.

The *combination* of labour market flexibility/deregulation and welfare state retrenchment has frequently been presented as part of a 'modernisation' of both economic and social policy. This term is often used in a vague way but, we would argue, the implicit claim is not only that these shifts in policy are adapted to contemporary conditions but also that the outcomes are at least as good or better than those which stemmed from more regulated labour markets and more extensive welfare provision. Such 'older' labour market and welfare regimes promised a reduction in social insecurity stemming, for example, from the loss of income due to unemployment or illness. Thus the key question addressed in the paper is whether 'modernisation' can deliver an alternative route to such security or whether it has a darker side which means that 'modern' labour markets and social policy will generate, for a substantial proportion of the population, a situation of increased social insecurity.

The paper discusses these issues with reference primarily to the British labour market and to British social policy. However, of course, the issues raised have relevance to the situation in all member states of the European Union (EU).

The paper is divided into five sections: the first discusses the role of the (1942) Beveridge report in producing a framework for the British social security system which embodied various key assumptions regarding the operation of the labour market. The second considers some of the key changes in labour markets since Beveridge and examines the approach to labour market regulation of both Conservative governments of the 1980s and 90s and the Labour Government elected in May 1997. The third section examines the approach of governments of both parties to welfare state retrenchment; the second and third sections conclude that, while there are important differences between the two parties, both can be seen to support a 'modernisation' agenda with some significant points of similarity. Part of this agenda is support for an enhanced role for private finance in the provision of social services. The fourth section considers the implications of such a shift of policy in two areas, pensions and health care. That section concludes that a shift in finance and provision of this type has significant potential for increasing social insecurity.

Finally a brief conclusion draws together the arguments presented in the paper.

The Beveridge Settlement

While the Beveridge report produced a 'plan for social security', its proposals were located in a series of explicit and implicit assumptions regarding the labour market. 'Assumption C' of the report required that government action should ensure 'maintenance of employment' which would involve '...the prevention of mass unemployment' (Beveridge, 1942, para. 440). In the 'plan' Beveridge had proposed a comprehensive social security system much more extensive than that operating at the end of the inter-war period and, inter alia, the prevention of mass unemployment was required to ensure that the cost of such a scheme was not 'insupportable'. The labour market was assumed to be dominated by male full-time employment. In the report Beveridge referred to the 1931 census as showing that 'less than one in eight of all housewives' were 'gainfully employed' (Beveridge, 1942, para 108). This pattern was expected to continue in the post-war period and thus Beveridge's later work *Full Employment in a Free Society* (1944) included an estimate of likely employment levels. What was expected was that the pattern of the post first world war period would apply, i.e. that in both cases war led to a large increase in the workforce participation of married women but this would fall back in the post-war period. Thus *Full Employment in a Free Society* contained an estimate that an additional 500,000 women would be in the immediate post-war workforce as against the additional 2,500,000 who had been drawn into the war economy (Beveridge, 1960, p.370). Thus the high level of married women's participation in war-time was treated as exceptional, the norm was that married women would be marginal to the labour force.

Central to the Beveridge scheme was the role of social insurance, so full employment would mean a buoyant source of contribution income that would limit the call on general taxation to finance benefits. However, given assumptions regarding the gendered pattern of employment, for Beveridge 'the archetypal insurance contributor was '...the adult male worker whose income was derived solely from earnings and who needed protection when such earnings were interrupted by unemployment' (Harris, 1977, p.392). The focus on the male worker did not just reflect Beveridge's view that relatively low levels of participation in the workforce by married women would continue, it also related to a normative conception of the male and female roles in marriage.

Male 'interruption of earnings' was undesirable but married womens' earnings were likely to be interrupted by childbirth and '...it is important that the interruption by children should be as complete as possible' (Beveridge, 1942, para.108). Thus for Beveridge it was not necessary to insure that married women have equal insurance benefits to male contributors since 'the housewife does not need compensating benefits on the same scale as the solitary woman because, among other things her home is provided for her either by her husband's earnings or benefit if her earnings are interrupted' (Beveridge, 1942, para.108). Beveridge did not conclude from this that women ceased to be vulnerable to risk on marriage since married women were then 'exposed to new risks, including the risk that her married life may be ended prematurely by widowhood or separation' (Beveridge, 1942, para.108). Thus he supported the idea of state insurance against such risks as part of a 'Housewife's Policy, endorsed or attached to her previous insurance document' (Beveridge, 1942, para.109). However, the argument for insurance against divorce or separation put him in a quandary since it involved a clash of two principles which he saw as central to social insurance. The first was that contingencies over which individuals could exert control raised major problems (of 'moral hazard') for social insurance (Harris, 1977, p.407). Potentially divorce or separation could be seen in this light and if they were to be 'covered' then this would require an investigation into responsibility for the divorce or separation. Yet this contradicted the view of insurance as an actuarially based relationship which should not involve any investigation into such personal circumstances (Harris, 1977, p.407). The Treasury used this tension successfully to push social insurance for such contingencies off the policy agenda (Land et al, 1992, p.20). Thus with the failure to implement specific cover for married women the Beveridge settlement effectively assumed a situation where male full-time employment, in a labour market without mass unemployment, generated earnings sufficient to sustain the income of the household which was, in turn, assumed to be a stable economic unit. Social security would deal with (mainly male) interruption of earnings, with income during retirement and, via family allowances, the effects of variations in family size.

The Breakdown of the Beveridge Settlement, Labour Market Flexibility and Deregulation

Labour Market Flexibility

The labour market conditions of the 1980s and 90s differ radically from those envisaged in the Beveridge report. The first key difference is the prevalence of much higher levels of unemployment. Thus whereas, measured by OECD standardised rates, the four largest European Union economies (UK, France, Germany and Italy) averaged an unemployment rate of 2.6 per cent over the period 1961-73; this had risen to 8.8 per cent over the period 1988-96 (Buchele and Christiansen, 1998, p.119).

There has also been a major shift away from a dominant pattern of full-time work on a permanent basis to one where 'atypical' forms of employment (part-time, fixed term contract and self-employment) are increasingly significant. For example, in 1951, 788,000 employees worked part-time in Great Britain, 3.9 per cent of the 19,940,000 employees in employment; the corresponding (seasonally adjusted) figures for March-May 1998 were 6,718,000, 28.6 per cent of the 23,486,000 employees in employment (Cutler, Williams and Williams, 1986, p.81; Office for National Statistics, 1999). Finally rates of household dissolution due to divorce have dramatically increased; in 1961 male and female divorce rates in England and Wales were 2.1 per 1,000 married population (over 16); by 1996 they had risen to 13.5 men and 13.4 women (Office for National Statistics, 1998, p. 51). These trends hit at a number of the pillars of the Beveridge settlement. His gendered division of labour in marriage raised the problem of an unacceptable patriarchal bias in access to benefits. Increased divorce and separation rendered this approach anachronistic particularly in the light of the failure to provide 'cover' for such contingencies. Finally the model of the regularly employed male full-time worker was overtaken both by increased unemployment and a more diverse pattern of employment relationships.

Labour Market Deregulation

There has been not only a major shift in labour market conditions but also in policy responses. A Keynesian approach to employment policy was implicit in 'Assumption C'. In contrast British Conservative governments post 1979 saw unemployment as a labour supply problem. This embodied the view that labour markets were excessively regulated and this was a major disincentive to employment creation. The response was to reduce such 'burdens on business' via employment law reforms (Davies and Freedland, 1993; Dickens and Hall, 1995) and other actions designed to create a more decentralised and competitive labour market.

In the area of employment law, wages councils, which set minimum wages in some sectors, were abolished and the period required to claim unfair dismissal was increased from six months to two years. A host of legislative reforms were also introduced to reduce the influence of trade unions and collective bargaining. These included the repeal of existing statutory procedures through which unions could claim recognition from employers; and the abolition of the Fair Wages Resolution and the removal of statutory provisions under which employers could be required to provide 'going rate' terms and conditions of employment; and the narrowing of union immunities from the common law legal liabilities associated with the organising of industrial action.

The above legal reforms were supplemented by a number of policy initiatives which, both directly and indirectly, acted to change the pattern of collective bargaining arrangements in the public sector. Thus the privatisation of electricity, water and railway industries resulted in the break-up of previously existing national negotiating machinery in them (Pendleton and Winterton, 1993). In addition, decentralised bargaining was encouraged through the creation of executive agencies in the civil service (Corby, 1993) and trade union bargaining power was challenged by the introduction of compulsory competitive tendering for a range of services provided by local authorities. This meant, inter alia, that unions came under pressure to accept deteriorations in pay and conditions in order to retain contracts 'in house' (Cutler and Waine, 1998, Ch. 4).

The current Labour Government has, in certain respects, moved away from this deregulatory position. Thus, following the report of the Low Pay Commission (LPC) in 1998 a minimum wage was introduced on Ist April 1999; and, in contrast to the Conservative policy of opting out of EU employment protection, Labour have signed up to the social protocol incorporated in the Treaty of Rome and has thus committed itself to bringing UK law in line with EU requirements on parental leave, part-time workers and the European Works Council Directive. Furthermore, proposals put forward in the White Paper *Fairness at Work*, and, at the time of writing contained in the Employment Relations Bill currently before Parliament, indicate a shift away from the approach taken by previous Conservative regimes (Department of Trade and Industry, 1998; Industrial Relations Services, 1999). Amongst the measures involved are a statutory union recognition procedure (McCarthy, 1999); the reduction of the unfair dismissal qualification period to one year; and the repeal of existing procedures under which employees on fixed-term contracts can waive their unfair dismissal rights.

However, Labour's position does not involve a repudiation of labour market flexibility but rather an attempt to temper such approaches with minimum standards. For example, the minimum wage, proposed by the LPC, and accepted by government (£3.60 per hour) for those 22 and over is 45 per cent of median earnings, a figure well below other EU countries (France 60 per cent; Belgium 58 per cent) (Low Pay Commission, 1998).

This is, perhaps, given added significance in the context of the fact, noted by the Low Pay Commission, that countries which have higher levels of minimum wage also tend to have less pay inequality (Low Pay Commission, 1998). In addition, employees under 18 are not covered and £3.20 is to apply to employees between the ages of 18 and 21; and the government has given no commitment to up-rate the figure for over 21 year olds. Thus while Labour policy is distinctive, it has not in any sense involved the repudiation of the pursuit of labour market flexibility.

Welfare State Retrenchment

Under the Conservatives, the view that public expenditure was too high went along with the objective of welfare state retrenchment. While this policy was uneven in its effects between services and did not achieve many of its original objectives (Pierson, 1994) there were a number of important changes. For example, the shift to indexing the basic state pension to prices rather than earnings has drastically reduced its value relative to average earnings and also greatly increased the significance of additional pensions for maintaining income during retirement (Pierson, 1994).

As in the case of labour market policy, Labour's approach to public expenditure and taxation exhibits both important continuities and significant differences with the Conservatives. In January 1997, prior to the general election, Gordon Brown, as shadow Chancellor, had pledged that neither the top nor the basic rate of income tax would be raised over the next five years (McGregor and Jones, 1998). 'Modernising' Britain would involve insisting that all parts of the public sector lived within their means. The 1997 Labour Manifesto also included a commitment to maintain Conservative spending limits (with the exception of the 'New Deal' welfare to work programme) (Hills, 1998, p.18). This commitment was undertaken even though, in particular, Conservative spending plans for the NHS were highly restrictive (Hills, 1998, p.23). Subsequently, following the Comprehensive Spending Review, there have been significant increases in planned health and education expenditure (Hills, 1998, p.25) but this has been achieved not by departing from overall spending restraints but rather by allocating resources to health and education to some extent at the expense of social security (Hills, 1998, pp. 24-5). The commitment to a prudent approach to public spending was also reflected in the Chancellor's approach to public borrowing. In June 1998, he stated that he aimed to reduce the ratio of government debt to gross domestic product over the next three years to a level roughly half that of the average level in the EU (*Financial Times,* 12 June 1998).

However, this does not mean that Labour policy has replicated the approach of the Conservatives. The New Deal welfare to work programme was funded by a £5.2billion windfall tax, with the water and regional electricity companies bearing the largest share. The fact that, in a context of overall expenditure constraint substantial funding was raised for this programme is indicative of a key emphasis in Labour policy. This is that the most important route towards a newly defined citizenship in contemporary society is through participation in paid employment. Recognising increases in poverty and inequality over the past two decades, the government has stressed the importance of encouraging people into work and keeping them there as the solution. Thus 'lack of work' is seen as 'the main risk factor for short-term and persistent low income' (Treasury, 1999, p.21) and thus government policy has focused on developing measures to get people back to work.

This has also been reflected in Labour taxation policies that have been designed to improve work incentives and to give more support to low-income working families. These include: the introduction of a 10 pence starting rate for income tax; the reduction in the basic rate of tax to 22 pence; a new Working Families Tax Credit and Childcare Tax Credit; a new Disabled Person's Tax Credit; a new Children's Tax Credit; and reform of national insurance contributions. Hence, while Conservative governments were often seen as willing to accept high levels of unemployment Labour has made the reduction of unemployment and increased access to the labour market a crucial aspect of its policy.

However, while many of these reforms may appear to contain a concern with improving the situation of the poor and intervening to prevent the cycle of deprivation, they markedly fail to address the fact that a major explanation for poverty lies in the low rate of pensions and other income support benefits. Thirty-seven per cent of those in the bottom 20 per cent of the income distribution are pensioners and 39 per cent are workless (Treasury, 1999, p.21). While waiting for these longer-term interventions to affect the opportunities available to the unemployed, there is one solution to poverty which is not contemplated and that is to raise the level of pensions and benefits above the poverty line. Increases in pensions would impact on the total social security budget and require income tax increases: and they believe that part of the explanation for detachment from the labour market is a culture of welfare dependency, which would be encouraged if the gap between income from benefits and income from paid work were to be reduced.

Labour's emphasis on redirecting resources, particularly to an emphasis on the labour market, within broad public expenditure limits similar to that of the Conservatives, means that alternatives to state finance and provision of social services could be viewed favourably. This, in turn, raises the issue of how far such non-state alternatives can function to protect the population against social insecurity. In the next section this issue is discussed in the context of non-state provision of pensions and health care.

Alternatives to the State? Pensions and Health Care

Pensions

The pensions system in the UK operates with a basic state pension and additional pensions. The latter are provided by the state, via the State Earnings Related Pension (SERPS) or by the private sector either through occupational schemes, which may involve a defined benefit (a proportion of final salary, i.e. at the end of working life) or defined contribution (where the employer guarantees a contribution level rather than a benefit level) or, since 1986, the Appropriate Personal Pension (APP). The APP was the alternative to membership of SERPS or an employer's scheme: it was not a new financial product. Prior to the 1986 Act, personal pensions were confined to the self-employed who did not have access to other forms of additional pensions. The APP, like personal pensions (PP) generally are individual money purchase schemes, where benefits are related to the outcome of the particular investment plan (see below). As it is usual to subsume discussion of the APP under the PP that convention will be followed here.

A justification of the addition of the PP was the claim that Britain was becoming an 'enterprise economy' in which both frequent job changes and people experiencing a range of employment relations over their working lives would become the norm: a flexible labour market required a flexible form of pension provision. Occupational pensions were associated with a pattern of employment involving long job tenures and were perceived as disadvantaging earlier leavers.

The publication of the Labour Government's Green Paper, *A New Contract for Welfare: Partnership in Pensions* (Department of Social Security, 1998) clearly demonstrates that it too is committed to 'modernising the pension system to meet the needs of the modern world' (Department of Social Security, 1998, p.25). In particular, it is argued that the system must adapt to changing work patterns – fewer people expecting lifetime employment with one or two employers, an increase in self-employment, more part-time and short term contract jobs, people experiencing periods on both low and high incomes over a working life (Department of Social Security, 1988, pp.25-6). In short a 'modern competitive economy requires a flexible and efficient labour market' (Department of Social Security, 1988, p.25) and a flexible pensions system. The key role in the modernised pensions system will be fulfilled by the private sector. Thus 'state pensions will *complement* private provision to give people a decent income in retirement' (Department of Social Security, 1998, p.42, emphasis added). While the basic state pension will remain, SERPS will be recast into a State Second Pension (SSP) for those who are not working (carers, disabled people) and low and moderate earners. However, the latter (earning between £9,000 and £18,500) will be encouraged to join private schemes via restructuring the SSP into a flat rate benefit scheme. This is planned to occur within five years of its introduction and attractive contracting out rebates are to be provided. Second tier provision for all other employees and self-employed will fall to the private sector via personal pensions, employer based schemes or the new stakeholder pension.

Labour's 'modernisation' programme thus continues the Conservative emphasis on a shift to private provision. However, this continuity itself raises a problem since Conservative pensions policy has been subject to considerable criticisms. These particularly focused on the failings of the PP which have been well documented both in the academic literature and by parliamentary investigations (Treasury Select Committee, 1998a and 1998b). Briefly, the PP is a money purchase scheme with the final pension being the result of a complex set of determinants including the level of contributions, administrative charges, the capital sum invested (contributions minus charges), the rate of return on the investment and the annuity which can be purchased with the final fund. Each of these elements is potentially problematic. Thus in a 1986 personal pension (unlike personal pensions generally), only a minimum contribution is required and this is the contracted out national insurance rebate (1.6 per cent for employees and 1.5

per cent for employers between the upper and lower earnings level, plus an additional 1 per cent for those over 30); tax relief is also given on employees' contributions. Thus, in a context in which contributions are likely to be low charges may be significant and can absorb up to a quarter of a member's savings (Department of Social Security, 1998, p.26). The capital sum depends on how well the premiums are invested and this is linked to the stability/volatility of the markets, as of course is the annuity which can be purchased with the fund.

By the early 1990s it became clear that many people had been inappropriately advised to purchase a PP. The nature of the PP means that they can be poor value for those on low or intermittent earnings or who cannot maintain the regular contributions required. This is due to the high costs of distributing and selling personal pensions. Charges reduce the value of the fund and hence the final pension: a third of the people who buy personal pensions cease contributing within three years (Department of Social Security, 1998, p.19, p.26, p.48). In addition employers are not required to provide more than minimum contributions to a 1986 personal pension scheme and it is the usual policy for employers to make substantially higher contributions to occupational schemes. (National Association of Pension Funds, 1997).

The Conservative 'modernisation' of the pensions system was thus argued to be likely to lead to insecurity in retirement. The key question is whether Labour's proposals (currently proceeding through Parliament in the Welfare Reform and Pensions Bill, 1999) will avoid such problems? Of central importance here is the Stakeholder Pension (SP).

The SP will be a money purchase scheme, but one, which it is argued, will be more secure than the PP. Firstly, all SP schemes must meet minimum standards, especially in respect of charges – this is to be achieved via a simple charging structure based on the percentage of the fund or contributions rather than a flat rate charge, a limit on the permitted level of charges and members being allowed to stop, restart and transfer their funds without penalty. Secondly, SP schemes are to be managed by trustees who will be required to run the scheme in the best interests of their members that is, be responsible for the investment strategy of the scheme (the government is prepared to consider alternative governance structures). Finally, SP schemes will be regulated by the Occupational Pensions Regulatory Authority and the Financial Services Authority.

The government's response to the defects of the PP have been those of minimum standards, improved governance and regulation. Will they be sufficient? If it is assumed that they all work as intended, would the SP be a more desirable product than its predecessor, the PP? Obviously the pre-requisites outlined are to be welcomed. However, the SP retains a key characteristic of its PP predecessor, namely, it is a money purchase, defined contribution scheme and thus there can be no guarantee of the level of the final pension: insecurity and uncertainty will remain. As Watson Wyatt Partners have commented, the SP make 'no mention of protection against market falls or poor annuity rates other than the minimum income guarantee' (Watson Wyatt, 1998).

Indeed it could be argued that Labour's pension regime might be even more insecure than that of the Conservatives. This is due to the abolition of SERPS. With the APP, employees could always return to SERPS if the APP became less attractive. Labour's proposals will, of course, remove this option. Furthermore, it is interesting that a government which was concerned to act swiftly to protect the pension rights of women and divorcees has been blind with respect to the impact of its pension proposals on women (the possible exception is the State Secondary Pension). There is a significant body of writing and research which convincingly argues that the privatisation of pensions is not in the interests of the majority of women (Williamson, 1997; Ginn and Arber, 1998). This follows from the combination of women's employment patterns and income profile. Thus while more women enter the labour force and remain in it for longer periods than previously, their participation has been disproportionately via part-time employment with implications for earnings both at a particular period and over a lifetime. Evaluation of the PP found that it had few advantages for women (Waine, 1996) and the SP, which in many ways replicates the PP is also likely to disadvantage women, (its one 'woman friendly' proposal is that members of SP schemes should be able to stop and restart their contributions without penalty) (Department of Social Security, 1998, p.51). Thus the Equal Opportunities Commission (1998) has commented that the SP is unlikely to produce an adequate entitlement for part-time workers because low contributions will mean a low pension fund. Initial low earnings will inevitably lead to low contributions, which combined with the conservative investment policy for women, who tend to be risk averse investors, (Williamson, 1997) will lead to small investment funds to be turned into annuities, even if it is assumed that these are not differentiated by sex. Thus non-state provision raises disturbing questions regarding its potential for generating social insecurity. Similar issues can also be argued to arise with respect to health care.

Private Medicine

In the UK, private medical care does not have a role of the same level of significance of occupational or personal pensions. The sector is primarily financed by health insurance and there is a long-term trend away from finance via direct payment of fees by users to insurance based cover. Thus Williams and Nichol (1994, p.1701) estimate that 75.1 per cent of men and 69.2 per cent of women in the UK financed their private medical treatment via insurance in 1981 but, by 1992-3 this had risen to 90 and 86 per cent respectively. The limits on overall coverage can be seen in two major sources of information: in their annual survey of the private health care market in the UK Laing and Buisson (1998, p.96) estimate UK population coverage for private medical insurance at 10.9 per cent in 1997; the UK General Household Survey puts population cover at 10 per cent in 1995 (Rowlands et al, 1997, p.124).

Coverage figures *per se* overstate the significance of the sector since cover is not usually provided, as is the case with the NHS for the range of medical treatments, but rather concentrates on acute care. Furthermore, given the commitment of increased funding to the NHS referred to earlier it might seem that private care will continue to have a marginal role in this area. However, one important development in health policy under Labour points potentially to a different conclusion. Labour inherited from the Conservatives the private finance initiative (PFI). Under PFI, public sector capital projects are undertaken by private providers who also continue to provide certain operational services in the facilities concerned. In return a regular leasing payment is made to the private provider from public sources.

A key theme in New Labour policy has been the emphasis put on 'partnership' between public and private sectors and it would appear that Labour have treated PFI as an exemplary instance of this approach. Thus not only have Labour taken over PFI but they have given it a much more salient role than it had under the Conservatives. Thus, for example, PFI projects are to account for 17 per cent of NHS capital expenditure in 1998-9 up from 3 per cent in 1997-8 (Froud and Shaoul, 1998). This would also be consistent with the Chancellor's emphasis on restraint on both public expenditure and borrowing.

A key point in criticisms of PFI in health is that projects have involved plans for hospitals which envisage drastic reductions in the provision of acute beds. Furthermore, while it is the case that there has been a long-term trend to reduce bed numbers in the NHS, increasing patient throughput per bed and reducing length of hospital stay, this process appears to be slowing down. Thus whereas PFI hospital projects in England plan for a reduction in bed numbers of *26* per cent over the next *5-7* years, the fall in bed numbers over the *14* years to 1996 was only *20* per cent and bed numbers actually increased marginally between 1994-5 and 1995-6 (Pollock et al, 1997, p.1267). This has led critics of PFI in health to argue that such plans involve unattainable throughput targets and therefore that they will result in reductions in the availability of acute care in the NHS. In this respect Pollock and Dunnigan (1998, p.2) have argued that the 'progressive downsizing' of acute hospitals 'may lead to...fragmentation of the NHS reshaping it as [a] safety-net service'.

In such a case it could be anticipated that the demand for private medical care would rise. Thus, for example, interviews with individuals with private medical cover indicate that such care is sought not because it is thought that the private sector provides a higher quality product but to obtain easier access to services (Calnan et al, 1993, p.41). New Labour has frequently argued that it has no bias in favour or public or private provision. In this respect, therefore, it might seem that a shift to a more significant role for private medical care could be seen as a satisfactory alternative, at least in some respects, to NHS provision.

However, as in the case of pensions, discussed in the last section, there are a number of aspects of private medical insurance (PMI) which suggests that it has a major potential to generate insecurity. To investigate this issue it is necessary to examine the pattern of PMI cover in the UK and the most useful source in this respect are the data given in the General Household Survey (GHS). The most recent survey which asked questions on PMI was that of 1997 which gave data for the UK for 1995. This showed that, while 22 per cent of professional and 23 per cent of managers had PMI cover, this fell to 4 per cent for skilled workers or non professional self employed people and to 2 per cent for semi-skilled workers or personal service groups (Rowlands et al, 1997, p.124). Gender differences in *coverage* were small but there were important differences in the percentages of men and women who were *policyholders*. Overall 9 per cent of men were policyholders but only 4 per cent of women (Rowlands et al 1997, p.124). This difference arises because a policyholder can obtain coverage not only for himself/herself but for members of their family. However, the gender difference in policy holding raises the 'Beveridge' problem of women being dependent on their spouses for their access to cover. GHS data are also significant in this respect since they show that, overall, PMI cover for married or cohabiting women was 11 per cent but for widowed, divorced or separated women it was 4 per cent (Rowlands et al 1997, p.123).

The GHS data show that 59 per cent of policyholders were in schemes organised by employers (Rowlands et al, 1997, p.125). These were broken down into four types: 37 per cent of policy holders were covered by schemes in which the employer paid the whole premium; in 10 per cent of cases the employee paid the whole premium (but probably benefited from a group premium discount); in 8 per cent of cases part of the premium was paid by the employer; and in 4 per cent the employer paid for cover for the employee but the employee paid for cover for dependants (Rowlands et al, 1997, p.125). The GHS data also showed that there were inequalities in the terms offered to policyholders through employer-based schemes. Thus, for example, whereas 44 per cent of employees and managers who were policyholders had the whole subscription paid by the employer, in the case of manual workers the figure was 29 per cent.

In many respects, these differences reflect the dynamics of an occupationally based welfare benefit. Thus, insofar as coverage reflects employer views of the value of an individual to the organisation, then both cover and the terms on which it is offered tend vary with position in the corporate hierarchy. This is also reflected in the concentration of such benefits on the workforce. Thus the GHS shows a sharp falling off of coverage at retirement: for 45-64 year olds overall population coverage is 12 per cent but over the age of 65 this drops to 5 per cent. A similar pattern has been found in company-based case study research. Thus an Income Data Services study of 1996 found that, of 33 large firms surveyed, only 3 gave coverage after retirement. Two of these were withdrawing this benefit by limiting it to those who retired after a certain date and the third restricted post-retirement cover to directors.

Of course, as has been pointed out, PMI currently in Britain is a 'niche' product. However, such structural inequalities can also be seen in health care systems such as the American where the dominant mode of funding is via private insurance. The American system has not been able to achieve universal population coverage and the US Bureau of Census concluded in 1996 that 40.6 million Americans were without health insurance cover throughout 1995 (Thorpe, 1997, p.352). Such lack of cover is, however, markedly unevenly spread. Johnson and Crystal (1997) analysed data from the US Health and Retirement Study; the data were for 1992-3 and households were included if one member was born between 1931 and 1941

(Johnson and Crystal, 1997, p.124). This middle-aged group of respondents could be argued to be particularly significant because of their greater health needs compared to younger age groups (Johnson and Crystal, 1997, p.123). Their analysis of the data from this study showed that African American respondents were twice as likely and Hispanic respondents four times as likely as white respondents to have no cover (Johnson and Crystal, 1997, p.126). They also found that divorced or widowed women were more than twice as likely as currently married women to have no cover (Johnson and Crystal, 1997, p.126) There was also a broadly inverse relation between cover and need, if measured by self-reported health status with those who described their health as 'poor' being twice as likely to have no cover when compared with those who described their health as 'excellent' (Johnson and Crystal, 1997, p.126). Equally, for those earning over $15 per hour 84 per cent had employment based health insurance cover whereas the corresponding figure for those earnings $6 an hour or less was 34.8 per cent (Johnson and Crystal, 1997, p.133).

What would appear to be clear, therefore, is that private medical insurance is not an alternative to the type of provision given by the NHS. The occupational basis of the benefit means that whether it is available and the broad terms on which it is made available are at the discretion of employers. This means that inequalities in access and terms of access reflect inequalities in the labour market on class, gender and ethnic lines.

Conclusion

As was indicated at the beginning of the paper, the 'test' for 'modernisation' policies was that they create an alternative route to the protection of the population against social insecurity which was an objective of the 'older' approach embodied in the Beveridge Report. The argument presented in the paper raises considerable doubts as to whether 'modernisation' is likely to pass this test.

Support for labour market flexibility and deregulation is usually based on the argument that such policies result in higher levels of employment and lower levels of unemployment. Such arguments are often advanced in the context of comparisons of the highly deregulated US labour market with the relatively regulated labour markets of the EU. However, the labour markets which are most 'flexible' are also those in which there has been a long term trend to increased pay inequalities and significant falls in real earnings. For example, in the American case there have been long term falls in even median income levels in real terms and sharper falls further down the pay distribution (Freeman, 1995). Furthermore there is little convincing evidence within the EU that higher levels of labour market flexibility improve employment creation. Thus, for example, Morgan (1996) has shown that job creation in the 'rigid' French labour market was superior to the 'flexible' British labour market in the recoveries from the early 1990s recessions. This suggests that labour market flexibility can involve marked problems of low pay which are not necessarily compensated for by increased employment opportunities.

Thus, where labour market deregulation policies are *combined* with welfare state retrenchment there is a likelihood of marked increases in social insecurity. Thus, as was argued in the fourth section, personal pension plans involve low rates of contributions and exposure in a number of respects to the risks of market volatility; occupational schemes are more secure but have never been a basis for universal coverage. Similarly private medical insurance involves problems of lack of cover and these are usually most marked for the most vulnerable and worst paid members of the workforce. Of course, it is also important to stress that the Labour position is ambivalent with respect to such issues. Thus while there is clear support for a continuation of welfare state retrenchment, which is particularly marked, as was shown in pensions policy, this is combined with a willingness to increase, to some degree the regulation of the labour market.

Labour has argued that while labour market deregulation is linked to a low wage economy its goal, via an emphasis on improved education and training of the workforce, is a high wage economy. However, critics of this more 'enlightened' supply side approach have questioned whether it can deliver the benefits which Labour claims for it (for a summary of such arguments, see Cutler and Waine, 1998, pp.159-161). If Labour's tempered approach to labour market flexibility does not succeed then, in the context of its willingness to support welfare state retrenchment, 'modernisation' is likely to equate with increased insecurity for a substantial proportion of the population.

References

Beveridge, W. (1942), *Social Insurance and Allied Services*, Cmd. 6404, HMSO, London.
Beveridge, W. (1960), *Full Employment in a Free Society*, Allen and Unwin, London (first published, 1944).

Buchele, R. and Christiansen, J. (1998), 'Do Employment and Income Security Cause Unemployment? A Comparative Study of the US and the E-4', *Cambridge Journal of Economics*, vol. 22, pp. 117-136.

Calnan, M., Cant, S. and Gabe, J. (1993), *Going Private: Why People Pay for their Health Care*, Open University Press, Buckingham.

Corby, S. (1993), 'How Big a Step is 'Next Steps'? Industrial Relations Developments in Executive Agencies', *Human Resource Management Journal*, vol. 4, pp. 52-69.

Cutler, T. and Waine, B. (1998), *Managing the Welfare State: Text and Sourcebook*, Berg, Oxford.

Cutler, T., Williams, K. and Williams, J. (1986), *Keynes, Beveridge and Beyond*, Routledge, London.

Davies, P. and Freedland, M. (1993), *Labour Legislation and Public Policy*, Clarendon Press, Oxford.

Department of Social Security (1998), *A New Contract for Welfare: Partnership in Pensions*, Cm. 4179, Stationery Office, London.

Department of Trade and Industry (1998), *Fairness at Work*, Cmnd. 3968, Stationery Office, London.

Dickens, L. and Hall, M. (1995), 'The State, Labour Law and Industrial Relations' in P. Edwards (ed.), *Industrial Relations: Theory and Practice in Britain*, Blackwell, Oxford.

Freeman, R. (1995), 'The Limits of Wage Flexibility to Curing Unemployment', *Oxford Review of Economic Policy*, vol. 11, pp. 63-72.

Froud, J. and Shaoul, J. (1998), 'Appraising and Evaluating PFI for NHS Hospitals', Paper presented at the *CIMA Public Sector Accounting Workshop*, University of Edinburgh, 24-25th September.

Ginn, J. and Arber, S., (1998), 'Prospects for Women's Pensions: the Impact of Privatisation', paper given at the *American Sociological Association Annual Conference*.

Harris, J. (1977), *William Beveridge: a Biography*, Clarendon Press, Oxford.

Hills, J. (1998), *Thatcherism, New Labour and the Welfare State*, Centre for the Analysis of Social Exclusion, London School of Economics, London.

Income Data Services (IDS) (1996), *Private Medical Insurance* (study no. 593), IDS, London.

Industrial Relations Services (1999), 'Employment Relations Bill Stumbles Out of the Blocks', *Industrial Relations Law Bulletin*, 611, pp. 2-3.

Johnson, R. and Crystal, S. (1997), 'Health Insurance Coverage at Midlife: Characteristics Costs and Dynamics' *Health Care Financing Review* vol. 18, pp. 123-148.

Laing and Buisson (1998), *Healthcare Market Review 1998-99*, Laing and Buisson, London.

Land, A., Lowe, R. and Whiteside, N. (1992), *The Development of the Welfare State 1939-1951: a Guide to Documents in the Public Record Office*, HMSO, London.

Low Pay Commission (1998), *The National Minimum Wage: First Report of the Low Pay Commission*, Stationery Office, London.

MacGregor, S. and Jones, H. (1998), *Social Issues and Party Politics*, Routledge, London.

McCarthy, Lord (1999), *Fairness at Work and Trade Union Recognition: Past Comparisons and Future Problems*, Institute of Employment Rights, London.

Morgan, J. (1996), 'Labour Market Recoveries in the UK and Other OECD Countries' *Labour Market Trends*, December, pp. 529-539.

National Association of Pension Funds (NAPF) (1997), *Annual Survey 1996*, NAPF, London.

Office for National Statistics (1998), *Social Trends*, 28, HMSO, London.

Office for National Statistics (1999), *Labour Market Trends*, February.

Pendleton, A. and Winterton, J. (eds) (1993), *Public Enterprise in Transition: Industrial Relations in State and Privatized Industries*, Routledge, London.

Pierson, P. (1994), *Dismantling the Welfare State: Reagan, Thatcher and the Politics of Welfare State Retrenchment*, Cambridge University Press, Cambridge.

Pollock, A., Dunnigan, M., Gaffney, D., Macfarlance, A. and Azeem Majeed, R. (1997), 'What Happens When the Private Sector Plans Hospital Services for the NHS: Three Case Studies under the Private Finance Initiative', *British Medical Journal*, vol. 314, 26th April, pp. 1266-1271.

Pollock, A. and Dunnigan, M. (1998), 'Public Health and the Private Finance Initiative', *Journal of Public Health Medicine*, vol. 20, no. 1, pp. 1-2.

Rowlands, O., Singleton, N., Maher, J and Higgins, V. (1997), *Living in Britain: Results from the 1995 General Household Survey*, Stationery Office, London.

Thorpe, K. (1997), 'The Health Care System in Transition: Care, Cost and Coverage', *Journal of Health Politics, Policy and Law*, vol. 22, pp. 341-361.

Treasury (1999), *The Modernisation of Britain's Tax and Benefit System. Number Four. Tackling Poverty and Extending Opportunity*, The Public Enquiry Unit, London.

Treasury Select Committee (1998a), *Report on the Mis-Selling of Personal Pensions, Ninth Report*, Session 1997/8, vol 1, HC 712-1, The Stationery Office, London.

Treasury Select Committee (1998b), *Report on the Mis-Selling of Personal Pensions, Minutes of Evidence and Appendices, Ninth Report*, Session 1997/8, vol 1, HC 712-2, The Stationery Office, London.

Waine, B. (1996), 'Security in Retirement: the Case of the Personal Pension', *Benefits*, 17, pp. 14-17.

Watson Wyatt Partners (1998), *Pension News: Green Paper: UK Pension Reform*, www.watsonwyatt.com.

Williams, B. and Nicholl, J. (1994), 'Patient Characteristics and Clinical Caseload of Short Stay Independent Hospitals in England and Wales, 1992-3', *British Medical Journal*, vol. 308, pp. 1699-1701.

Williamson, J., (1997), 'Should Women Support the Privatisation of Social Security?' *Challenge* vol 40, no.1, pp 97-108.

PART II
EMPLOYMENT
UNCERTAINTY AND
ECONOMIC SECURITY

7 Mobility of Manpower in Europe and the Transfer of Social Rights

ELAINE JAOUI-PYLYPIW

Introduction

Mr Aldewereld, a Dutch resident, worked in a firm located in Germany. He was sent to Thailand by his firm and worked there for one year. During that year, his employer deducted from his salary the contributions to pay for sickness and unemployment benefits, old age pension and industrial accidents. At the same time, the Dutch Inland Revenue asked him to pay the compulsory contributions which any resident must pay, in accordance with Dutch legislation. Mr Aldewereld refused to do so. Which legislation was to be implemented as regards Mr Aldewereld? The legislation of the country in which he was employed (i.e. Germany), or that of the country in which he lived (i.e. the Netherlands)?

In 1961, Mr Belbouab, a French miner of Algerian descent, went to work in Germany, after 13 working years in France. Algeria became independent in 1962 and Mr Belbouab lost his French nationality. When he asked for the retirement pension available to German miners, he was not considered eligible since he did not have the nationality of an EC member, and could not, therefore, be protected by the law of the Community.[1]

These cases, examined, among many others, by the Court of Justice of the European Communities (CJEC) clearly indicate the necessity for European social legislation. Indeed, the Single Market implies the free circulation of people, goods and capital. This free circulation has immediate consequences : the nationals of one of the member states, whether tourists, students, wage-earners, or self-employed, etc., must be confident, if they move within the European Union (EU) that they will be provided with a social coverage similar to that which they obtain in their own country.

This chapter proposes to study the case of people who move within the EU, more precisely the case of those called 'migrant workers' by the

97

Social Security Agency. The conditions of transfer of their social rights, in the context of a continuously changing social Europe, will then be analysed.

This type of research implies a precise definition of each of the categories concerned, as well as a study of the 'social rights' granted to each. These rights may vary according to the definitions of each member state and to those of the official European texts that apply.

Past difficulties in harmonizing and implementing a common social policy will be retraced. This will lead to an analysis of the current social coverage of this particular category of workers (Hill, 1996).

The various systems of social security and welfare of each country are noticeably different. European committees are working to bring in solutions which should be adopted by all the EU member States. The most recent proposals and their possible implementation will be examined here since they are all part of the creation of the future 'European Social Area'.

Definitions and Area of Research

- The term migrant worker means 'a national of a Contracting Party who has been authorised by another Contracting Party to reside in its territory in order to take up paid employment'.[2]

This term is fairly general, and consequently, more precise definitions have been added, thus:[3]

- Workers on assignment who work in one country but can be sent abroad to work for a maximum temporary period of 12 months (exceptionally, an extra period of 12 more months can be granted). They are under the social security scheme of the country in which they usually work or on a scheme determined by an international agreement of social security. Regulations vary according to the length of the assignment – less than 3 months, from 3 months to a year, more than a year and within a two-year limit.
- Workers who are not on assignment are under the social welfare scheme of the country in which they work as wage-earners or as self-employed. Community regulations apply to them if they are members of the EU or of the European Economic Area (EEA).

- Frontier workers can be wage earners or self-employed. They work in one of the member States and go back to their county of residence at least once a week. They are insured in the country in which they work.
- Seasonal workers work in the country or countries of work for a maximum period of 8 months. They are insured in the country(ies) of their work and benefit from Community regulations, except for the specific provisions on unemployment benefits.
- Pension holders who live in another EU or EEA member state have the same rights as migrant workers, whether they are granted retirement pensions, disability or survivor benefits.

All these categories of European citizens are eligible for various social security benefits, in cash or in kind.

- Cash benefits replace wages lost because of sickness, disablement, maternity, etc. They are generally granted by the country in which the worker in insured.
- Benefits in kind include all types of care delivered by doctors, dentists, etc. in case of sickness, at home, in hospital and in emergency cases. They also include direct payments to refund these expenses.

As Community activities have developed, the rights and duties of workers have been specified in official documents.

Regulations have been made more precise in the field of social security. At the level of the European Community, social assistance – or, rather, solidarity – is a more recent and more limited phenomenon, as we shall see.

Towards a Social Europe : the Major Steps

In 1958, the member states signed the Treaty of Rome which envisaged the creation of a common market in order to facilitate and increase trade and commerce between member countries. The social dimension was not forgotten altogether but was rather scanty, and no general overall plan was to be found. In the early stages, and over the next twelve years, the six member states of the European Community did not include the elaboration of a social policy among their top priorities.

Community documents dealt with citizens, first and foremost, as *workers*. Typically, workers were the people who had social rights, and as a result, their families were granted some social benefits. Social coverage could vary, according to the category that workers belonged to, such as civil servants, employees or self-employed.

Community regulations made it possible to deal with a number of questions. It became possible, for instance, to determine which country was accountable for the unemployment benefits of borderers; who was responsible for hospital costs in the case of accidents abroad; the way to proceed when a person who had worked in one or several member states outside of the state of residence became eligible for a pension, etc.

The Common Market had to promote 'the harmonizaton of social systems' (*Treaty of Rome*, art. 117). The member states must see to the social coverage of all migrant workers:

> The Council, …shall adopt such measures in the field of social security as are necessary to provide freedom of movement for workers … to secure for migrant workers and their dependents: (a) aggregation, for the purpose of acquiring and retaining the right to benefit and of calculating the amount of benefit, of all the period taken into account under the laws of several countries; (b) payments of benefits to persons resident in the territories of the Member States (Art. 51).

The European Social Fund (ESF) must help job seekers to find adequate training, and must fight against long-term unemployment (art. 123 to 127; see Carraud, 1994 for more detail).

In 1968, the European Code of Social Security,[4] despite its title, did not create a single level system of social security at the European level: even today, the system of each signatory country is too specific for such an ambitious project to be achieved in the immediate future. Nevertheless, this code determines a series of norms and minimum provisions which have to be granted by member states in specific areas: medical care, sickness and maternity benefits, unemployment benefits and industrial accidents, retirement pensions, family allowances, disablement, etc.

These regulations, which were made more precise in 1972 by the European Convention of Social Security (ETS No.78) entitle all European workers to the same rights as nationals. The code was to be revamped once more in 1990.[5] It now offers new allowances, increases in rates of coverage, in levels and lengths of benefits, broadens the conditions of eligibility and bans discrimination on the basis of sex in the allocation of benefits.

The regulations of the European Economic Community (EEC) No. 1408/71 and 574/72 established the co-ordination of social security schemes in 1971 and 1972. They set out a number of common definitions as regards eligibility for benefits and the terms 'workers', 'migrant workers' and 'family members'. Appendix 1 of Regulation 1408/71, which lists the definitions of 'wage-earners', self-employed, members of the family' in the various member states, demonstrates what a complex task it was. This regulation, and the measures taken to implement it, have been modified more than twenty times. In addition, numerous directives provide rules concerning various professions, the diplomas required and recognised by member states, and the equivalent degrees in vocational training (Guggenbülh and Leclerc, 1995).

As a rule, the wage-earner or the self-employed must have a professional activity covered by the social security system of one or several member states in order for him and his family to benefit from the Community regulation (see Ogus, Barendt and Wikeley, 1995, Ch.18, for an analysis of these regulations). Various forms make it possible to apply for various benefits. For example, any European citizen who travels in the EC, might be familiar with the E111 form which testifies to his/her eligibility to benefits in kind during a stay in a member state.

The European Convention on the legal status of migrant workers of 1997[6] stated that a migrant worker is 'a national of a Contracting party who has been authorised by another Contracting Party to reside in its territory in order to take up paid employment' (art.1). The Convention does not apply to a number of people such as frontier workers, artists, seasonal workers, seamen, etc., as these categories are often subject to special regulations. Despite the restrictive meaning of the term, the social rights of migrant workers have been made clear, particularly in the field of a transfer of savings, of social security, of welfare and medical care.

The Community Charter on basic Social Rights of 1989 and the protocol annexed to the Treaty of Maastricht of 1993 on the European Union were adopted by 11 countries (The United Kingdom only signed the Social Charter under the government of Mr. Blair[7]). The jurisdiction of the member states in terms of welfare was made explicit : some measures would, from then on, be adopted with a qualified majority – unanimity would not be compulsory any longer. Yet, it is noteworthy that the decisions in the areas of social security and social welfare still require unanimity (Guggenbülh and Leclerc, 1995, p.6). Many states are still hesitant : they want to remain in control of policy in these matters and dread a leveling downwards if the EU were to conform to the schemes of member states in which social coverage is less comprehensive. Today, the fear of 'social dumping', i.e. a shift of production from the North to the South of Europe, where social costs are lower, is less apparent than it was in the 1980s, but currently, some states feel mistrustful of the hegemony of Brussels, whose regulations might influence national decisions.

Obviously, all the legal measures of the European Union have not succeeded in creating what some people had dreamt of: a '13th social security scheme, supplying all European citizens with a minimum number of rights, thanks to a Community law of social security' (Dumont, 1988, p.354). Nevertheless, the European institutions have managed to implement a co-ordination of the various national schemes, which remain the only ones to be applied. Yet, this co-ordination has had an effect upon the national schemes which must now be modified since Europeans who move to another member state cannot be discriminated against, and, as Article 12 of the European Social Charter states:

> The Parties undertake ... to ensure: (a) equal treatment with their own nationals of the nationals of other Parties in respect of social security rights, including the retention of benefits arising out of social security legislation, whatever movements the persons protected may undertake between the territories of the Parties; (b) the granting, maintenance and resumption of social security rights by such means as the accumulation of insurance or employment periods completed under the legislation of each of the Parties.

Article 4 of regulation (EEC) No. 1408/71 applies to social security but explicitly excludes a number of sectors, in particular social and medical assistance. This aspect of the European social policy will be examined later.

In 1995, the European Commission adopted its third programme of action since the 1970s, for the 1995-97 period. This ambitious plan suggested a closer correlation between social and economic policies and presented programmes 'for action in the social field, covering employment, legislation, equality of opportunity for women, the idea of a society that belonged to all its citizens and the need for studies and research in the social area'.[8]

Thanks to the European Economic Area, social coverage has even spread from 15 to 18 countries. The same Community regulations concerning social security now apply to Norway, Iceland and Liechtenstein. The nationals of these countries benefit from the same rights as the EU workers when they come to work in the EU and vice versa.[9]

Some of these rights will now be examined, chiefly to consider the principles which have guided the lawmakers. The obstacles or hurdles they met with will be retraced and the most recent proposals to improve the system will be presented.

European Social Security in 1998

General Background

Ever since the construction of the European Community, the 12, now the 15, member states, have come up against the same problems: poverty, immigration issues, worsening unemployment rates, declining fertility rates, aging populations - with an increasingly large very-elderly group (Henrard and Veysset-Puijalon, 1997; Jaoui-Pylypiw, 1997). All these parameters weigh on the working population and inflate social welfare budgets (De Montalembert, 1997) : costs have been soaring, whether the welfare state patterns are mainly of a Beveridge type (i.e. tax-based, as in the United Kingdom), or inspired by Bismarck (i.e. with a contributory base levied on wages, as in Germany) or a combination of both, as in the French pattern (Dupeyroux, 1993; Viossat, 1997).

Consequently, many states have been decreasing the amount of benefits granted, such as unemployment benefits, or have modified the conditions of entitlement, e.g. entitlement to retirement pensions.

Community Regulations

In any given case, Community regulations relevant to social security prevail over national ones. They are generally acknowledged and applied by member states. They override national regulations in conflicting cases. A migrant worker in the EU cannot be put at a disadvantage in comparison with a worker who has always lived in one state. Community legislation thus makes it possible to solve various types of problems:[10] Social security schemes are either based on insurance, on employment, or on residence conditions, as the case may be, in each country.

- Community law decides which legislation the migrant worker comes under. As the latter must neither be insured twice nor utterly uninsured, he can only be under the law of one member state at a time.
- He is insured in the country in which he works.

In each state, there are 'waiting periods', i.e. a number of contributions required or a given time in work, or a given time in the country of residence, are compulsory before a claimant can receive benefits. These waiting periods can vary from a few months to several years, according to the countries or the benefits paid. But a migrant worker must not lose his rights because he moved within the EU.[11]

- Community law has therefore instituted a cumulative aggregate of periods of insurance, work or residence, in any EU or EEA state.
- When the amount of a benefit is reduced because of national legislation, on account of non-residence conditions, Community law intervenes so that seasonal workers, frontier workers, members of the family or migrant workers are not penalised.

Social Security Benefits

Obstacles

In some member states, a number of practices make the situation of migrant workers difficult; they are the victims of red tape, through no fault of their own. Entitlement to social security benefits is often conditional on the possession of a valid residence card. Migrant workers sometimes cannot get a pension payable by another member state, for instance, even when it constitutes their only financial resource, if their residence card has not been renewed in due time, in accordance with regulation (EEC) No. 1408/71 and the pension is paid via the competent agency of the host country. Now, to be registered in a social security institution, a valid residence card is compulsory. However, to obtain a residence card, a minimum level of financial resources is required. This conundrum constitutes a vicious circle which undermines the very existence of the right of residence.[12]

The Commission and the European Parliament adopted different proposals and resolutions in July 1998 to facilitate the free circulation of *citizens* (which implies that not only workers, but also family members should freely move within the EU) and to facilitate access to social security benefits.

Unemployment Benefits

Nearly all the EU member states have high levels of unemployment. On the whole, unemployment affects around 10 per cent of the working population. This issue has been a great cause of concern economically, politically and socially and Community law is therefore particularly important in this regard.

Despite the legislation (art.7, directive 68/360) which guarantees that a citizen who is not voluntarily unemployed has a right to stay in the host country, some states are reluctant to renew the residence card in such cases, even when the period of validity has not yet expired.

The conditions of entitlement to unemployment benefits are rather stringent, when compared to other Community rules. Periods of insurance *and* periods of work are taken into account.

- A claim for unemployment benefit is receivable only if it is registered with the state in which the worker was insured just before losing his job, and he must have worked there for a minimum period of 4 weeks. The amount of payment depends only on the wages he earned before losing his job.
- When the claimant loses his job, he must be at the disposal of the employment agency for at least 4 weeks.
- If the claimant goes to another state to look for work, he must register with the unemployment benefit office in this other state within a 7 day period. He must be available to the control proceedings of this country in order to receive the unemployment benefits which will be payable for a maximum period of 3 months.
- The unemployed worker has 3 months to find a job. If, before the end of this time, he has not found any work, he will have to go back to the state which pays him his unemployment benefits, if he wants to go on receiving these allowances. After this 3 months period, and without permission from the employment agency of that country, he will lose his entitlement to benefits.
- 'The maintenance of unemployment benefits between two periods of work will be secured only once'.[13]

(These provisions do not apply to frontier workers who are subject to specific regulations).

In many cases, unemployed people are disqualified from receiving unemployment benefits because of a lack of information: they either do not register with the employment agency of the country before leaving it to go and try to find work elsewhere, or they do not register in time in the new state, or they stay over the 3 month period before coming back to the country which grants them the benefit.

The Court of Justice (CJEC) was already quite aware of the restrictive provisions of regulation 1408/71 and had indicated in a 1991 decision that a 6 month period, instead of 3, would be beneficial to unemployed European workers seeking employment in another state. The Commission has adopted a proposal which aims at conditionally extending the maintenance of benefits over the 3 month period, but, according to the Veil report, it is difficult to determine the consequences of this proposal (Veil Report, 1997).

Apart from the strict implementation of social security benefits, the increase in unemployment and the necessity of adapting the labour force to the transformation of business structures, have given birth to various measures in favour of professional training and reintegration. For instance, the European Social Fund (ESF) spent 5.6bn euros in 1995 to develop employment opportunities, and, between 1994 and 1999, the Union budget granted the ESF 47bn euros to fight against long-term unemployment, to help young unemployed workers to join the labour market and to train workers for changes in manufacturing.

Family Allowances

The unemployed who are paid unemployment benefits are eligible for family allowances in the same way as workers. A member state cannot enforce a law which would disregard members of a family in the calculation of benefits simply because they live in another state.[14]

Actually, all the member states make provisions for family allowances, which include 'all benefits for dependants, whether in cash or in kind'.[15] However, the amounts and conditions of entitlement are significantly different from country to country and can be based on periods of insurance or periods of employment. Waiting times can also vary.

Community law specifies that member states must take into account the periods of insurance or of employment performed in other states, as is the case for other social rights. When a migrant worker is entitled to these allowances in accordance with the schemes of several countries, Community law states that the highest amount granted by one of these states will prevail. It is as if the family lived in the country with the most favourable legislation. This principle sounds simple but is not so easy to implement. Besides, the payment of family allowances can either be linked to the occupational activity and/or the legislation of the country of residence; if paid twice, the allowance might be suspended and would entail complex administrative procedures.

Sickness/Maternity Benefits, Industrial Accidents and Diseases

The provisions relating to sickness or maternity, industrial accidents and diseases give the workers and the unemployed a broad protection. Sickness benefits in cash are paid in accordance with the law of the country of work and benefits in kind are granted by the country in which the claimant lives or stays.

A frontier worker can choose to receive sickness benefits in kind in his country of residence or in the country in which he works. In some member states, this optional right is even available to family members.

When a citizen cannot get sickness benefit in kind in his country of residence, he can go to another country to be cared for, provided he was first granted permission by the country of residence. The country in which he is insured will refund the competent institution of the country in which the benefits in kind were granted. This procedure might shorten possible waiting lists. Yet, it might also trigger a phenomenon of 'medical tourism', which could even accelerate, because of the uneven quality of hospitals, and bring about a disequilibrium in the financial balance of some national social security systems.

Nevertheless, the conditions of access to health care should be made more flexible in cross-border regions. Agreements between social security institutions of neighbouring states should be developed to enable a more efficient use of equipment. Furthermore, as the Veil report underlines, this would reduce the difficulties of former frontier workers and of their families : they are only entitled to health care in their country of residence.

Disablement Pensions

There is a considerable number of regulations concerning pensions for disabled people in the EU and the EEA.

In some states, these pensions are linked to the number of insurance contributions (Type B legislation). The longer the period of insurance, the higher the amount of disability pension. The same thing can apply to a retirement pension. In other countries, the disablement pension is not a function of the period of insurance.[16] The duration of insurance does not matter, the claimant must be insured when the disablement occurs (Type A legislation). A citizen who stopped being insured before a disablement occurs gets no pension. Finally, in some states, there is no insurance against occupational accidents or diseases.

European regulations have been instituted so that a migrant worker who would alternatively pay contributions in countries of Type A and of Type B, would not be disadvantaged. Other arrangements aim at preventing double payments, (or conversely, at favouring them) in some cases of disablement and old-age pensions.

A migrant worker who has been insured for a minimum period of a year (waiting time) in the country in which he claims the pension, will be granted it, in accordance with the principle of cumulative aggregate of work periods, if he paid contributions in other states.

If he is entitled to a disablement pension from one state while living in another member state, he will be paid the pension after a medical examination.

Lastly, some regulations make it possible to reinstitute disablement benefits that have been interrupted or to have these benefits transformed into retirement/old-age pensions.

It must however be noted that disability rates, which determine pension rates, can be very different from one country to another. Up to now, it has not been possible to co-ordinate them since mutual recognition between member states on the matter has not yet been achieved.

Retirement Pensions

Retirement pensions are part and parcel of social security benefits.[17] They are likely to be more and more significant since the number of people over 60 which, in Europe, was estimated at 77 million in 1995, will increase by

2020 by a minimum of 29 million and by a maximum of 44 million persons.[18]

The principle of unicity governing the above-mentioned benefits - namely, the legislation of only one state is implemented - does not apply to retirement and widows' pensions. The migrant worker reaching pensionable age will receive pensions from the countries in which he has paid contributions for at least one year, wherever he lives. It must be observed that this compulsory one-year period may penalise some workers who paid contributions in member states for shorter periods of time : these periods will not be taken into account and consequently, claimants will be paid lower pensions.

The amounts of pensions are calculated according to the years of insurance or years of residence in each state (cumulative aggregate principle). When calculations yield different results, depending on the periods spent in other member states, the competent institution is compelled to grant the migrant worker the highest amount of pension.

As the social security systems have not yet been harmonised, pensionable ages vary from country to country. A migrant worker, reaching pensionable age in one country (60 for instance), may be paid a low pension if (s)he contributed in this country for only a few years; (s)he will have to wait until (s)he reaches the legal pensionable age (67, for instance), in other countries in which (s)he paid contributions before (s)he can receive the pension from these other states.

Early Retirement and Additional Pensions

Early retirement pensions, though included in social security benefits, are not covered by regulation (EEC) 1408/71. This gap is all the more important since, over the last decades, there has been a rising trend towards a shorter occupational life. The number of people over 55 still in employment has noticeably decreased, and various schemes enable workers to stop working at an early age : specific allowances for elderly workers, early retirement schemes, disablement pensions, early payments of pensions in cases of unemployment, graduated retirement benefits and so on.

The proposal of the Commission, renewed in 1996, to ensure that early retirement pensions would be exportable, has not yet been put into practice.

Meanwhile, the report on Employment in Europe in 1997 stressed the potential advantages and the problems of a gradual transition to retirement.

The green paper (1997) on additional pensions put forward a legal framework at the European level to guarantee an efficient administration of additional pensions based on capitalisation. This loophole in Community law has not yet found a satisfactory solution. The Commission has been pondering over a Bill which the parliament approved in July 1998, aimed at preserving the rights to additional pensions (COM (97) 486).

From Social Security to Welfare/Solidarity

Non-Contributory Benefits

Specific non-contributory pensions for the elderly constitute another stumbling block for the Community legislation. These benefits, which are paid only when income falls below a given limit, depend on conditions of residence. Thus, the Belgium basic income for the elderly, the French national solidarity fund, and the Italian supplement to basic minimum pensions, for instance, are deferred if the claimant moves to another country.

These non-contributory pensions fall somewhere between social security and assistance (The very term 'assistance' tends now to be replaced by the terms 'social welfare' or 'solidarity').

In recent years, the increase in the number of dependent elderly has given rise to much debate. A new branch of social welfare may be emerging, which would account for these new needs. A new type of insurance might supply benefits in kind or in cash, delivered either by social security services and/or by personal social services. Compulsory contributions from the population against the risk of dependence has both an economic and a social interest. The dramatic increase of social needs offers potential opportunities in terms of employment and a strict policy is necessary if costs are to be kept under control. The specific links between social policy and economic performance were in fact underlined during the Conference of Amsterdam. Furthermore, the existence of some legal framework would guarantee equal opportunity in terms of sex as well as in terms of socio-economic category. It would also safeguard the principle of solidarity and reduce the anti-redistributive aspect of the current European schemes (the wealthy being more favoured than the poor) (European Commission communication, 1997, pp. 14-15).

Exclusion and Solidarity

The number of European citizens living at or below the poverty line has been increasing. This phenomenon does not affect just the elderly. Thus 'the combined effect of unemployment insurance schemes, which pay benefits for a limited period, and assistance schemes, whether for unemployment or as part of a minimum income guarantee can be inappropriate' and put the unemployed in a poverty trap. The latter must therefore be helped to acquire new skills 'within a framework of social protection that prevents a drift into poverty, and exclusion from the labour market and society in general' (European Commission communication, 1997, p.9).

The EU cannot ignore the needs of its citizens, but, as already mentioned, and in accordance with the regulation 1408/71, only social security benefits come under community legislation and can be exported. Up to now, assistance has exclusively been a national matter. However, the report of the High Level Panel rightly stated that a number of publicly-financed non-contributory benefits are hybrid: their characteristics include both insurance and assistance elements.[19] Since 1992, some of these benefits can no longer be exported and this clause is being challenged before the Court of Justice.[20]

Although assistance falls within the jurisdiction of each state, migrant workers should nevertheless be granted the 'same social advantages as national workers'.[21] For instance, they should theoretically be granted the discount cards on public transport delivered to large families, paid maternity leave and child benefits, minimum living standard allowances etc. The difficulties encountered in enforcing these rights, in particular in the case of large families, demonstrate that the distinction between social security and assistance/solidarity is indeed tenuous.[22]

In many countries entitlement to benefits is conditioned by work. However, unemployment has noticeably decreased the number of eligible people. The growing number of people cut from the labour market subsequently induced member states to establish a guaranteed minimum income, generally tax-based. France created the minimum living allowance (revenue minimum d'insertion or RMI) in 1988. It thus eventually joined other countries following a Beveridge pattern (8 member states out of 15 have a minimum living allowance, which has become a basic principle instituted by the European Social Charter). Solidarity, with a 'European minimum living allowance', might become the 'spearhead of the future European policy to fight against poverty' (French Institute of International Relations, 1996, pp. 202, 203).

Conclusion

The systems of public social protection of the member states represent more than 28 per cent of the aggregate GDP. However, this rate ranges from 16 per cent to 35 per cent in the EU,[23] which explains the variations in the rates of social rights granted to migrant workers.

The mechanism of co-ordination of the EU social security schemes (No. 1408/71) has tremendously improved the free circulation of people. This regulation has been continuously modified, yet, it was implemented more than 25 years ago and should be utterly updated. Social security schemes, which used to be mainly contributive, have become more and more state-funded and less contributory, while the distinction between insurance, assistance and taxation has become more blurred than in the past. These elements will have repercussions on the Community legislation of the next decades.

Member states are free to establish their social security norms. They should try to work on a common definition of entitlements to benefits and avoid large discrepancies between their respective schemes, so that all EEA citizens benefit from the same social rights.

As far as migrant workers are concerned, the sectors which particularly require updating include, as it has been shown, the conditions of maintenance of unemployment benefits, additional pension and early retirement schemes, and the conditions of eligibility to cross-border medical care.

Numerous modifications are being studied by the European authorities. Their aim is to offer EU workers greater protection, to simplify administrative proceedings, to try to iron out obstacles, eliminate reluctance on the part of member states, and to make the European legislation concerning social protection more comprehensive. For instance, the regulation does not apply to the special schemes for civil servants, but national civil services have been opened up to nationals from other member states. The High Level Panel, chaired by Mrs Simone Veil, mentions that the Commission proposal to include these special schemes is still pending. The Council has consequently resumed working on this matter to try to extend the scope of the regulation to civil servants.

Up to now students, retired persons and other people who lawfully live in another member state, who have sufficient resources and sickness insurance, are still excluded from the co-ordination of social security schemes. The Commission would like to fill this gap and speed up the work of the Council.

Among the current proposals, specific plans have been produced
- to extend the rights of the unemployed
- to include early retirement schemes in the regulation
- to ensure that any insured person can receive medical treatment and medicine anywhere in the EU
- to implement the use of social security 'smart' cards, readable all over the EU, 'which, besides their own finality, would demonstrate, together with the euro, the advantages of European integration'.[24]

The question of unanimity in the field of social security and social rights does, however, act as a brake upon the modernisation of the system of co-ordination. The European Parliament has deeply regretted that 'once more, the European Council applied art. 51 of the Treaty of Rome, in the Treaty of Amsterdam, so that co-decision requires the unanimity of the Council for the European Parliament... (It) reasserts that this constitutes one of the main hindrances to the implementation of a common scheme of social security for migrant workers'.[25]

The transfer of social rights of migrant workers alone was the subject of this paper. It should be emphasised that the current scope of the legislation covers neither non-active persons nor third country nationals, even though they are lawfully insured in a member state. In some cases, however, the CJEC has ruled in favour of third country nationals, as for example, in Mr Belbouab's case, mentioned in the introduction. A recent resolution of the Parliament now enables third country nationals, married to an EU worker to be granted the same cultural, fiscal and social rights as their spouses even if they divorce, provided they can prove they have been residing for 3 years in a member state.

Finally, a resolution proposal envisages extending the scope of the regulation to third country nationals who come under the social security scheme of one of the member states.

This enlargement to third country nationals testifies to a clear move on the part of the EU towards a policy of opening up the Community. Nevertheless, an efficient and consistent system for a European social policy - which must still be improved - will also have to cope with a possible enlargement of the European Community. How can all the citizens who move and work in this enlarged Europe be granted a high level of social protection, when there are no longer just 15 member states, but 20 or 30, each with different economic and social standards? This is a considerable challenge, which will, no doubt require prolonged effort to overcome.

Notes

1   These cases are excerpts from the book by Alan Guggenbülh and Stéphane Leclerc, *Droit Social Européen des Travailleurs Salariés et Indépendants*, Bruylant, Brussels, 1995, p. 285 and p. 254. In the first case, the European Court of Justice stated that a wage-carner paying contributions in a member State in which he worked could not be asked to pay for social security contributions by the member State in which he lived. As to Mr Belbouab, he was granted the right to benefit by the Community Law since he had the nationality of one of the member States during his period of work and insurance (Guggenbülh and Leclerc, 1995).

2   Article 1 of the *European Convention on the Legal Status of Migrant Workers*. Council of Europe (CE), ETS 93, Strasbourg, 24.11.1977, came into force in 1983.

3   See *La Protection Sociale des Français à L'Étranger*, Centre de Sécurité Sociale des Travailleurs Migrants, état au 1er janvier 1998.

4   *European Code of Social Security*, EC European Treaties ETS no. 48, Strasbourg, 1964, came into force in 1968.

5   *European Code of Social Security (revised)*, CE, ETS no. 139, Rome, 1990.

6   *European Convention on the Legal Status of Migrant Workers*, CE, ETS 93.

7   Munday and Ely (eds) provide a British point of view on the part played by the United Kingdom in the treaties of the European Union. (See Munday and Ely, 1996).

8   See *Employment and Social Policy*, http://europa.eu.int.

9   *Vos Droits de Sécurité Sociale Quand Vous Vous Déplacez dans l'UE*, Commission Européenne, Emploi et Affaires Socials, Guide Pratique, 1997, p. 32.

10 See the 1997 European Commission handbook, op cit, blue pages.

11 For example: a worker, insured for a 4 year period in a state where the waiting period is 5 years, who goes to work for 14 years in a state where the waiting period is 15 years, would not be entitled to any disablement pension, although he contributed for 18 years. See the 1997 European Commission handbook.

12 See Report of the High Level Panel on the free movement of persons chaired by Mrs Simone Veil, presented to the Commission on 18 mars 1997, Ch. 1. (Veil Report, 1997).

13 Art. 69.3 of regulation (EEC) no. 1408/71, and see Guggenbülh and Leclerc, 1995.

14 Decision of the Court of Justice of the European Communities (CJEC) 2 August 1993.

15 See Art. 72 to 76 of regulation (EEC) no. 1408/71.

16 As is the case in Belgium, France, Greece, Ireland, The Netherlands and the United Kingdom – except for specific categories, Guggenbülh and Leclerc, 1995, pp. 313-314.
17 In France they are at the top of the list in terms of social spending: in 1994, they represented 40 per cent of social benefits, i.e. FF900bn, see Maquart, 1987. In the United Kingdom, in 1994, benefits for old-age people (pensions, housing benefits and income support) represented 45 per cent of social welfare, see Glennerster, 1997, p.266. In 1995/96, retirement pensions alone represented £30,156bn, i.e. 32.4 per cent of social security benefits (Annual Abstract of Statistics, London, HMSO, 1997).
18 *Modernising and Improving Social Protection in the EU*, European Commission communication, 1997, file: A/socprot.htm.
19 The notion of social security, as defined by the CJEC, has a broad definition: any benefit granted on account of a legally defined situation, earmarked for the coverage of a risk listed in regulation (EEC) 1408/71, comes under the heading of social security. An allowance paid 'disregarding any individual or discretionary assessment of the personal needs of the beneficiary' is a social security benefit, so long as it is linked to sickness, old-age, death, disability, accidents at work, etc. It can therefore be exported, in principle. (Veil Report, 1997).
20 Court of Justice of the European Communities, Case 20/96 'Kelvin Snares'.
21 Art. 7§2 regulation (EEC) 1612/68.
22 For instance, in the case-law Hughes v. Chief Adjudication Officer, the CJEC confirmed that, although the family credit claimed by Mrs Hughes was a non-contributive benefit – granted in Northern Ireland to poor families – this benefit was to be considered as a family allowance, which had to be paid to the claimant, as any other social security benefit. Case C-78/91, quoted by Guggenbülh and Leclerc, 1995, p. 394).
23 The figures come from *Modernising and Improving Social Protection in the EU*, European Commission communication, 1997.
24 All these proposals can be found in the report of the European Commission on the free circulation of people, dated July 22, 1998, http://europa.eu.int.
25 § 14 of the Parliament resolutions on the Commission communication '*Action Plans for the Free Circulation of Workers*', July 3, 1998, COM(97) 0586-C4-0650/97

References

Carraud, M. (1994), *Droit Social Européen*, Publisud, Paris.
De Montalbert, M. (1997), 'L'Europe Sociale', in *La Protection Sociale en France*, La Documentation Française, Collection Les Notices, Paris.
Dumont, J.P. (1988), *Les Systèmes Etrangers de Sécurité Sociale*, Economica, Paris.
Dupeyroux, J.J. (1993), *Droit de la Sécurité Sociale*, Dalloz, Paris.
French Institute of International Relations (1996), *Rapport Annuel Mondial sur le Système Economique et les Stratégies*, (Ramses 96) Dunod, Paris.
Glennerster, H. (1997), *Paying for Welfare Towards 2000*, Harvester Wheatsheaf, London.
Guggenbülh, A. and Leclerc, S. (1995), *Droit Social Européen des Travaillers Salaries et Indépendents*, Bruylant, Brussels.
Henrard, J-C. and Veysset-Puijalon, B. (1997), 'Les Personnes Agées et la Dependance', in *La Protection Sociale en France*, La Documentation Française, Collection Les Notices, Paris.

Her Majesty's Stationery Office (1997), *Annual Abstract of Statistics*, HMSO, London.

Hill, M. (1996), *Social Policy: A Comparative Analysis*, Prentice Hall/Harvester Wheatsheaf, London.

Jaoui-Pylypiw, E. (1997), 'L'Etat Providence Sous le Gouvernement Conservateur: le Cas des Personnes Agées': L'Etat Providence: Bilan de 18 Années de Gouvernement Conservateur', *Revue Française de Civilisation Britannique*, vol. IX, no. 4, Université de Provence, Aix-Marseille I, Aix en Provence.

Maquart, B. (1997), 'Les Régimes de Retraite', in *La Protection Sociale en France*, La Documentation Française, Collection Les Notices, Paris.

Munday, B. and Ely, P. (eds) (1996), *Social Care in Europe*, Prentice Hall/Harvester Wheatsheaf, London.

Ogus, A., Barent, E. and Wikeley, B. (eds) (1995), *The Law of Social Security*, Butterworths, London.

Veil, S. (1997), *Report of the High Level Panel on the Free Movement of Persons*, presented to the Commission on 18th March 1997.

Viossat, C-C. (1997), 'Protections et Institutions Sociales', in *La Protection Sociale en France*, La Documentation Française, Collection Les notices, Paris.

Other documents cited:

Centre de Sécurité Sociale des Travailleurs Migrants, *La Protection Sociale des Française à l'etranger*. État au 1er janvier 1998.

Commission Européenne, Emploi et Affairs Sociales: Guide Practique (1997), 'Vos droits de sécurité sociale quand vous vous déplacé dans l'UE'.

European Code of Social Security, EC European Treaties ETS No. 48, Strasbourg 1964.

European Code of Social Security (revised). CE ETS No. 139, Rome 1990.

European Commission communication (1997), *Modernising and Improving Social Protection in the EU*.

European Convention on the Legal Status of Migrant Workers, Council of Europe (CE), ETS 93, Strasbourg 24th November 1977.

The Treaty of Rome 1958.

8 Flexible Labour Markets, Citizenship and Pension Provision: a View from the UK

RUTH HANCOCK AND CLAUDINE MCCREADIE

Introduction

In the UK, achieving an adequate income in retirement depends crucially on having built-up good pension rights during one's working life. On its own, the basic state pension - the first tier of the UK pension system - does not provide an adequate income. It is already below the social assistance level and on current policies will fall further behind it in future. Although more pensioners now have income from a second tier pension, many still do not or have only small amounts. Patchy work histories, frequent job changes and self-employment are all likely to lead to poor retirement incomes. In common with France, the present UK Government is currently conducting a pensions review. One fact is clear. In relation to all aspects of social welfare, the Government stresses the importance of paid work (Stationery Office, 1998a). It argues among other things that paid work provides people with the best opportunities for saving for their retirement. Its proposals for pension reform are based partly on the principle that those who have spent their lifetimes in paid work should be able to retire with a pension above the social assistance level (Stationery Office, 1998b). Whether the new so-called flexible labour market will undermine this work-based strategy for pension provision is an open question.

This paper considers the different forms that labour market flexibility can take, the implications of each of them for the accumulation of pension rights, the true extent of labour market flexibility in the UK and its relationship to trends in forms of activity other than paid work. Evidence is drawn from existing studies and from original analysis of one of the UK's nationally representative household surveys. We discuss the merits of alternative routes to pension provision in the light of this evidence. The next section gives a brief overview of pensions in the UK. Section two discusses labour market trends and in section three we consider how greater labour flexibility interacts

117

with the accumulation of pension rights. Policy responses are discussed in section four. Section five concludes.

Pensions in the UK

In the UK, people accumulate pension rights through the state pension scheme, through schemes run by their employers ('occupational' schemes) and through personal (individual) pension arrangements with an insurance company. The state pension is in two parts: a flat-rate 'basic' pension and an earnings-related component, the State Earnings Related Pension Scheme (SERPS). Rights to the basic pension derive from contributions when in employment or self-employment and 'credits' when unemployed involuntarily or prevented from working due to ill-health or disability. Since 1978, 'home responsibilities protection' means that periods spent out of the labour force looking after children or caring for elderly or disabled relatives do not necessarily result in reduced rights to the basic state pension. In general, people can now earn a full or near-full basic state pension even if they do not spend all their working-age lives in paid work. This was not the case for the current generation of pensioners. In particular, many of today's older married women rely on their husband's pension contributions to earn them a married woman's state pension which is only 60 per cent of the full rate. Rights to SERPS are accumulated by paying contributions on earnings as an employee but are not earned when self-employed. SERPS acts as a form of limited compulsory second-tier pension for periods spent in employment: all employees earning above a minimum must contribute to SERPS or to an employer-run scheme or to a personal pension.[1] There is no similar compulsion for periods spent self-employed or out of the labour force. In retirement, social assistance (paid on a means-tested basis) acts as a safety net. Currently the basic state pension is below the minimum income for older people as defined by social assistance (Income Support). Anyone without a second-tier pension is therefore entitled to a means-tested supplement.[2]

The UK pension system works well for people who spend most of their working lives in full-time employment, especially if they have belonged to the same employer-run pension scheme for most of it. In the private sector this generally means staying with the same employer because there are relatively few industry-wide occupational pensions schemes. Most occupational schemes are of the 'final salary' type in which the pension which is paid on retirement is related to the employee's earnings near the time of leaving the scheme. Under this sort of scheme frequent changes of job and pension scheme result in lower pension rights than if the same earnings had been earned in one job, assuming that during their lifetimes, people experience real increases in salary, through promotion for example. To counteract this effect there have been some improvements in arrangements for transferring rights between schemes and in protecting the value of preserved pension rights against inflation.

The introduction of personal pensions in 1987 aimed to address some of the rigidities within employer-run schemes and in principle facilitate a more flexible labour market. At the same time it became illegal for employers to compel employees to join their pension scheme, giving employees the choice of being in SERPS or a personal pension instead. However, personal pensions have not proved successful for those who can afford only small contributions which can be absorbed by insurance companies' charges. Personal pensions have also been tainted by the 'mis-selling' scandal in which some employees ill-advisedly left their employers' schemes and took out less favourable personal pension schemes instead. The level of pension which can be earned through SERPS has been cut substantially since its introduction in order to reduce its cost to the tax-payer. In the present context one of the most significant changes was to make SERPS rights dependent on earnings averaged over the whole of one's working lives (currently 44 years for women and 45 years for men) rather than the best 20 years' of earnings. The 'best 20 years' rule would have been particularly beneficial to those with spells out of the labour market or in part-time low paid work.

At the time of writing, the UK Government is consulting on its proposals for pension reform (Stationery Office, 1998). There are three main aspects to these proposals. A greater commitment than before now to increase the social assistance level for pensioners (to be called the Minimum Income Guarantee in future) according to annual earnings growth. SERPS will be replaced with a new Second State Pension (SSP) which will give greater state pension rights to employees on low lifetime earnings. Finally, it will be possible to contract-out of second-tier state pensions via a new form of personal pension provided by the private sector. These so-called Stakeholder Pensions will be subject to a simple (and, for those with earnings below a given level, generous) form of tax-relief and must conform to regulations concerning charges and governance. They are aimed at those on modest earnings without access to an occupational pension and for whom existing personal pensions are too costly. It is the proposals to replace SERPS with SSP which are of most concern here and we return to them in section four below.

Labour Market Trends

Setting the Scene

At between 58 and 59 million people, the sizes of the French and UK populations are now very similar, although the UK has an older age structure. The main trends in the labour market over the past 25 years have also been very similar:

- More women are working.
- Within their working age populations, fewer younger and older people work.
- A shift in employment from the manufacturing to the service sector. The service sector now accounts for 70 per cent of employees in both countries.
- Higher unemployment since the end of the 1970s. Both countries have experienced two sharp recessions, one at the end of the 1970s and the other in the early 1990s, although the precise timing of the recessions has been rather different.

The most obvious differences in the two labour markets relate to the continuing existence in France, until 2002, of compulsory military service for young people; differences in pension age between the two countries - 60 in France for both men and women, and 65 in the UK for men and 60 for women (by 2020 it will be 65 for both); and the pattern of female employment in the two countries. Fewer women overall were employed in France in 1996 (about 10 million compared with 12 million in the UK), but those who are employed are very much more likely to be in full-time work. Around two-thirds of French women work full time, compared with just over half in the UK (Lee, Midy, Smith and Summerfield, 1998).

However, these apparent similarities may mask underlying differences between the two countries. For example, while UK and French unemployment among males has moved very similarly, unemployment in France among women has not only been higher overall, but has moved

120

upward whereas in the UK it has fallen steadily since 1984. Secondly, in the UK, compared with other EC countries, there has been a faster growth in self-employment and more experience of self-employment. Finally, a higher proportion of UK households have low incomes and at a time when the gap between those on low and high wages has increased in the UK, in France it has decreased.

Some of these changes are more relevant to the issue of labour market flexibility and its implications for pension provision than others. Salient trends discussed below include changes in the distribution of work between households, the related growth in part-time employment, self-employment, accompanying changes in income and its distribution and changes in job security and tenure.

Changes in the Distribution of Work Among Households

A revolutionary change has occurred in the UK in the distribution of work across households. The proportion of working age *individuals* in employment was similar in 1990 and 1975 but the proportion of individuals living in *households* containing no-one in work roughly doubled in that period and had trebled by 1993. The reason is that the number of households with two earners and the number with no earners had risen at the same time. This is gender related - employment among women has risen but it has risen largely in households where the other partner is working. The number of two adult households in which only a man works has declined steadily from 27.4 per cent of all households in 1975 to 13.6 per cent in 1993.

At the same time, unemployment among men has risen but in households where no-one else is working. Between 1975 and 1993, the proportion of all households which were households consisting of two adults in which neither worked rose from 2 per cent to more than 6 per cent. There has been no change in the proportion of women working whose partners were not in work (around 40 per cent in 1975 and 1993). In fact, the severity and intensity of unemployment has increased. Non-employed members of households where no-one works are less likely to find work than those where another member of the household has work (Gregg and Wadsworth, 1996).

Part-Time Working

There has been a substantial growth in part-time employment. In 1975 part-time work accounted for 17 per cent of all employment and self-employment. By 1993, 23 per cent of all employment was part-time and over 40 per cent of people entering work from non-employment entered part-time work (Gregg and Wadsworth, 1996). Women remain much more likely than men to work part-time. Our own analysis of General Household Survey data (Table 8.1) shows that although the proportion of working-age men employed for under 16 hours[3] a week more than doubled between 1985 and 1995 it did so from a very low base to stand at only 2 per cent in 1995. In contrast the proportion of working-age women employed for fewer than 16 hours stayed at about 10 per cent.

Self-Employment

The numbers of self-employed people in the UK grew very rapidly during the 1980s and these new entrants were disproportionately likely to be young and female. By 1995, they constituted 17 per cent of those in work (Spencer, 1996, reporting Labour Force Survey figures). The nature of self-employment has also changed as work which used to be undertaken by employees has been contracted-out to the self-employed (Pension Provision Group, 1998). It is clear from research that in the UK, self-employed people are a very diverse group with very diverse incomes. The distribution of earnings from self-employment is more unequal with concentrations at both ends of the distribution. Having been self-employed strongly increases a person's chances of being in a low income group, of having minimal savings and no occupational pension in retirement (Meager, Court and Moralee, 1996).

Implications for Income Distribution

Employment polarisation has been accompanied by increasing wage inequality in the UK (Gosling, Machin and Meghir, 1994). A fundamental consequence of these changes has been the impact on incomes. There has been a very substantial increase in inequality in the UK. Between 1975 and 1990, the income of the poorest 20 per cent fell by 10 per cent while the income of the top 20 per cent rose by 45 per cent (Gardiner, 1993, quoted in Gregg and Wadsworth, 1996).

Compared with those in full-time employment, part-time employees and the self-employed have a greater chance of being in the bottom decile of the income distribution, as do women compared with men, even controlling for employment status (Meager, Court and Moralee, 1996).

Mobility Between EU Countries

A key aspect of European Union policy is to facilitate the mobility of labour between member countries. Pension schemes, indexation rules and so forth vary substantially between countries and the co-ordination rules are very complex. The result is that there is a real possibility of financial loss being incurred by moving within EU countries (Luckhaus and Moffat, 1996).

Job Security and Tenure

There is only incomplete information on the extent to which people have less secure jobs than they used to have, or change jobs more frequently, although the changes discussed above, all suggest that this is likely to be the case. One problem in this area is the difference between *ex-ante* and *ex-post* security. Short-term contracts may be renewed with the effect that job tenures change little but for the individual concerned there is still considerable uncertainty.

Some evidence on changing job tenures is contained in Table 8.1 which presents an analysis of General Household Survey data for 1985 and 1995. It shows the distribution of length of time in present job according to employment category: employed for at least 16 hours a week; employed for under 16 hours a week; and self-employed. Figures are shown separately for men and women. Also shown are the percentages of working-age men and women in each of these employment categories. The latter confirm the reduction in full-time employment and growth in self-employment for men. For women, this definition of part-time work shows no growth between the period but there is an increase in the proportion working at least 16 hours a week from 45 per cent to 51 per cent and an overall increase in the proportion in paid work from 60 per cent to 67 per cent. The data do not enable us to provide a comparison of the duration of jobs which have lasted more than 10 years but comparison is possible for shorter durations. Overall there have been only small changes. Within the employment categories there has been more change. Among men employed at least 16 hours a week, more have held their current jobs for under 1 year and fewer for 10 or more years. However, for the self-employed and to some extent those who work under 16 hours a week, there is some evidence that durations have become longer. This is consistent with the greater prevalence of self-employment and part-time work. It suggests that such jobs can no longer be regarded as temporary and people's pension behaviour and pension policies need to recognise this.

For women, changes in job durations also appear small although overall durations have become longer if anything. Again this is consistent with more women participating in paid work. It emphasises the need for pension policies which are suited to their working patterns which are still very different from those of men. Women are still more likely than men to be working shorter hours and to have been in their jobs for shorter periods of time. In 1995, 37 per cent of all men in paid work had been in their jobs for at least 10 years. This was the case for only 22 per cent of women. The table also shows (last row) the proportion in each employment category accounted for by women. In 1985 women made up 42 per cent of all working-age people in paid work, 10 years later they accounted for 45 per cent. The increase among those working at least 16 hours a week was even greater. Although they continue to make up the large majority of those employed for under 16 hours a week, this has fallen from 98 per cent to 81 per cent as more men are now in this category.

Increased Flexibility and Pensions

These labour market changes have significant implications for retirement income, and therefore for pensions policy. 'Flexibility', despite its resonance of the desirable in the English language can be a euphemism for any or all of the following developments, which have the potential to interrupt a smooth flow of adequate earnings from which to save for retirement:

- more job changes and shorter job durations
- more fixed-term employment contracts and fewer permanent jobs
- more part-time jobs, possibly with people having several part-time jobs at the same time

Table 8.1 Length of time in present job by employment category and gender, people of working-age (16-59/64), Great Britain 1995 and 1985

	Employed 16+ hours per week		Employed < 16 hours per week		Self-employed		All employed self-employed	
	1985 %	1995 %	1985 %	1995 %	1985 %	1995 %	1985 %	1995 %
Men								
< 6 months	8	10	38	30	7	5	8	10
6 months – 1 year	6	7	16	17	6	4	6	7
1 - 5 years	26	26	38	39	30	24	26	26
5-10 years	22	22	3	5	17	19	21	21
10+ years	39	36	5	9	40	48	39	37
All durations	100	100	100	100	100	100	100	100
Sample size	5198	4221	81	172	841	962	6120	5355
% of all working-age men in employment category	66	60	1	2	11	14	78	76
Women <6 months	12	10	19	19	12	6	13	11
6 months – 1 year	9	9	14	14	10	8	10	10
1 - 5 years	32	32	40	39	37	33	34	33
5-10 years	24	26	15	16	21	26	22	25
10+ years	24	24	11	13	21	27	21	22
All durations	100	100	100	100	100	100	100	100
Sample size	3312	3449	4371	743	277	344	4371	4536
% of all working-age women in employment category	45	51	11	11	4	5	60	67
% of all in employment category who are women	39	45	98	81	25	26	42	45

Source: General Household Surveys analysed through the Gerontology Data Service

- more self-employment and/or more people experiencing self-employment at some time
- work which would previously have been carried out by employees being contracted-out as a new kind of self-employment
- more people experiencing unemployment at some time in their lives, for example, between finishing one fixed-term contract and starting another
- more low paid and non-pensionable jobs.

Consideration of these changes supports the view that employment policy is quite as important to protection in old age as pensions policy (Luckhaus and Moffat, 1996). The Pension Provision Group, which recently carried out an independent review for the government of pension provision in the UK, concluded that pension policy in isolation could only go so far in resolving the pension problems of women and the self-employed (Pension Provision Group, 1998). The developments in the UK labour market which we have outlined all point to the relevance of these comments. Women, who live longer, and, to this extent, face a higher risk of living with disability, are disproportionately represented in those employment groups for whom future income security is least assured. Their chances of being in low paid jobs, of being below the government's threshold for contributing to a state pension, of not being in an occupational pension scheme, are all significantly higher than those of men.

Short durations and frequent changes of jobs and traditional 'final-salary' employer pension schemes do not mix well. Fixed-term and temporary jobs may deter people from joining an employer's schemes. The decision to join an employer's pension scheme because one might remain in the job, or not to join it, because one might leave is a difficult one. Anyone leaving an employer pension scheme after belonging to it for less than two years is not entitled to a preserved pension but to only a refund of his or her contributions and so loses the benefit of the employer's contributions. Low earnings - whether due to part-time work, self-employment or poorly paid full-time employment - and unemployment make affording pension contributions difficult. Short-term contracts, even if renewed, exacerbate this problem.

Current Policy Responses

How far do the UK Government's proposals for improved retirement income address these issues of labour market changes? At the level of the safety net, a small increase in the level of social assistance is proposed which is payable to pensioners whose resources fall below this level; the commitment to increase the level in line with earnings growth will also confer some benefit. However, in terms of citizenship rights to pensions without means testing, there are two major planks to the Government's proposals. First, in response to the risk of poverty during working life and in retirement, the Government places great emphasis on participation in paid work through welfare-to-work policies. The proposal for new Stakeholder Pensions to be run in partnership with the private sector stems from the recognition that occupational pensions are not open to everyone in work, and may be less suitable for a more flexible labour market. The Government view is that they will be more suitable (less costly) than personal pensions for people who can afford only small contributions while being portable from one job to another. Secondly, in response to the recognition that these pensions will not be suitable for the lowest paid, the new Second State Pension (SSP) will confer higher state pension rights for lower paid workers. Essentially the proposal is to replace pension rights which are purely proportional to earnings (between a lower and upper limit) with rights which will represent a higher proportion of lifetime earnings for the lower paid than for the higher paid. At first, this will still entail some earnings-relation, although ultimately this second tier of state pension may become flat rate. As with the present system of SERPS it will be possible to opt out of this second tier of state pension via an occupational, personal or stakeholder pension and pay lower state pension contributions as a result.

It is interesting to consider who might benefit from the first two proposals and who might still be reliant on social assistance in later life. To do this it is necessary to consider in more detail how the new SSP is proposed to operate. All employees earning above a lower limit (approximately £3,000 a year) will be treated as if they have earnings of £9,000 a year. If their average lifetime earnings are between these two limits and they do not opt out of SSP, their total state pension on retirement will be at the social assistance level for a single person[4]. A lifetime, in this context is 49 years, from the age of 16 to the age of 65. Credits of equivalent value will be given to certain periods out of the labour force or earning below the lower limit. Credits will be available in respect of periods looking after a child aged 5 or under, or spending at least 35 hours a week providing care for someone in receipt of disability benefits. Unlike the first tier of pension, credits will not be available once the youngest child is aged 6, or for periods of unemployment.

Table 8.2 categorises today's working age population according to their present pension coverage, so far as this can be deduced from the data. Again it is based on the 1995 General Household Survey. Overall 35 per cent of working age men and 31 per cent of women are currently contributing to a pension scheme run by their employer (an occupational scheme). Membership is highest among the 25-49 year old age group and lowest among the under 25s. 23 per cent of men but only 12 per cent of women are contributing to a personal pension but not to an occupational scheme. Ten per cent of men and 13 per cent of women are not contributing to either an occupational or personal pension but are earning enough to be contributing to SERPS. Over 20 per cent of the under 25s are in this category. Altogether 68 per cent of working age men and 62 per cent of working age women appear to be currently contributing to a pension beyond the basic state pension. Of those who are not, some may have done so in the past, and others, especially those currently under 25, are likely to do so in the future. But some of those currently contributing may not have done so for all their working lives and may cease to contribute or have breaks from contributing before they retire.

The main groups who are currently earning rights to a basic state pension but to no second tier pension are the self-employed, those looking after children (and in receipt of Child Benefit) and the unemployed. Six per cent of men and 4 per cent of women are in the first group. Only 1 per cent of men, but 20 per cent of women are in the second. Only very small proportions of working age men and women are in receipt of Invalid Care Allowance which at present is the main route to home responsibilities protection for people caring for disabled adults or older people, although some people who do not receive this benefit may qualify if they spend at least 35 hours a week caring for a disabled person. Eight per cent of working age men but only 3 per cent of women class themselves as unemployed. Providing they are available for work and actively seeking it they will be being credited with contributions for the basic state pension. Altogether 14 per cent of men but 23 per cent of women appear to be earning rights to the basic state pension alone. Finally there are those not currently earning any pension rights. The main groups are the young in education or earning below the minimum needed to contribute to the state pension. But some 6 per cent of women aged 50-59 are in work but earning less than this amount. Another 17 per cent of women in this age group classify themselves as 'looking after the home/family' but do not receive the main benefits which qualify them for home responsibility protection.

Table 8.2 Pension coverage among the working-age population, by age group and gender, Great Britain 1995 - men

	Men aged:			
Currently contributing to a 2nd/3rd tier pension:	16-24	25-49	50-64	All aged 16+
Employed and in an occupational scheme	11	44	29	35
Not in an occupational scheme but employed/self-employed in a personal pension scheme	9	28	22	23
Not in an occupational or personal pension but employed and earning enough to contribute to SERPS	24	8	7	10
Currently earning only the basic state pension (1st tier):				
Self-employed, not contributing to a personal	4	6	7	6
Other, receiving Child Benefit and so eligible for home responsibility protection for the basic state pension	*	1	*	1
Other, receiving Invalid Care Allowance so eligible for home responsibility protection for the basic state pension	*	1	*	*
Other, unemployed so eligible for credits for the basic state pension	16	7	6	8
Other, man aged 60-64, eligible for credits for basic state pension	0	0	14	4
Not currently earning 1st/2nd tier pension*				
Other, earning below the minimum for the basic state pension and SERPS	10	1	*	2
Other, in education or training	23	1	*	4
Other, retired	0	0	4	2
Other, looking after home/family	0	*	1	*
Other	3	4	9	5
Total	100	100	100	100
Sample size	1027	3871	1858	6756

* Some may be earning 1st tier pension rights if they are spending at least 35 hours a week caring for someone in receipt of relevant disability benefits.
Source: General Household Survey, analysed through the Gerontology Data Service

Table 8.3 Pension coverage among the working-age population, by age group and gender, Great Britain 1995 - women

	Women aged:			
Currently contributing to a 2nd/3rd tier pension:	16-24	25-49	50-64	All aged 16+
Employed and in an occupational scheme	14	31	24	27
Not in an occupational scheme but employed/self-employed in a personal pension scheme	5	14	11	12
Not in an occupational or personal pension but employed and earning enough to contribute to SERPS	22	15	14	16
Currently earning only the basic state pension (1st tier):				
Self-employed, not contributing to a personal pension	1	4	4	4
Other, receiving Child Benefit and so eligible for home responsibility protection for the basic state pension	12	27	4	20
Other, receiving Invalid Care Allowance so eligible for home responsibility protection for the basic state pension	*	*	1	*
Other, unemployed so eligible for credits for the basic state pension	8	2	2	3
Other, man aged 60-64, eligible for credits for basic state pension	0	0	0	0
Not currently earning 1st/2nd tier pension*				
Other, earning below the minimum for the basic state pension and SERPS	12	1	6	4
Other, in education or training	22	*	0	4
Other, retired	0	0	7	1
Other, looking after home/family	2	3	17	6
Other	2	2	10	4
Total	100	100	100	100
Sample size	995	4176	1299	6470

* Some may be earning 1st tier pension rights if they are spending at least 35 hours a week caring for someone in receipt of relevant disability benefits.
Source: General Household Survey, analysed through the Gerontology Data Service

Table 8.4 Pension coverage among the working-age population, by age group and gender, Great Britain 1995 – men and women combined

	Men and women combined, aged:			
Currently contributing to a 2nd/3rd tier pension:	16-24	25-49	50-64	All aged 16+
Employed and in an occupational scheme	13	37	27	31
Not in an occupational scheme but employed/self-employed in a personal pension scheme	7	21	18	18
Not in an occupational or personal pension but employed and earning enough to contribute to SERPS	23	12	10	13
Currently earning only the basic state pension (1st tier):				
Self-employed, not contributing to a personal	3	5	6	5
Other, receiving Child Benefit and so eligible for home responsibility protection for the basic state pension	6	15	2	10
Other, receiving Invalid Care Allowance so eligible for home responsibility protection for the basic state pension	*	*	1	*
Other, unemployed so eligible for credits for the basic state pension	12	4	5	6
Other, man aged 60-64, eligible for credits for basic state pension	0	0	8	2
Not currently earning 1st/2nd tier pension*				
Other, earning below the minimum for the basic state pension and SERPS	11	1	3	3
Other, in education or training	22	1	*	4
Other, retired	0	0	5	1
Other, looking after home/family	1	2	7	3
Other	3	3	9	4
Total	100	100	100	100
Sample size	2022	8047	3157	13226

* Some may be earning 1st tier pension rights if they are spending at least 35 hours a week caring for someone in receipt of relevant disability benefits.
Source: General Household Survey, analysed through the Gerontology Data Service

131

It is hard to see how stakeholder pensions could help many of those currently not contributing to a second tier pension apart from the self-employed. The other categories have no or only very low earnings from which to make contributions. Stakeholder pensions *may* provide better value for people currently contributing to SERPS or to a personal pension or more portability than occupational pensions. But that does not help people not in a position to contribute to them. The proposed changes to state second tier pensions are therefore a crucial part of the Government's pension policy. Although they will not help people who continue to earn below the lower earnings limit (unless they also qualify for credits), the proposed changes do provide a substantial incentive to earn just above this lower limit (Pension Provision Group, 1999), increasing the pension rights earned by so doing. In fact, at the national minimum wage, 17½ hours a week of paid work will be sufficient to earn SSP rights, whereas if the work is unpaid in the form of caring for a disabled person, 35 hours is required.

The Government's proposals therefore reinforce a lifetime of paid work as a route to adequate retirement incomes. They provide improved pension rights for a lifetime of low paid employment. Although acknowledging some other forms of citizenship, in practice those with broken work records still look likely to be dependent to some extent on social assistance in retirement.

A fourth route, which is not currently attracting support within government, would be a true citizen's pension to provide everyone with a basic income in retirement, ideally at an adequate, if modest, level. Possibilities for a citizen's pension for the UK have recently been examined (Sutherland, 1998) and this work suggests that it is not prohibitive in terms of cost as long as the costs are spread across all citizens including pensioners.

Conclusions

It is probably fair to say, that within the European Union, there has not been a great deal of interest in population ageing. Despite the Maastricht treaty and the existence of European wide measures on both state and occupational pensions, harmonisation of pension policies appears extremely unlikely in the foreseeable future (Luckhaus and Moffat, 1996). Matters concerning benefits and pensions are amongst those over which member states retain the widest discretion. Perhaps this may be related to the extent to which social policies are embedded in particular national, political and economic contexts (Maddox, 1992) and to their great diversity. The relationship of occupational pension schemes to capital markets is only one example of this. Although a strong degree of humility is required in thinking about the transferability of policies, one of the most valuable aspects of cross-country comparisons is in challenging national customs and conventions. There seem to us to be at least three challenges from our examination of the implications of changes in UK labour market "flexibility" for pension provision. These are:

1.   What are the key areas for retirement income that need to be tackled through employment policy, as opposed to pensions policy?

2.   How can citizenship in its broadest sense be acknowledged in retirement, where pension rights depend largely on uninterrupted paid employment?

3.   What is the proper balance between pension rights and means-tested safety nets in retirement, bearing in mind that those whose citizenship has been other than through a lifetime of paid work are most at risk of dependence on the latter in old-age?

Acknowledgement

Material from the General Household Survey, made available by the Office for National Statistics and the Data Archive has been used with permission. Analysis of the General Household Survey was undertaken through the Gerontology Data Service at the Age Concern Institute of Gerontology, King's College London. All responsibility for the analysis reported here and its interpretation rests with the authors

Notes

1   Personal pensions and most private sector occupational pensions are funded pension schemes. State pensions – the basic pension and SERPS – are financed on a pay-as-you-go basis. That is state pensions being paid today are paid for from contributions from today's working-age population.
2   Means-tested help with rents and local taxes are also available and can be received by pensioners even if they have incomes above the social assistance level.
3   16 hours is a threshold which is relevant for some social security benefits. It does, however, represent a lower definition than is usually used.
4   Because state pension rights will be increased only in line with price inflation during retirement and because the social assistance level increases at older ages, they would, however, fall below this level during retirement.

References

Gardiner, K. (1993), *A Survey of Income Inequality Over the Last Twenty Years - How Does the UK Compare?* STICERD/LSE, London, Discussion Paper WSP/100.

Gosling, A., Machin, S. and Meghir, C. (1994), 'What Has Happened to Men's Wages Since the Mid-1960s?', *Fiscal Studies* 15(4), pp. 63-87.

Gregg, P. and Wadsworth, J. (1996), 'More Work in Fewer Households?' in, Hills, J. (ed.), *New Inequalities: The Changing Distribution of Income and Wealth in the United Kingdom*, Cambridge University Press, Cambridge, pp. 181-207.

Lee, P., Midy, P., Smith, A. and Summerfield, C. (1998), 'French and British Societies: A Comparison', *Social Trends*(28), Stationery Office, London, pp. 15-28.

Luckhaus, L. and Moffat, G. (1996), *Serving the Market and the People's Needs? The Impact of European Union Law on Pensions in the UK*, York Publishing Services, York.

Maddox, G. L. (1992), 'Long Term Care Policies in Perspective.' *Ageing and Society*, 12, pp. 355-368.

Meager, N., Court, G. and Moralee, J. (1996), 'Self-employment and the Distribution of Income' in, Hills, J. (ed.), *New Inequalities: The Changing Distribution of Income and Wealth in the United Kingdom,* Cambridge University Press, Cambridge, pp. 208-235.

Pension Provision Group (1998), *We all Need Pensions - the Prospects for Pension Provision*, The Stationery Office, London.

Pension Provision Group (1999), *Response of the Pension Provision Group to the Green Paper on Pensions*, PPG/AON CONSULTING, Harrow.

Spencer, P. (1996), 'Reactions to a Flexible Labour Market' in, Jowells, R. (ed.), *British Social Attitudes Survey 13th Report*, Dartmouth, Aldershot.

Stationery Office (1998a), *New Ambitions for our Country: A New Contract for Welfare*, Cm. 3805, The Stationery Office, London.

Stationery Office, (1998b), *A New Contract for Welfare: Partnership in Pensions,* Cm 4179, The Stationery Office, London.

Sutherland, H. (1998), *A Citizen's Pension,* Microsimulation Unit, Department of Applied Economics, University of Cambridge.

9 Are Proposals for Pension Reform Compatible with Adaptation to Employment Flexibility?

MICHAEL HILL

Introduction

Contemporary debates about pension policies have been very influenced by the World Bank's analysis of them in terms of three pillars:
1. A mandatory publicly managed pillar.
2. A mandatory privately managed pillar.
3. A voluntary pillar.

The World Bank's view that efforts should be made to develop mandatory privately managed pillars has been picked up by many pension reform advocates. This chapter will look at the relevance of that approach in France and the United Kingdom, with particular reference to employment flexibility but does so in the context of Hancock and McCreadie's treatment of the issue elsewhere in this collection.

The chapter begins with a brief description of current pension policies in the United Kingdom and France, showing that at present neither country has a mandatory private pillar. Rather, France has a strong corporatist second pillar whilst the United Kingdom combines a weak first pillar and a strong third pillar with problems in between.

It will then explore the current debates about pension reform, which are driven by proposals that systems should be designed in which the second and third pillars are more central, evaluating the arguments used for both funding and private management. It will suggest that the threat of the so-called 'demographic time bomb' has been widely misused in those arguments, particularly inasmuch as it is not related to changing patterns of employment.

It will be argued that whilst growing employment flexibility seems to provide support for the view that citizens should each have separate funded pension accounts, in fact the solidarity which was seen to be of great importance to the pioneers of state pension schemes may be of even greater importance in a flexible labour market. This is because the road to a flexible labour market is in many respects an unplanned one in which flexibility is rather more forced upon workers by economic and family circumstances than chosen by them.

Pensions in the United Kingdom and France

France is difficult to classify in terms of the World Bank model set out above. It has two distinct pillars - the first of which is public. But its second pillar can only be described as 'private' inasmuch as it is corporately managed by representatives of both sides of industry. It is certainly not managed by private entrepreneurs and, even more importantly, it is not funded. It embodies important elements of cross-occupational solidarity in that nearly all employees are within the two main schemes, the split being between manual workers and cadres. The French second tier scheme is a strong one, offering good benefits to those who are able to be long term labour market participants. Accordingly private third tier schemes have not developed to any great extent in France.

This situation has not inhibited the proponents of second tier schemes along World Bank lines, such as insurance companies and banks. A number of private legislative bills have been put forward. But 'successive governments ... have been very cautious on the matter. The consensus concerning the pay-as-you-go technique is high in France and funding with regard to pension provision is a touchy issue' (Reynaud, 1997, p.93).

The position in the United Kingdom is very different. Beveridge's proposals for pensions, enacted in the 1940s, very clearly envisaged the state as only the provider of a basic first pillar. Supplementary pensions arrangements were seen as matters for individual choice (essentially third pillar schemes). At the same time large organisations, including the civil service and other state employers, had their own schemes which - notwithstanding the fact that a public employer was underwriting them - were to all intents and purposes private schemes. Their special features were however that they were 'final salary' based schemes rather than contribution based.

Big employers very largely followed this lead from public employers. From the late 1950s onwards governments sought ways to extend supplementary pension coverage to those employees whose employers would not or could not develop schemes. The political compromise eventually developed was an unfunded state second pillar (the State Earnings Related Pension Supplement - SERPS) set up in 1976 for all employees not able to join private schemes at least as good as SERPS.

The Thatcher government then went back on that political compromise, seriously weakening SERPS and offering tax incentives to individuals to join third pillar money purchase schemes. Unscrupulous selling of such schemes and evidence (most particularly from the misdeeds of Robert Maxwell) demonstrated a need for tighter state regulation of private pensions. This was done in the Pensions Act of 1995. The whole incident (which is very well discussed in Waine, 1995) illustrates many of the pitfalls of pension privatisation. However, the position today is that there are still large numbers of pensioners, and future pensioners, whose protection is very limited.

Shortly before they fell from power in 1997 the Conservatives developed outline proposals for legislation very much along World Bank lines to establish a mandatory privately managed second tier to replace the messy mix of the inadequate SERPS and private schemes of varying quality. The Conservatives fell from power before they were able to legislate on this, but the new Labour government has picked up the theme, rejecting the alternative of restoring the value of SERPS to its originally proposed levels because of the costs involved. They are introducing, in the Welfare Reform and Pensions Bill, an optional Stakeholder Pension system to give relatively low paid workers the chance to contribute towards a private second pension under strict state regulation (see also Department of Social Security, 1998). They are proposing to back this up, though in this case the legislation has not yet been published, with a scheme to replace SERPS which will offer a better deal, but only to very low paid workers.

Thus, in France, while the arguments for new funded approaches to pension provision are gaining strength they have to counter strong public preferences for a relatively strong unfunded public system. By contrast, in the United Kingdom, the long standing failure to fill in the gap between the flat rate Beveridge pension and the plethora of good private schemes for well paid employees has left the field open to a private pillar. However, whilst this will be strongly recommended by the government it will not be compulsory. However the mandatory state provided alternative will only be a 'good buy' for the very low paid.

The Argument for a Private Pillar

The World Bank makes the case for its second pillar in the following terms:

> A second mandatory pillar - one that is fully funded and privately managed - would link benefits actuarially to costs and carry out the income-smoothing or savings function for all income groups within the population. This link should avoid some of the economic and political distortions to which the public pillar is prone. Full funding should boost capital accumulation and financial market development (World Bank, 1994, p.16).

The World Bank's critics (see, for example, Beattie and McGillivray, 1995) challenge the assumption that political instability is a bigger threat to pensions than economic instability. There also are difficulties that stem from the fact that the safest investments from pensioners' points of view may not be the best ones to promote national economic growth (indeed they may even be investments in other economies). The assumptions here about the economic advantages of this approach are beyond the concerns of this paper. But the argument most widely used, in a succession of presumably pensions industry inspired newspaper articles, to support the case for private and funded pension schemes is the so-called 'demographic time bomb' (for an example of this literature see Taverne, 1995).

The demographic data on falling death and birth rates in many societies, creating a steadily deteriorating ratio between the so-called active and inactive population is a rare example of 'hard' evidence in the social sciences which it may seem unwise to challenge. But there are two ways it needs to be challenged. First, it is not self-evident that, if there is a 'burden' of dependency, funded private pensions help to solve the problem. Certainly they lift the burden directly off the public exchequer, but funded pensions are just as much transfers between the generations as unfunded ones. Pension contributions are not simply put away in bank vaults to be taken out later. Money is invested by pension funds. When those investments are realised they are a charge on future profits, to be paid out of the returns to the productive activities of the workers at that time. Again that argument is something of a diversion from our main theme, but it is a point that is so often ignored that it needs saying over and over again.

But the second point about the 'demographic time bomb' is very relevant to the concern of this book. Data on the age structure of the future population are often cited in terms of an alleged problem of dependency without regard to the fact that it is to a considerable extent the availability or unavailability of work which determines dependency in the later years rather than age as such. Hence figures on the proportion of the population over 65, or expected to be over 65 at certain dates in the future are widely quoted to illustrate this so called 'burden of dependency'. Yet there is no necessary correspondence between a specific chronological age and the age at which an individual is unable to make an active contribution to society. Even if the idea of making an active contribution is given a more specific meaning - to correspond with formal employment - there are great differences within and between societies in the extent to which individuals participate in the labour market either above or below the formal pension age.

In any case the issue of 'dependency' in a society needs to be looked at in relation to the population as a whole, not just the numbers of the elderly. Table 9.1 shows something rather surprising: that despite the fact that the numbers of the elderly have been rising in England and Wales, the proportion of the population in the workforce has not been falling. Until 1971, it we count the potential workforce as the employed plus the unemployed, it was constant at 47 per cent of the population. Then in 1991 it was up to 52 per cent, though in fact the rise of unemployment brought the actual workforce back down to 47 per cent.

Table 9.1 shows a dramatic fall between the first two and the last two dates, in the 'others' - neither young nor old but not in (or trying to get into) the labour force. What accounts for this is clear if we look at census data for women. Table 9.2 shows how important has been the shift of women from the category 'other' to labour force participation. Even in 1991 moreover these 'participants' were mostly in work (only 3 percent were unemployed). However, a significant amount of this work was part-time. Hence, I would argue from the British data that the issue of the 'burden of dependency' - derived from an examination of crude demographic data has been much exaggerated. I feel sure French data would show many similar features (some relevant figures are quoted in Table 9.3). There is a need to take into account issues about participation in the labour force.

Table 9.1 Employment status etc of the population of England and Wales at various census dates

	1931	1951	1971	1991
In full-time education	23	23	27	19
Retired	2	4	14	16
Unemployed	5	1	2	5
Others	26	26	12	13
Employed	42	46	45	47

Sources: population and occupation tables from the census reports for England and Wales 1931, 1951, 1971 and 1991.

Table 9.2 Employment status of women in England and Wales at various census dates

	1931	1951	1971	1991
In full-time education	22	21	25	18
Retired	1	1	19	18
Others	51	49	22	22
Labour force participants	26	29	34	42

Sources: population and occupation tables from the census reports for England and Wales 1931, 1951, 1971 and 1991.

Once we do this two trends seem evident. One is increased labour market participation by women whilst the other is increasing early withdrawal from the labour force (particularly by men) as formal unemployment has grown (see Table 9.3 for recent economic activity rate data for France and the United Kingdom). There is a third set of changes that might be taken into account, but which will not be here, that is changing participation in the education system by persons over the minimum school leaving age.

Juxtaposing the two issues highlighted above may seem to prompt a conclusion – but one that I would certainly not want to draw - that there is a certain trade off here between the interests of women and the interests of elderly men.

Table 9.3 Economic activity rates of men and women aged between 15 and 64 in France and the United Kingdom

	French men	UK men	French women	UK women
1986	78.9	85.9	57.8	61.3
1996	75.7	83.1	61.3	66.5

Source: Eurostat Yearbook 1997

The alternative conclusion that could be drawn is that if there are difficulties in providing work for all who want it, more attention needs to be paid to questions about how it is shared between the various competitors for it. Another phenomenon that has certainly developed in the United Kingdom is a tendency for the numbers of single earner households to fall relative to both two-earner and no-earner households (Hills, 1993). That trend is partly explained by the regional and social class distribution of job opportunities, but it has been enhanced by social security benefit rules which tend to penalise female earners in situations in which their husbands are out of work. A related concern is the difficulties female single parents have in entering the workforce, because of a lack of support for child care and rules relating to other benefits which deter earning. Going more widely, there are questions that could be addressed about opportunities for job sharing that would reduce the stresses upon double earner households.

What this adds up to is a need to qualify the demographic time bomb argument with reference to questions about the extent to which there will be work for all who want it. If there were to be a demographic situation in which there seemed to be insufficient numbers in the so-called prime age groups then a number of things might happen - older people might work longer, young people might enter the work force earlier and people in between (particularly women) might choose to work more hours.

There are therefore various labour market assumptions that need to be used to modify the scenarios constructed solely on the basis of demographic assumptions:

- work opportunities may increase, an improbable scenario

- work opportunities may remain much as at present, in which case the adaptations highlighted in the last paragraph may be necessary
- work opportunities may decline, in which case a fall in the numbers wanting to work may be welcome
- work opportunities may decline rapidly, in which case the demographic issues become rather irrelevant.

In that last case, pension arrangements which are premised upon the notion that all should be contributors to their own pensions will increasingly collapse. And surely, there is evidence that this is already happening. Increasing numbers, particularly of men, have left the labour force before retirement age. In the British case the reaction to this was a reluctant one, no adaptations were made to retirement ages but for a while a strong shift of men from dependence upon unemployment benefits to the more generously conceived long-term invalidity benefit was tolerated. In France, on the other hand, there were definite efforts to facilitate early retirement including the reduction of the retirement age from 65 to 60 in 1983 and the enactment of a variety of 'early exit' provisions (see Guillemaud, 1991).

In both countries governments subsequently came to regret their generosity. In the French case the reaction was to strengthen contribution conditions for the insurance based pensions, in the British, to replace long-term invalidity benefit by a new benefit which imposed a much stricter disability test, incapacity benefit.

All this may be regarded as taking the discussion a long way from issues about the pension implications of employment flexibility but in fact the early retirement issue illustrates very clearly two things. One is that very often employment flexibility, far from being 'chosen' by people, is something imposed by labour market conditions. The 'imposition' of early retirement upon many people without the private resources to make this a tolerable option illustrates this very clearly. The second is that the political reaction was, initially, generous (particularly in France) but subsequently has involved a falling back upon ways of tightening eligibility conditions. It goes without saying that funded personal pensions offer no contribution to the alleviation of this particular problem.

Clearly the argument in this paper rests upon the evidence that employment flexibility is rather more something imposed by labour market conditions than freely chosen. Of course, flexibility does not have to involve a sharp contrast between those in and those out of the labour force. It is sometimes presented in more attractive terms as involving options at various points in the life course to move in and out of work. In that case the implications for funded pensions are more complex, depending upon both levels of income when in work and government willingness to offer subsidies at others. These issues are further explored elsewhere in this volume (see the chapter by Hancock and McCreadie).

Conclusions

In both the British and French cases at the moment there is a social insurance based first pillar with quite strong labour market attachment conditions (that is contribution conditions) regulating access. Behind that sit means-tested benefits for those with little or no other sources of help. These two countries can be contrasted with the Scandinavian countries in which the qualifying contribution conditions for the basic minimum pension are really very slight. Advocates of 'basic income' measures (who very often draw their arguments from predictions of increasing labour market flexibility) see this as the way forward. The problem lies in the levels of income likely to be offered by governments with basic income guarantees of this kind. There are no signs that the British government would accept this sort of approach. Rather the New Labour government's position on social security issues is to stress the importance of labour market participation. As far as pensions are concerned therefore the government has opted for an approach which stresses the private pillar, with a public 'safety net' back up. That may be satisfactorily if flexible employment carries with it only risks of temporary unemployment, it is clearly not if it brings endemic difficulties for many people.

References

Beattie, R. and McGillivray, W. (1995), 'A Risky Strategy: Reflections on the World Bank Report "Averting the Old Age Crisis"', *International Social Security Review*, vol. 48, no. 3/4.

Department of Social Security (1998), *Partnership in Pensions*, HMSO, London.

European Commission (1997), *Eurostat Yearbook*, European Commission, Brussels.

Hills, J. (1993), *The Future of Welfare: A Guide to the Debate*, Joseph Rowntree Trust, York.

Kohli, M. et al (eds) (1991), *Time for Retirement. Comparative Studies of Early Exit from the Labour Force*, Cambridge University Press, Cambridge.

Reynaud, E. (1997), 'France: A National and Contractual Second Tier' in Rein, M. and Wadensjö, E., *Enterprise and the Welfare State*, Edward Elgar, Cheltenham.
Social Trends (1996), HMSO, London.
Taverne, D. (1995), *The Pension Time Bomb in Europe*, Federal Trust, London.
Waine, B. (1995), 'A Disaster Foretold? The Case of the Personal Pension', *Social Policy and Administration*, vol. 29, no. 4, pp.317-334.
World Bank (1994), *Averting the Old Age Crisis*, Oxford University Press, New York.

10 Minimum Wages, Flexibility and Social Exclusion

ALAN GORDON

Introduction

This paper aims to link together the introduction of a national minimum wage in the United Kingdom, and its anticipated and forecast impact, with three key labour market concepts that are at the heart of the pan-European policy debate about the role of the state in regulating the labour market and intervening in the economy: labour market flexibility, active labour market policies and social exclusion. The paper starts by discussing the tradition of minimum wage legislation in the UK from 1909 onwards. The establishment of the Wages Councils, and their more recent abolition is then considered. In July 1997 the incoming Labour Party government established the Low Pay Commission, charged with making recommendations on a National Minimum Wage - its report and the later legislation implementing government plans are discussed. In April 1999 the first ever National Minimum Wage was introduced in the UK, with a range of fears and hopes and anticipated effects. The paper therefore considers the impact of minimum wages on labour market flexibility, especially the impact on young people's employability. Where relevant, selective, comparative international research on impact is cited from the USA and from OECD and from the countries of the European Union. The paper ends by discussing the links between labour market rewards, welfare benefits and social exclusion.

The discussion is firmly located in the current debate taking place in Europe about the benefits and costs of changing minimum wage arrangements and the impact of any such change on beneficiaries. Of particular importance is the way minimum wages can inhibit labour market flexibility and, for young people at least, may exacerbate the severe social problem of social exclusion. It was mainly because of concerns over this latter point that the 1999 arrangements for a National Minimum Wage in the United Kingdom at its full rate (£3.60 per hour) apply only to those aged 22 years old and over.

The UK Tradition of Minimum Wages : Winston Churchill

Even before the (then) radical creation of the Trade Boards in the first decade of the 20th century, there had been a recognition that low pay was a serious labour market and social problem. In order to prevent private companies from using low pay to undercut rivals so that they could successfully bid for government contracts, the Fair Wages Resolution was passed in 1891, ensuring that private sector employing organisations bidding for public sector contracts should pay wages of accepted parity throughout the sector (Field, 1984).

> It is a serious national evil that any class of His Majesty's subjects should receive less than a living wage in return for their utmost exertions. ..... Where in the great staple trades in the country you have a powerful organisation on both sides, where you have responsible leaders able to bind their constituents to their decision, where that organisation is conjoint with an automatic scale of wages or arrangements for avoiding a deadlock by means of arbitration, there you have a healthy bargaining which increases the competitive power of the industry, enforces a progressive standard of life and the productive scale, and continually weaves capital and labour more closely together. But where you have what we call sweated trades, you have no organisation, no parity of bargaining, the good employer is undercut by the bad, and the bad employer is undercut by the worst; the worker, whose whole livelihood depends upon the industry, is undersold by the worker who only takes the trade up as a second string, his feebleness and ignorance generally renders the worker an easy prey to the tyranny of the masters and middlemen, only a step higher up the ladder than the worker, and held in the same relentless grip of forces. Where these conditions prevail you have not a condition of progress, but a condition of progressive degeneration (Churchill, 1909).

It was with this speech in the House of Commons in April 1909 that the President of the Board of Trade, Winston Churchill, introduced the second reading of the bill that was to become the Trade Boards Act 1909. Churchill explained that Trade Boards, which were to be introduced to put in place minimum wages and regulations in industries noted for the prevalence of cheap labour, were essential to provide a 'living wage'.

Four Trade Boards in the manufacturing sector were established under the Act.

Churchill himself stated that, 'We believe that decent conditions make for industrial efficiency and increase rather than decrease competitive power' (Pond and Winyard, 1983): beliefs had changed by the 1980s. There was also a continuing concern about poverty: according to Spender, 'The tendency of our wage system is to always drive down the price of their labour to the lowest level of life livable'. He wanted to ' ... limit the extent of peril and suffering to which a worker is to be liable (Spender, 1912).

The Wages Councils

The Trade Boards remained in place until 1945 when the Wages Councils Act established the Wages Councils, consisting of independent members and representatives of both sides of industry - employers and trade unions. Wages Councils had the power to set minimum rates of pay and holiday entitlements for different ages and types of worker in the sector for which they were responsible. At the time of the Coronation in 1953, Wages Councils were at their peak, with 66 Councils setting minimum pay rates for some 3.5 million workers (Lourie, 1995; Employment Department, 1988). Consolidation, mergers and changing labour market structure shrank the number of Councils from 66 to 26 in 1986. A further 400,000 farm workers came under the auspices of the Agricultural Wages Boards (Metcalf, 1999). The powers of the Wages Councils were extended by the Employment Protection Act 1975, put into place by a Labour Party government

With the election of the first of four consecutive Conservative Party governments in 1979, the attitude towards state regulation of the UK labour market in general, and minimum wages in particular, changed. As part of its declared programme of deregulating the labour market a Consultation Paper published in 1985 proposed that Wages Councils be radically reformed or abolished: at that time the opposition in many quarters to abolition meant that the option initially selected was reform. While the Wages Act 1986 kept in place the 26 Councils still existing, it removed their authority to set wages and conditions for those workers under the age of 21 years to establish holiday entitlement, pay rates for shift work, pay rates for 'unsociable' hours, and the legislation stopped any new Wages Councils from being set up.

While the 1992 Conservative Party's general election manifesto did not contain any proposals for abolishing the Wages Councils altogether (Lourie, 1995), the Trade Union Reform and Employment Rights Bill (November 1992) contained provision for their abolition. On the 30th August 1993, the remaining Councils were no more: they had covered 2.5 million low paid workers with a minimum hourly pay rate, a minimum overtime rate and specified when overtime rates must be paid. All that remained was the separately established Agricultural Wages Board, the maintenance of which was strongly supported by both employer and employee representative organisations. So, outside the agricultural sector, from 1993 to 1999 there was no minimum wage in existence in the UK, neither nationally nor by sector. This state of affairs contrasts sharply with minimum wages in Europe and in the USA. Examples are shown below.

The figures in Table 10.1 relate to 1994, near to when the UK abolished its Wages Councils. While other comparative data are discussed below, it is worth noting at this stage that the value of the national minimum wage in France (SMIC) from July 1st 1998 was 40.22 francs per hour for workers aged over 18 years (c. £4.10) (at http://www.msa86.fr/cot/smic.htm), and in the United States the recent increase has raised it to $5.25 per hour (c. £3.30), after falling in real terms throughout the 1980s (Gregory and Salverda, 1999).

The Low Pay Commission

In its 1997 general election manifesto, the Labour Party committed itself to introducing a National Minimum Wage (NMW), if elected to government. The level at which it was to be set, and the groups in the labour market to whom it would apply would be 'decided not on the basis of a rigid formula but according to the economic circumstances of the time' (Labour Party, 1997). This contrasts with the earlier, 1992, manifesto pledge, where the Labour Party asserted that it would, if elected:

> ... end the scandal of poverty pay and bring Britain into line with the rest of Europe by introducing a statutory minimum wage of £3.40 an hour. This is a major but long overdue reform which will benefit around four million low paid people, 80 per cent of whom are women.

Table 10.1 Minimum wages in Europe 1994: examples

Country	Type	Uprating	Minimum	Coverage
Belgium	Central Legal	Two years Inflation	Over 21s £760 month	4% applies where no industry/ company deal
France	SMIC Legal	Annual 1st July	£4.19 hour	9% of workforce on min
Ireland	15 sectors no national	Regular review	eg waiters £117 week	12% workforce covered
Luxembourg	Stat min	Two years Interim	Skilled £847 mth, Unskil. £729 mth	10.7% on min ('89)
Netherlands	Stat min	Reviewed Periodically	£799 mth	5% workforce on min
Portugal	Stat min	Annual	Main-£200 Mth.	8% affected
Spain	Stat min	Annual	£313 mth	10% affected
UK	Agriculture	Annual	£145 week	217,00 farmworkers 1% workforce

Source: Lourie 1995

Two months after winning the 1997 general election with a large majority the Labour government set up the Low Pay Commission in July. Its main terms of reference were to recommend the level at which a NMW might be introduced, and to make recommendations about exemptions or the introduction of lower rates for those aged 16 to 25 years of age. The Low

Pay Commission was explicitly required to take into account a number of NMW impact factors (Metcalf, 1999):

- the wider economic and social implications
- the likely effect on employment
- the likely effect on inflation
- the impact on the competitiveness of business, especially small firms (SMEs)
- the potential impact on the costs of industry
- the impact on costs to the Exchequer

The first report of the Low Pay Commission made recommendations that were to cover all regions of the country and all business sectors (Low Pay Commission, 1998a). The Summary Report expressed its concern over inequality, welfare dependence and the location of low pay, *viz*:

> Over the past twenty years there has been a growth in earnings inequality. This has led to a substantial degree of in-work poverty and dependence on social security benefits to supplement low wages.

> Low pay is more prevalent among certain groups of individuals, especially women and young people. It is closely associated with particular working patterns, such as part-time work and home-working. And low pay is concentrated in certain business sectors - particularly service industries, such as hospitality, retail, business services and social care - and in small firms. Low pay is found in all regions (Low Pay Commission, 1998b).

The Low Pay Commission estimated that around two million people would benefit from their proposals if introduced, about nine per cent of employees: three-quarters would be women, over one half of whom were part-time workers. The Commission argued that:

> The NMW should be introduced at a rate which offers real benefits to the low paid, while avoiding unnecessary risks to businesses and jobs (Low Pay Commission, 1998b).

There were, in all, over twenty recommendations, the main ones being:
- a NMW of £3.60 an hour from April 1999, rising to £3.70 in June 2000
- NMW at this rate applying to those aged 21 years old and over
- a £3.20 NMW development rate for those aged 18 to 20 years of age

- the development rate applying for six months for those on training courses aged 21 and above
- the self-employed to be excluded
- apprentices to be excluded from coverage
- 16 and 17 year-olds to be excluded

The Commission produced detailed figures on the number and proportion of workers who would benefit by the full implementation of their recommendations, by age, gender and employment status, as well as changes to the wages bill. With these proposals, the UK's wages bill would rise by just over 0.5 per cent: even with some restoration of wage differentials 'the total cost is unlikely to be over 1%' (Metcalf, 1999). Estimates are given in Table 10.2.

It was estimated that other beneficiaries would include:

- over one-third of home-workers
- one-fifth of single parents
- over one in ten ethnic minority workers

The Government Response and the April 1999 NMW

Just as in 1909 it had been the President of the Board of Trade who introduced the policy aimed at producing a 'living wage', so, in 1998, it fell upon the incumbent of the same government position to provide the government's response to the Low Pay Commission's recommendations. In her statement, Margaret Beckett reiterated the concern about fair competition among employing organisations and the provision of a decent standard of living to those in the workplace:

> Such low levels of pay mean that taxpayers provide massive sums of income subsidy, and businesses, large and small, striving to compete, as Britain must, on quality and value for money, see their position undermined, not by fair competition, but by cut-throat cowboys. ....

> This government believes in decent minimum standards, as a spur to competing sustainedly on quality, to tackle social exclusion and to make work pay (Department of Trade and Industry, 1998).

Table 10.2 Coverage of the National Minimum Wage – commission recommendations

Type of Worker	No's Covered (000s)	% of group affected	Increase in wage bill %
All aged 18+	2050	9	0.6
18 - 20	235	21	3.9
21+	1815	8	0.6
Male f.t. workers	320	3	0.3
Male p.t.workers	240	26	3.0
Female f.t	340	5	0.7
Female p.t.	1150	22	2.7

Source :: Low Pay Commission, 1998b

In welcoming the report, the concern about likely impact, contained in the guidance to the Commission, was repeated in the speech, with the President of the Board of Trade emphasising that the NMW had to be set at a level that 'avoided the risk of adverse effects' on:

- employment
- inflation
- the Public Sector Borrowing Requirement
- the position of young people

The labour market situation of young people was a special concern, and mindful of this the government would introduce a main NMW rate of £3.60 an hour for those aged 22 years and above (rather than 21) with the development rate of £3.00 an hour applying to 18 to 21 year olds inclusive, rising to £3.20 in June 2000. The Commission would be reviewing the position of 21 year-olds during 1999. Sixteen and 17 year-olds were confirmed as exempt groups. The main rate of £3.60 is one half of median wages.

The numbers of beneficiaries with the NMW as implemented by the government thus deviates somewhat from the Commission's estimates, but are nevertheless substantial. These include 1.4 million women workers, more than 1.3 million part-time workers, 200,000 young people, 110,000 home workers, 175,000 lone parents who work and some 130,000 ethnic minority workers (Department of Trade and Industry, 1998).

According to members of the Commission, the issue of lower rates or exemptions for those aged 16 to 25 years ' ... took up a disproportionate amount of time' (Metcalf, 1999). While the youngest of the young people participating in the labour market should be exempt, according to almost all those providing evidence or expressing a view, more complex was the issue of the age at which the main NMW rate should start. A particular concern is that while minimum wages might assist the low paid in work (of whatever age) the risk of continued exclusion from the labour market might be a particular risk for lower productivity young people experiencing multiple disadvantages.

Labour Market Policies and Flexibility

In the last twenty years, and especially during the Conservative government years from the mid-1980s, the United Kingdom has gained something of a reputation within the European Community of having the most 'flexible' of labour markets, in the sense of experiencing historically sharp increases in employment during the upturn and boom years of the business cycle, increased labour turnover and expansion of part-time, contracted and self-employed jobs, home-working and other developments. These changes have resulted from a range of engineered alterations to labour market regulations, the differentiated status of workers, and action on labour supply, including quantity and quality of labour issues, but especially action on the price of labour. Key government-initiated changes have included:

- as noted above, first altering the terms of, then abolishing the Wages Councils, which set minimum wages and other conditions for workers in key sectors
- exempting small businesses from a range of labour market and health and safety regulations
- curbing the power and influence of the trades unions in a variety of ways, including compulsory balloting, abolition of the 'closed shop', privatisation of the public utilities,
- the abolition of the forum for government, employing organisation and trades union representatives to discuss policy (NEDO)

- permitting part-time and contract staff to operate with different terms and conditions of employment from full-timers
- social security reforms

While the actions of the European Commission and some of the changes introduced by the incoming Labour government (including minimum wage legislation) have altered the regulations pertaining to the labour market somewhat, many of the Conservative-induced changes remain in place.

Although the UK is often taken as an exemplar of enhanced flexibility within the European Union, there is some evidence that the European economy and labour market as a whole has become more flexible recently:

> While the ... evidence suggests that there is more flexibility in the European economy than ten years ago, the impact of this so far on employment creation is not apparent. This may suggest that some barriers to job growth still exist (European Commission, 1996).

While this flexibility may improve the position somewhat in Europe, there is evidence that it lags substantially behind the USA, Canada and Australia in creating new jobs over the past twenty years. Employment in the USA, for example, rose by more than 50 per cent between 1970 and 1995, but grew by less than 10 per cent in France, the UK and Germany (Department of Education and Employment, 1997). Within Europe, there are particular concerns over 'flexibility in working patterns' and 'flexibility in wages and salaries', as well as some identified shortcomings in education, training and skills acquisition, the remedying of which would assist in creating a more flexible labour market (European Commission, 1997).

The 1994 OECD Jobs Study (Organisation for Economic Co-operation and Development, 1994) came up with ten main recommendations to attempt to overcome the 'jobs deficit': the extent to which the recommendations have (or have not) been put into effect by OECD member states has been monitored (Organisation for Economic Co-operation and Development, 1997). While many of the policy proposals have gained wide support and are being implemented, Gregory and Salverda note that:

> A number of member countries, notably in the EU, have however been reluctant to implement the recommendations relating to labour market flexibility. As the OECD itself acknowledges, this is due to concern that policies to achieve greater flexibility in the labour market would be at odds

with objectives concerning equity and social cohesion. The trade-off posed is clearly a difficult one (Gregory and Salverda, 1999).

The 'buzz-word' of flexibility can cover a whole host of labour market policy issues, including:

- the wage-setting process
- collective bargaining procedures
- the level of social benefits
- the eligibility criteria for social benefits
- employment protection legislation
- in-work benefits (private and public)
- new types of employment contract
- the (re-) organisation of working practices
- multi- and re-skilling

The 'European view' of these issues often stresses that the causes of weak economic growth and unbalanced development are the regional problems of low local workforce skills and inadequate local infrastructure. These factors '... may be as important as wage flexibility' (European Commission, 1997). It is this perspective that assists an understanding of just why most of the European members of the OECD have been reluctant to act upon the Jobs Study proposals in relation to labour market flexibility, especially on wages. This is in spite of some evidence in the 1990s of the adverse consequences of minimum wages on the employability of certain labour force groups, especially young people. In its 1990-91 Economic Survey of France (Organisation for Economic Co-operation and Development, 1991) the OECD pointed out that the French national minimum (SMIC) was paid to 2 million workers, some 12 per cent of all dependent employees, and, importantly, that the gap between the SMIC and the average industrial wage had fallen by 14 percentage points in the first half of the 1980s. The conclusion was:

Indications are that the increase in the relative value of the SMIC in the 1980s is likely to have reduced employment levels, especially for youths (Organisation for Economic Co-operation and Development, 1991).

For the Netherlands, the relative decline in the real value of the minimum wage in the 1980s was accompanied by - the OECD used the phrase 'contributed to' – '... the significant increase in the number of workers employed in the lowest age category'. Metcalf, in his summary of the evidence of the impact of NMWs on employment and unemployment concludes that:

> International evidence also points to adverse labour market consequences for younger workers if their minimum wage is set too high (Metcalf, 1999).

He cites Dolado et al (Dolado, 1996) and the case of Spain, which raised minimum youth wages relative to adults: The evidence is unambiguous. The employment of those aged 20-24 rose and that of 16-19 fell.

With the UK government having taken the decision to exempt 16 and 17 year-olds from the NMW completely, and having a lower rate for 18, 19, 20 and 21 year-olds (Department of Trade and Industry, 1999), this initially cautious approach is most likely to minimise the employment consequences for young people, especially for those young people already disadvantaged in some way or socially excluded.

Minimum Wages and Social Exclusion

As noted above, one particular aspect of labour market inflexibility in evidence in both the USA and many European Union countries, including France, and from April 1999 the UK, is the presence of a national statutory minimum wage. The existence of such a floor below which wages cannot legally be paid is held by some commentators and some researchers to be partly responsible for the high levels of unemployment and relatively low levels of employment among certain groups in society, such as youth labour. There is a concern that a NMW impacts most harshly upon already disadvantaged and socially excluded groups:

> We regard the minimum wage as one of the most, if not the most, antiblack laws on the statute book (Friedman and Friedman, 1980).

Although, in terms of raised wage rates, the UK NMW will benefit ethnic minority workers, young people, home-workers and lone parents in work (Department of Trade and Industry, 1998), there is a concern about job losses among these groups, partly due to the discrimination that prevails in the UK labour market, partly due to productivity levels (perceived or actual) and partly due to other reasons. Young people represent a special 'worry' group.

At the same time that many EU countries are debating the current impact of prevailing wage levels on job creation, and are actively considering the levels and coverage of minimum wages, the UK government has taken a step that will reduce its labour market flexibility. But it has rejected the pattern of minimum wages related to age embraced by many EU neighbours. It is interesting to compare the levels of the SMIC rates in France to the UK, and the age groups to which they apply (Table 10.3).

It can be seen that the main SMIC rate applies to those aged over 18 years (UK 21), with a lower rate for 17 and 18 year-olds (UK lower rate 18 to 21 inclusive), and a still lower rate for those under 17 years. Even with this age structure for the NMW in the UK, more young workers are being affected by the introduction of the minimum wage than those aged 22 years and over. According to Metcalf, 'Over one seventh of those aged 18-21 will receive a pay rise, causing the overall pay bill of this group to increase by 2.4%' (Metcalf, 1999).

Table 10.3   Valeur du SMIC (Salaire horaire)

Ouvriers de plus de 18 ans	- 40,22F	(39,43F)
Ouvriers de 17 a 18 ans	- 36,20F	(35,49F)
Ouvriers jusqu'a 17 ans	- 32,18F	(31,54F)

Source: At http://www.msa86.fr/cot/smic.htm

[Note: values in French francs from July 1997 are shown in brackets. An upgrade took place on the 1st July 1998, with a 2 per cent increase for each group]

There exists a policy concern, shared in Europe, that minimum wages hinder the process of promoting social inclusion, especially among young people. It is recognised that:

... poverty and social exclusion remain significant problems in the EU. The new employment strategy ... will contribute to overcoming these problems by targeting those at risk of exclusion from the labour market and by encouraging the reform of social protection systems to enhance people's employability. (European Commission, 1998).

And recent research has concluded '... that employment for young people in some European countries with relatively high minimum wage standards could be improved by lowering the minimum wage ... without creating permanent poverty problems' (Westergaard-Nielson, 1998). One of the continuing tasks of the UK's Low Pay Commission is to monitor and evaluate the impact of the NMW on young people (Low Pay Commission, 1998c).

Interestingly, at the 1998 New Start Conference held under the auspices of the UK Presidency of the European Union (Insight, 1998), focusing on the European Commission's approach to youth unemployment, the main reasons listed for high youth unemployment did not include actions on youth wages. Out of 18 million people unemployed in the EU, it was estimated that five million were young people, with almost two-thirds having been unemployed for over six months. The main explanations given were poor preparation by education and training systems, low economic growth, changing labour market conditions and an increase in the size of the working population.

It is argued here that while minimum wages may help to alleviate poverty for the low paid in work, they may simultaneously make worse the risk of continued exclusion from labour market opportunities, especially for young people. Socially excluded young people often suffer from multiple disadvantages and disaffection, making them unattractive to potential employers. If they are then made expensive, or more expensive, to hire, this makes inclusion that much more difficult. Young people who fall into this 'excluded' group do tend to suffer from one or more of the following disadvantages:

- lack of basic skills
- low educational achievement
- low levels of work skills
- inability to cope with work discipline
- disrupted family life
- low self-esteem
- homelessness
- drug, alcohol and substance abuse
- criminal record

(Central London Training and Enterprise Journal, 1997).

Clearly, the implementation of creative and effective wide-ranging social policies are needed to respond to this range of disadvantages, in the areas of education and vocational training, health policy, housing , family support and the law and rehabilitation. In the UK, a national strategy to tackle social exclusion is being developed by eighteen action teams, co-ordinated by the Social Exclusion Unit: a programme of policy development is to be completed by December 1999 (Insight, 1999). One of the five major themes being worked on by the action teams is 'building a future for young people'. With the range of disadvantages currently being experienced by socially excluded young people, participation in the labour market may only be a small part of the solution. However, the fewer the number of barriers that are in place inhibiting young people from being offered employment the better: minimum wages may be one such barrier.

Conclusions

This paper has reviewed the development of minimum wage legislation in the United Kingdom from the first decade of the 20th Century through to the introduction of a National Minimum Wage in 1999. It discusses the proposals of the Low Pay Commission and the way in which the recommendations were received by government, and how the implemented NMW deviated in some key respects from the Commission's recommendations. These changes reflected a continuing concern in the UK and elsewhere in Europe about the impact of minimum wages on employment opportunities, especially for young people. The different concepts of labour market flexibility are considered, with a special emphasis on wage flexibility and inflexibility. National minimum wages introduce an inflexibility that has the potential, at least, to make the employment of young people, in particular, less attractive to employing organisations. Of particular concern are the prospects for socially excluded young people who may be experiencing and suffering from a range of disadvantages, many of which will be unrelated to their labour market status. Effective social policies on a number of fronts are required to respond to these disadvantages and to promote social inclusion: labour market participation may be only a small part of the solution. However, the smaller the number of barriers inhibiting young people from being offered jobs, and the lower their height, the better: minimum wages for young people represent one such barrier.

References

Central London Training and Enterprise Council (1997), *Excluded Youths*, FOCUS, London.

Churchill, W. (1909), House of Commons Debate, 28th April, c388, House of Commons, London.

Department of Education and Employment (1997), 'Job Creation in the USA and Europe Compared', *Labour Market Trends*, May, pp. 173-4, Department of Education and Employment, London.

Department of Trade and Industry (1998), *The Government's Response to the First Report of the Low Pay Commission*, Statement by Margaret Beckett, President of the Board of Trade, Thursday 18th June 1998, Department of Trade and Industry, London.

Department of Trade and Industry (1999), *A Detailed Guide to the National Minimum Wage*, DTI, London.

Dolado, J., Kramarz, F., Machin, S., Manning, A., Margolis, D. and Tealings, C. (1996), 'The Economic Impact of Minimum Wages in Europe', *Economic Policy*, 23, pp. 317-372.

Employment Department (1988), *Wages Council 1988, Consultation Document*, December, Employment Department, London.

European Commission (1996), *Employment in Europe 1996*, European Commission, Luxembourg.

European Commission (1997), *Employment in Europe 1997*, European Commission, Luxembourg.

European Commission (1998), *Social Action Programme 1998-2000*, European Commission, Luxembourg.

Field, F. (1984), *The Minimum Wage – Its Potential and Dangers*, Heineman, London.

Friedman, M. and Friedman, R. (1980), *Free to Choose*, Secker and Warburg, London.

Gregory, M. and Salverda, W. (1999), 'Employment and Wages: Summary Report', in *Wages and Employment*, EC/DG V – OECD/DEELSA Seminar, European Commission, Luxembourg.

Insight (1998), 'Youth Unemployment – the European Perspective', *Insight*, 42, Summer 1998, p. 28.

Insight (1999), 'Tackling Social Exclusion', *Insight*, 44, Spring 1999, p. 30.

Labour Party (1997), *Because Britain Deserves Better*, (The Labour Party 1997 General Election Manifesto), The Labour Party, London.

Lourie, J. (1995), 'A Minimum Wage', *House of Commons Library, Research Paper 95/97*, House of Commons, London.

Low Pay Commission (1998a), *The National Minimum Wage*, Cm. 3976, The Stationery Office, London.

Low Pay Commission (1998b), *The National Minimum Wage, Summary Report*, The Stationery Office, London.

Low Pay Commission (1998c), *National Minimum Wage: Monitoring and Evaluation*, Paper presented to the Education and Employment Economics Group, 30th October 1998, The Stationery Office, London.

Metcalf, D. (1981), *Low Pay, Occupational Mobility and Minimum Wage Policy in Britain*, American Enterprise Institute, Washington.

Metcalf, D. (1999), 'The Low Pay Commission and the National Minimum Wage', *Economic Journal*, February.

Organisation for Economic Cooperation and Development (1991), *Economic Survey 1990-91 : France*, Organisation for Economic Cooperation and Development, Paris.

Organisation for Economic Cooperation and Development (1994), *Jobs Study : Evidence and Explanations*, Organisation for Economic Cooperation and Development, Paris.

Organisation for Economic Cooperation and Development (1997), *Implementing the OECD Jobs Strategy : Lessons from Member Countries' Experience*, Organisation for Economic Cooperation and Development, Paris.

Pond, C. and Winyard, S. (1983), *The Case for a National Minimum Wage*, Low Pay Unit, London.

Spender, H. (1912), Preface to: Snowden, P., *The Living Wage.*

Westergaard-Nielson, N. (1998), 'Wage Dispersion, Employment and Unemployment : Possible Trade Offs', in *Wages and Employment*, EC/DG V–OECD/DEELSA Seminar, European Commission, Luxembourg.

PART III
CITIZENSHIP RIGHTS AND EMPLOYMENT SECURITY

11 Labour Market Flexibility, Security and Self-Respect

DAVID MIDDLETON

Introduction

Flexibility is promoted as a means to an end, that end often being the reduction of unemployment. Flexibility, used in this way, has come to mean deregulation of the labour market. Whether this is good for the economy is debatable; whether creating an insecure workforce is a necessary evil is certainly contestable. In this chapter I will argue that whilst flexible working can have positive affects, the attempt to create insecure workforces is inimical to social justice. This analysis is based on a view of social justice which is, in its essence, Rawlsian, that is to say that social justice here is conceptualised as being concerned with creating self respect. Self respect means being taken seriously. This means being treated as an active citizen, and being able to fund, usually through a wage income, a lifestyle that is on a par with others of the same community. Much of this chapter is concerned with philosophical issues which are cross-cultural, however, the empirical evidence is almost entirely drawn from the British context.

Flexibility - For Whom?

> This increase [in flexible working] has been associated with government measures to promote labour deregulation and encourage the greater use by employers of jobs with non-standard conditions of employment (Equal Opportunities Review, 1996).

Whether flexibility is a good or a bad thing very much depends on who is proposing the flexibility and what its underlying purpose is (Konsta, 1997). What I will refer to as 'negative flexibility' will be the flexibility proposed and supported by employers organisations and government bodies with a view to 'deregulating' the labour market. In general this type of flexibility is popular with employers because it allows them 'to engage workers in such a way that labour regulations - and their associated costs - are avoided'. (Jeffery, 1997). In other words, it creates a labour market which can respond quickly to fluctuations in the globalised economy. The emphasis here is on being able to hire and fire quickly, although it can mean the ability to reduce wage costs. 'Positive flexibility', by contrast, has long been a demand of the trade union movement, particularly those engaged in gender equality promotion (Evetts, 1994). This type of flexibility has as its aim a labour market which is responsive to the individual demands of workers, particularly those, predominantly women, who try to balance a career with a family (Lewis, 1994). The absence of such policies has been blamed for the high turnover rates among women managers (Brett and Stroh, 1994). In this chapter the concepts of 'negative' and 'positive' flexibility will be differentiated on the basis that one undermines self-respect and the other may help to promote it.

Positive flexibility includes such measures as flexi-time, part-time work, voluntarily reduced time (V-time), and career break schemes (Davidson and Cooper, 1992). The benefits of such schemes, for Davidson and Cooper, are primarily in terms of maintaining the confidence of individuals who do not become estranged from their workplace due to family commitments. The benefit here is for the individual worker, who for good reasons, may need to reduce their working commitments, but who still finds their work important and does not want to be identified purely in terms of their familial role. Whilst it is clear that this is primarily aimed at working mothers, there is no inherent reason why such schemes should not extend to fathers, those who have elderly relatives who require care, enticing 'discouraged' workers back into the workforce, or those who wish to pursue further training and education whilst maintaining a commitment to their employer. Davidson and Cooper argue that the employer benefits from such schemes by attracting younger women with talent and ability, who might otherwise have to choose between family and career. It can also mean reversing a trend where trained female workers are lost at no small financial cost to the company (Davidson and Cooper, 1992, p.159). Positive flexibility is concerned primarily with the organisation and distribution of work, whereas negative flexibility also addresses issues of remuneration.

The move toward negative flexibility has been conceptualised as part of a wider move toward what Jessop (1994) has called the 'post-Fordist state'. Fordism promoted state intervention in the market to produce the stable economic environment on which it was predicated, in partnership with employers and 'responsible' trade unions. In contrast, post-Fordism is characterised by a flexible production process and workforce. Post-Fordism, according to Jessop, places a greater emphasis on flexibility in internal and external labour markets. This is so particularly in regard to wages where there is a marked polarisation between skilled and unskilled workers. (Jessop, 1994, pp. 257-260). It is interesting that Jessop regards post-Fordism as having moved away from the partnership of employers and employees as it is this 'partnership' which is at the heart of the New Labour rhetoric I examine below. Jessop argues that it was the crisis of the Fordist state, which began in earnest in the 1970s, which provided the rationale for the transition to post-Fordism and attempts to reimpose unity of economic and social policy. The shift toward negative flexibility demanded by the post-Fordist state has seen the decline of what Veneziani (1996) calls the 'permanent labour contract based on unity of space (workers employed by one given company), of action (workers having one professionally defined job) and of time (workers having one job lasting in time)' (Veneziani, 1996). The development of such modes of production is of course uneven and it is important here to recognise that many workers continue to have relatively stable and secure employment patterns.

As Marx noted, labour power is a commodity and we tend to evaluate commodities by their exchange-value, as well as their use-value (Marx, 1954). There is very little doubt that for the majority of people being outside the labour market undermines their self respect, although it is important to note that 'status', in this sense, can be reflected, as for example, where women with high earning husbands (and these days the reverse may also be true) derive their status from the occupational position (and earning power) of their spouses. However, even among relatively high earners the dual income family is now the perceived norm, and this, I would argue, is as much to do with self-respect as it is with the ability to earn a wage. It may be argued however, that whilst the money is important, there is also a sense in which neither partner wants to be seen to be 'dependent' upon the other, with all the negative connotations that implies.

Government economic policy, for eighteen years was predicated on a belief that inflation and unemployment were linked and that the only way to reduce unemployment was to reduce inflation. The cause of inflation was supposedly inflexible trade union practices (among other things) which prevented employers from managing and which also kept workers wages artificially high. The 'grip' of unions was weakened by a series of Employment and Trade Union Acts, which made it more difficult for unions to pursue 'excessive wage demands'. The 1985 White Paper on Employment ditched the post-war consensus that Governments had a 'moral' responsibility to promote low unemployment, by claiming that the role of government was to create an environment in which enterprise could flourish. This was shorthand for weakening worker security. The idea of a 'job for life' was undermined and is now less apparent in the cultural landscape. Workers are encouraged to think of themselves as peripatetic, moving from job to job, from sector to sector and being responsible for upgrading their own skills. It relied on a commitment to an atomised individuated workforce, and was summed up by Mrs Thatcher's now famous declaration that there is no such thing as society.

The rationale behind the move toward negative flexibility was constantly changing in the flexible political environment in which it was born. At various times it was supposed to unleash the competitive sector, to protect jobs from overseas markets, to prevent undemocratic unions from running the country, and to be able to respond to changes in the global economy by moving quickly and efficiently avoiding unemployment by increasing competitiveness (Siddorn, 1996). Standing (1986) has examined the evidence of this last claim for the International Labour Organisation and found it less than convincing (Standing, 1986). A more convincing explanation perhaps is that negative flexibility has served to weaken the confidence of the union movement at a time when international capital itself was restructuring. The result is a reduction in self respect among individual workers caused by the removal of their ability to have some minimal control over their lives. At the same time, so it could be argued, negative flexibility undermines consumer confidence and therefore has a tendency to create the very unemployment it ostensibly prevents.

Fairness (At Work) - For Whom?

> Flexibility need not be bought at the expense of fairness: the two can
> - and should - go together (Commission on Social Justice, 1994:
> 208).

Before the General Election of 1997, the Labour Party declared its intention to abandon the deregulatory policies of their predecessors in favour of what they called 'fairness at work'. This was part of a wider commitment to creating a more just society. Part of this commitment was to be the implementation of various directives from the EEC, most notably the Working Time Directive limiting the working week to 48 hours, the part-time workers equal rights agreement which effectively prohibits discrimination against part time workers, and the parental leave agreement which allows parents up to three months unpaid leave on the birth or adoption of a child.

The Commission on Social Justice, chaired by Sir Gordon Borrie QC (and therefore referred to by the shorthand term 'Borrie Commission') was established in December 1992 by John Smith and reported its findings in 1994, three years prior to the General Election. They argued that social justice is concerned with equal citizenship rights which themselves are concerned with increasing self-respect. They argued that those who become marginalised lose their self-respect. Marginalisation was conceptualised in terms of the relationship to the labour market. Hence social justice, for the Commission, was concerned with creating jobs. It was important however that the jobs created should pay a 'living wage' and therefore the Commission supported proposals already firmly established in the labour movement for the establishment of a national minimum wage.

> Deregulators claim that minimum wages interfere with individuals freedom to price themselves into work. But power is not evenly distributed between employers and employees, especially at a time of high unemployment. Many employers seeking labour at the bottom end of the labour market exercise 'monopsony' power: as the only employers offering jobs to people with few skills, they can drive wages down *below* the level which would operate in a properly functioning labour market where employees had some choice of employers. A modern, still wealthy country should outlaw the worst forms of exploitation (Commission on Social Justice, 1994: 201).

Social justice could only be achieved, in the view of the Borrie Commission, by 'constructive partnership', a phrase much in use in New Labour rhetoric.

The Labour Government on taking office, and under the leadership of Tony Blair, set about a programme of welfare and tax reform through a number of initiatives, including the Low Pay Commission.[1] The Low Pay Commission, which reported in June 1998, one year after the election of a Labour Government with a massive majority, endorsed a minimum wage of £3.60 an hour for adult workers, and £3.00 an hour for young workers, with the exception of 16-18 year olds who the Commission notes 'should not be regarded as full participants in the labour market; they should be in education or training'. (Low Pay Commission, 1998: 5.10). We should note here that the very existence of a Low Pay Commission is a large step forward from the previous administration who abolished the Wages Councils which had offered some minimal protection for the low paid. However, we might also note that the rate is considerably below that endorsed by workers organisations, including the Trades Union Congress and even quasi-Governmental bodies such as the Equal Opportunities Commission who believed a rate closer to £4.50 was appropriate.

A major consideration of the Low Pay Commission was '.. to make recommendations which business could afford. No one wants a wage that cannot be paid'. (Low Pay Commission, 1998: Foreword.6). One of the assertions made by the Low Pay Commission is that workers are not merely commodities, and yet in one sense they are exactly that. Employers themselves talk of human resources in terms of human capital. Marx argued, in my view correctly, that labour itself is a commodity to be bought and sold like any other on the free labour market. Wages represent our evaluation in the social world. Different wage rates supposedly represent different skills and abilities, but often it is the person rather than the skill which is evaluated. Work done by men, for example, is nearly always valued more highly than work done by women, even when the skills necessary for carrying out the specific tasks are the same. To be 'low paid' is to be marginalised. Marginalisation is an aspect of lowered self-respect (Young, 1990). To be marginalised is to know that you are less valuable than others. The wage rate you can command, along with how secure your employment, is a constant reminder of your place in the social hierarchy. In this sense, paying people less than a 'living' wage is morally unjust.

A living wage is connected to the Rawlsian concept of pursuing the good life. In other words a living wage is not one which merely allows people to subsist but also allows them to take part in whatever citizenship rights they may possess, including the right to some form of leisure activities commensurate with what other people in their community partake. According to the Office for National Statistics,[2] the average gross hourly earnings of full-time adults, in April 1998, was £9.54. This figure represents 265 per cent more than the proposed Low Pay threshold for adults. Of course, this average hides significant differences between full time and part time workers, the latter's wages tending to be lower than the formers. It also hides differences between manual and non-manual workers, with the latter group tending to earn around 1.8 times the amount paid to the lower group. Finally, it hides the difference between women and men, with women tending to earn around 80 per cent of men's wages (Equal Opportunities Review, 1997b, no. 76, p 35).

Prior to the rate being announced by the Low Pay Commission, the *Equal Opportunities Review* (1997a, no. 73, pp.13-22) carried out an analysis of the Labour Force Survey to assess the potential impact of the national minimum wage proposals. They showed that some 6.5 million workers in the UK were paid at a rate less than half the average hourly rate. When people are valued so lowly it is difficult to see how they can be considered to be anything other than peripheral or marginal in our society. Low wages are often accompanied by the worst working conditions and the least job security. Their place in the wage hierarchy will also affect their view of the way others see them, and hence their self respect. Table 11.1 gives an idea of the percentages and numbers involved:

Table 11.1 Numbers and percentages of low paid employees in the UK 1996

Hourly rate of pay (£)	Percentage of all Employees	Number of employees affected (millions)
Less than £2.50	3.9	0.9
Less than £3.00	7.1	1.6
Less than £3.50	14.2	3.2
Less than £4.00	21.3	4.7
Less than £4.50	29.3	6.5

Source: Analysis of Labour Force Survey 1996 by Equal Opportunities Review 1997a, no.73

The emphasis on partnership in the Government's own bodies is undermined by a casual glance at this table. Almost 1 million people were paid *less than* £2.50 an hour in 1996. At some point these workers must have entered into a contract of some description with their partners - their employers - which both felt was to their mutual advantage. For the employees, any wage can often be better than no wage. For employers however, to employ people on such low wages is at best amoral, and at worst immoral. It could be argued that such employers are only a minority but almost one-third of employees were paid less than £4.50 an hour. In other words, the imbalance in what people need to survive and what they can actually earn is not an anomaly affecting a small part of the labour market, but appears to be an endemic feature of a capitalist labour market. No amount of rhetoric about partnership can take away from the fact, that one side of the so-called free labour bargain is in a far stronger position than the other to impose its will. Besides, this bargain is not 'free' in any conventional sense of the word, but is the result of the balance of class forces which, for various reasons, have shifted dramatically in favour of employers.

A rate of £4.50 equates to a wage of £180 per week, or £9360 per annum. Given that the average wage is now £384 per week we might feel that a wage of less than half that amount is not an unreasonable demand. However, we should bear in mind that the Low Pay Commission was not simply interested in whether a particular rate would be socially just, but whether business could afford to, or were prepared to, bear the costs. The implication is that the creation of jobs is merely a by-product of how much labour costs. In general, labour is employed not as a social service but because somebody has a job they are prepared to pay somebody else to do for them. That need for labour does not disappear because the rate of pay goes up or down by a few pence. The rate of pay is a bargain struck between employers and employees, and it is in the interests of employers to pay as little as they can get away with, whilst it is in the interest of employees to extract as much pay as they can. It is tempting to argue that the Labour Government, in placing too much emphasis on the employers side have let down the low paid. However, a commitment to increase the wages of around three million workers is not to be dismissed out of hand, but given the low rates, it should perhaps be regarded as one small step on a very long journey.

The other main plank of the Government's strategy is its 'Fairness At Work' legislation, the Employment Relations Bill (1999). The

Government introduced the White Paper into the House of Commons on 21 May 1998. It was introduced by the then President of the Board of Trade and Secretary of State for Trade and Industry, Margaret Beckett. In her opening comments she argued that the proposals would '.. foster and support a new culture in the workplace - a culture of partnership'. Whilst it is clear from her comments that the Government felt that in some companies a 'culture of partnership' already exists it is also clear that were this partnership real there would be no need for a White Paper on fairness. The Bill endorses parts of the European Social Chapter including giving full rights to part time workers and extending maternity leave from 14 to 18 weeks. The Bill also allows parents up to three months (unpaid) leave on the birth of a child, and gives employees a 'reasonable amount of unpaid time' to deal with 'domestic incidents'. In addition, an unspecified amount of money is to be provided to promote 'partnership at work'.[3] In discussing the issue of trade union recognition Margaret Beckett made the point that '..the Government recognise that these arrangements may not suit the circumstances of small firms. The statutory procedures will not therefore apply to firms with 20 or fewer employees'. This means approximately 5 million workers will not be covered by legislation giving them the right to have a trade union recognised for collective bargaining.

None of this is to be viewed entirely negatively. After 18 years in which Government was hostile to employee rights, and refused to sign the Social Chapter, any commitment to fairness must be welcome. The question here is not whether these are an improvement on the previous Government, but whether they will promote the type of society which will increase the primary social good? To put this another way, are they likely to make workers feel more secure?

Self-respect and Security

It is clear why self-respect is a primary good. Without it nothing may seem worth doing, or if some things have value for us, we lack the will to strive for them. All desire and activity becomes empty and vain, and we sink into apathy and cynicism (Rawls, 1971, p.440).

The primary sphere of social life in our society remains the economic. Work is what defines us. This is not to say that other spheres, including personal identity are unimportant. Indeed, there is a growing literature which claims it is equal to, if not more important, than the economic

(Phillips, 1992; Fraser, 1995). My assumption here is that identity is in part a reflection of our economic position and therefore the way in which we believe others perceive us at work is a vital indicator in areas of self-respect. Being outside the labour market is to be outside the commodified social world which most people take for granted. It is easy to understand how unemployed people come to regard themselves as value-less. They come to see themselves as having fallen below their own self imposed standards and therefore they lose self respect. Worse still they come to regard themselves as the cause of their own misfortune, effectively internalising the value-less opinion they think others have of them, until it becomes a badge they wear in public. The effects of long term unemployment have been the subject of a number of studies, but there has been less research on the effects of fear of job loss.

Hartley et al's (1991) innovative approach to this topic shows that fear of job loss can be as stressful as actually losing one's job. They show that as job insecurity increases an environment of uncertainty among many workers is created (Hartley, Jacobson, Klaudermans and Van Vurren, 1991). Among the causes of this uncertainty, according to Jacobson and Hartley (1991) is the new labour market flexibility. It is this which according to some theorists, for example Pfeffer and Baron (1988), has created a dichotomised workforce consisting of a core and a periphery, the former relatively secure and the latter, by its nature, insecure and often casual. This flexibility, promoted by Governments, has been embraced by employers keen to restructure, and to 'downsize', (a euphemism for 'sacking workers'). The most vulnerable workers in the restructuring have been those employed in the 'peripheral labour market': foreign labour, immigrants, ethnic minorities, older workers, women with small children, free-lance workers, those employed on short term contracts and those who are new to an organisation.

Whilst it might be argued that restructuring is a natural phenomenon within the business World, and necessary to maintain the profitability of companies in an increasingly competitive global market, this is to ignore the simple fact that those who are 'downsized' are real people, with their own commitments, and their own life plans. Those who actually become unemployed may or may not be reabsorbed into the labour market, however, the very threat of unemployment, which now hangs over huge numbers of workers on a semi-permanent basis has been shown to be detrimental to both personal and organisational effectiveness. Studies indicate that insecurity decreases commitment and job satisfaction and increases absenteeism. The prospect of losing a job can be as devastating as a bereavement for some people. Three attitude states have been found to exist where jobs are threatened: firstly, suspicion, external anger and self-blame; secondly, feelings of loss of control and helplessness; and thirdly, by contrast to the first two, an optimistic belief that the problems posed by job insecurity can be resolved (Hartley et al, 1991, p.13).

In these attitudes we see feelings of loss of confidence, loss of self worth, loss of autonomy and a sense in which life has spiralled out of control. All of these, I would argue, undermine self-respect. Security is important because it allows us to plan a future, and to have some confidence that the plan may become a reality. Of course, not all plans are equally likely to succeed, but to have any kind of plan for one's life involves some measure of certainty, if only of the income necessary to finance the plan, hence also the importance of a 'living' wage. People like to feel some control over their lives, being made to feel insecure reminds workers that they are subjects rather than objects, means rather than ends. Feeling that we are more than a means to someone else's end is important for self respect, it reminds us that we are an equal citizen with a right to expect to be taken seriously. When workers jobs are insecure, whether through flexible working or other reasons, it means that they are not being taken seriously as rational beings with ends of their own, but rather are merely means to another end, usually profit. To leave a job is to weigh up options and to make a decision about the way your life is heading. To be forced from a job is to be denied a say in decisions which affect your life, and leaves you without the means for autonomy.

Insecurity, lack of control, and not being taken seriously all affect the way in which we perceive ourselves, and thereby can have the effect of reducing self-respect. This relationship between insecurity and self-respect is important in that it is intricately related to questions of labour market flexibility. Whilst positive flexibility might offset some of the insecurity by giving workers new opportunities to try new modes of working; negative flexibility is concerned entirely with undermining whatever security workers feel. It is this insecurity that I would argue is responsible for reducing self-respect.

Self-respect, it should be noted, is a phrase often used rhetorically, but less often adequately conceptualised sociologically. For some theorists, including Rawls (1971) it is the primary social good. It is often confused with self-esteem. But, whilst self-esteem is an aspect of self-respect, it should not, in my view, be reduced to it (for a psychological discussion of self-esteem see Baumeister, 1993). Self-respect is essentially socially constructed. It is constructed in the interactions from which we gain our sense of self. As Goffman (1959) has discussed, the presentation of the self is an act mediated by the presence of others. Self-respect originates in the interaction we have with others. Self-respect is a concept which contains a number of overlapping and interconnected dimensions related to work, family/home, body image/psychological self-assessment etc.

A few theorists have made explicit use of the term self respect and I draw upon them here in an attempt to bring out its essence. For Rawls, self-respect is a person's sense of their own value and their confidence that their 'life plan' is recognised by others in a similar position (Rawls, 1971, p.440). It is concerned with an expectation that we can develop our talents and abilities in a way which is recognised by a community of our peers (Rawls, 1971, p.426). Rawls argues that self-respect is connected to a recognition that what we do well is evaluated both by ourselves - hence our self worth - and by others - hence mutual respect. Only when we are confident in our own sense of worth can we pursue our life plan safe in the knowledge that others in our community recognise our plans as rational and worthwhile. At the same time, the mutual aspect demands that we also evaluate their plans in the same way (Rawls, 1971, p.442). According to Hill (1991), those who lack self-respect, are often those who have allowed their standards to fall below those which would be evaluated positively by an outside audience. Hill also argues that people who adopt an attitude of servility are lacking in self-respect. A person who constantly defers to another is ignoring their own moral worth. It is not simply the act of deference, we all defer to others at times, but the justification in which the deferential person believes themselves to be of less worth than those to whom they defer (Hill, 1991, p.6). Williams (1964), following Kant (1952), refers to self respect as being regarded as an end in your own right, and not merely the instrument of another's will. To be treated as an end it is necessary for others to recognise that you exist not merely for their benefit. This means that your life plan is as important as anybody else's life plan and should be accorded equal respect.

The essence of self-respect then can be conceptualised within three broad themes: 1) Being treated as an end; 2) Self worth; and 3) Public recognition. The first of these is at the base of most theories of respect and is to be found in Kant's work on respect. It is often what people mean when they talk of 'equal respect'. We can see how treating people as ends and not merely means is connected with personal autonomy, which connects with Rawls view of the 'life plan'. To have a 'life plan' is to have an end of ones own regardless of whether you are also the means to someone else's end. This view that we should have ends is connected to our sense of self worth. This is partly concerned with confidence, the confidence to say that your opinions matter, and furthermore you matter as an individual. It is also concerned with the confidence to formulate life plans, and to regard oneself as an end in your own right. This aspect of self worth also connects to Hill's suggestion that self-respect is connected to the standards that we set ourselves. It is when we reach those standards, and these are often expressed in terms of the life plan, that we can affirm our self-respect, whilst falling below our own standards can have the affect of reducing our self-respect. Finally, and of equal importance, is public recognition. Self-respect is concerned with being able to present our life plan publicly, and for it to be evaluated as rational by an outside audience of our peers. The outside audience is important for it is not simply that they are the judge of our standards, more importantly they are the mirror by which we judge ourselves. It is not simply how they judge us that affects our self-respect, but how we think they judge us. This, of course, raises the possibility of more than one audience, evaluating our 'standards' in different ways. Peer groups, family, workmates, employers may all evaluate us differently. Indeed, they may not evaluate us at all, but the fact that we think they do, means that we are constructing self respect from the respect we believe we have from others.

Self-respect can be summed up in the phrase 'being taken seriously'. To be taken seriously is to be confirmed as a rational thinking person, but more than this it is to be accorded respect. Knowing that you are taken seriously and therefore respected increases self-respect, which by corollary increases self-confidence and self-esteem, all of which help in the presentation of self to the outside world. Self-respect is therefore affected by the way in which we see ourselves, and is likely, it would seem, to be affected by everyday happenings. There is a strong sense in which perceived injustices undermine our sense of self-respect. Clearly, this depends somewhat on the nature of the injustice. Losing one's place in the supermarket queue is likely to have rather less affect on our self-respect than being the victim of sexual harassment. Self-respect is concerned with the way we feel about ourselves, but what mediates those feelings is the way that others feel about us. The woman executive (or office junior, for that matter) who is sexualised by male colleagues is constantly reminded that she is first and foremost a sexual object, and only if she can overcome that can she be taken seriously as a member of the labour force (see Collinson & Collinson, 1996).

Increasing Self-respect Through Security

...by relying on a Commission to establish and monitor the promised minimum wage, Labour has substantially reduced the potential the minimum wage question has to create difficulties now it is in office (Whitton, 1998, p.175).

The British Government in common with other centre-left Governments declares itself as dedicated to the promotion of social justice. Its legislative programme claims to be a programme in which active partnership will promote both fairness and flexibility. If what the Government were promoting was simply positive flexibility then it is possible that their claims would stand up to scrutiny. But as the Low Pay Commission has declared, its aim was to fix a rate 'which business could afford'. Whilst the Employment Relations Bill does little more than implement European legislation giving people *unpaid* time off for maternity and family leave. The exemptions to legislation are at least as important as those who are included. By not including 16 and 17 year olds in the low pay regulations and by exempting companies employing less than 20 employees from the 'fairness at work' legislation, millions of workers remain without basic protections. The flexibility that the government are keen to promote appears to be a hybrid of the positive and negative flexibilities which are described above. What this means is that the goal of promoting social justice relies on the voluntary partnership of employers who in the past have opposed every step taken to improve working conditions. Of course, some employers will embrace the rhetoric which is currently popular in political circles, but the test is whether they will continue to embrace it should the political context change. Past experience suggests that most employers are willing advocates of negative flexibility regardless of the effect on social justice. In this scenario, workers' insecurity seems set to remain a feature of the labour market.

It is not difficult however, to imagine a set of policies that might serve to increase security. The Government could, for example, make it unlawful for profitable companies to dismiss any worker in order to increase the profits of the company, or to increase bonus payments to senior staff or to pay dividend to shareholders. Such a policy would certainly create more security than exists at present. Downsizing, that euphemism of the eighties, often meant profitable companies sacking workers in order to be more profitable. These were not redundancies, for the work still needed to be done and was simply shifted to the remaining workforce. Such a policy is ultimately self-defeating. The workers left become overworked, over-stressed and de-motivated. Those who are sacked lose spending power, and become a further 'burden' on the over-stretched welfare state meaning that those left in work have to pay more taxes - either directly, or more often these days, indirectly - in order to support them.

But, as I have argued, it is not simply having a job but having one which pays a 'living' wage. A minimum wage is one half of the equation, but there is also an argument that social justice should concern itself with relative values, and in this sense perhaps income differentials should be of interest to us. Vastly different incomes are a crude but effective measure of social inequality. Of course, increasing people's incomes can be beneficial socially. After all, people work in order to consume. The things they consume must be produced by somebody. The more money they have the more they will spend. Up to a point. At some level of income there must be a decline in marginal utility, so that more money simply means more saving. For those at the lower end of the income spectrum every penny is accounted for, often using complex patterns of debt displacement, or what is more colloquially known as 'robbing Peter to pay Paul'. At the higher income level, however, the problem is the exact opposite. If you 'earn' millions in a year, there are simply not enough things to spend it on. If this money was used to create productive work for others it might be morally justified, but often the only intention of those with high incomes is to generate more money for themselves. In this sense, their rational self interest leads them to pursue the highest rate of return, which can often mean 'gambling' on the international money markets, which produces no product that could realistically be described as of use to anybody, particularly those at the lower end of the income scale.

Therefore, whilst tackling poverty wages is obviously important, social justice in some of its forms will require that income differentials should also be tackled. What is needed is a ratio of top to bottom earners, modelled somewhere along the lines of Rawls's 'difference principle', with the emphasis being on improving the life of those at the bottom of the scale. In pursuit of justice, the Government could make it economic policy to reduce the differential in income from its current ratio of

179

top:bottom which must be in the millions, to say 1:100. In other words, if the lowest paid person, in a given organisation, was paid £144 per week, the top paid person could earn no more than £748,800 per annum. Over time, the aim might be to reduce the differential to perhaps 50:1, or even 25:1. Of course, the very wealthy would feel that this was extremely unjust, for how could they possibly be 'adequately' rewarded at such a level of remuneration. This is not necessarily a fetter on the earnings of the 'top' jobs, but can be achieved by a higher minimum wage rate. At a ratio of 100:1, if the managing director of a company thought they were worth £1 million a year, the lowest paid person in their organisation would have to earn £10,000 (or whatever the pro rata rate was for part-timers). At 25:1, the lowest paid person would be on £40,000 a year. Such a policy would force organisations to examine their pay differentials, and to justify both high and low wages in something more than the usual 'what the market can bear' terms. Of course, for a Government to enact such policies would require a commitment to a radical transformation of the distribution of wealth and income. It is highly unlikely that the present British Government would be prepared to incur the wrath such policies would no doubt engender, and therefore the present 'partnership' will continue. Flexibility will continue to be promoted as if it were an adjunct of social justice rather than, in its negative forms at least, its antonym.

Flexibility and partnership have come to be buzz words accepted by Governments of both right and left. The Blair Government are keen to promote flexible working patterns, flexible life styles, flexible pension arrangements etc. The message is: flexibility is the key word to the restructuring of a Britain made bad by years of Tory misrule, and partnership between employers and employees is the means to this end. It is not just the British government who espouse such policies; across Europe, including the Jospin Government in France, flexibility is promoted as the rational choice in politics, employment and life style. At the same time governments are aware that most people expect to be treated as more than just a means to an end. To this end, in Britain and France, as in much of Europe, Government has tried to balance the conflicting interests of business, on the one hand, and employees, on the other. Mostly, this has been achieved through the rhetoric of social justice particularly the idea of 'constructive partnership'. In Britain, the Borrie Commission and in France, the Minc Commission, both had similar frames of reference (for a discussion see Leydier, 1998). The Minc Commission, proposed a supposedly new paradigm based around equity, where 'equity equals justice which means coherence which implies efficiency' (Leydier, 1998, p.15). The Borrie Commission was similarly weak on how to achieve its goals and placed an emphasis on the creation of a genuine equal opportunity society, based on 'partnership' between Government, employers and the wider community. As Townsend points out: 'What is the point of all this stress on improving opportunities when the occupational and class positions to which these opportunities supposedly give access are being inexorably driven apart? There is little point in enhancing people's opportunities to climb ladders if the ladders grow ever longer, the gap between rungs wider, and chances of falling greater'. (Townsend, 1995, p.145).

To be fair to the Labour Government, within the rather narrow focus in which it operates, attempts are being made to promote a fairer welfare capitalism. The 'Fairness At Work' and Low Pay legislation are examples. However, the emphasis on 'partnership' between employers and employees ignores the tension between the desire of business for an unregulated labour market where profitability is the key, and the desire of the wider community for social justice, which means the opportunity to be an active citizen, supported by a living wage.

Social justice is concerned implicitly with the creation of an environment where self-respect can flourish. Self-respect flourishes where people are regarded as ends in their own right. Where they have choices, where they are taken seriously, and treated with respect. But labour market flexibility is primarily concerned with denying workers the opportunity to have any rights to a job, and in some cases extends to the denial of the 'right' to a home life (see Lavalette & Kennedy, 1996). Whilst positive flexibility can have beneficial consequences for workers, for capital, flexibility has a rather more narrow meaning. It is concerned with cutting costs by controlling the supply and flow of labour. From the employees perspective such a vision can only have negative consequences. Workers, according to Hartley et al. respond in a predictable way to insecurity. Most workers need a sense that the future is relatively stable, and this helps to create a sense of psychological security, which generates a more committed and productive workforce. Insecurity, which is an inevitable side effect of labour market flexibility, has the effect of reminding workers that they are first and foremost means to an end. In simple terms they are not taken seriously as individuals, and are rather seen as part of an undifferentiated mass to be hired and fired at will. Clearly this state will not affect all workers, some will continue to have better working conditions than others. But for those whose labour becomes increasingly casualised, and this is most likely at the semi- and unskilled end of the labour market, insecurity will have the affect of weakening their concept of self, particularly their self-respect.

Notes

1   The findings of the Low Pay Commission can be downloaded from the Internet at *http://www.lowpay.gov.uk/*
2   The Office for National Statistics places information on a variety of subjects at *http://www.ons.gov.uk*
3   For the full text of the Bill see *http://www.parliament.uk/commons/hsecom.htm*

References

Baumeister, R. F. (1993), *Self Esteem. The Puzzle of Low Self Regard*, Plenum Press, New York.

Brett, J. M. and Stroh, L. K. (1994), 'Turnover of Female Managers' in Davidson, M. and Burke, R. (eds), *Women In Management. Current Research Issues*, Paul Chapman, London.

Collinson, M. and Collinson, D. (1996), '"Its Only Dick": the Sexual Harassment of Women Managers in Insurance Sales', *Work Employment and Society*, vol. 10, no. 1, pp.29-56.

Davidson, M. J. and Cooper, C. L. (1992), *Shattering The Glass Ceiling*, Paul Chapman, London.

Equal Opportunities Review (1996), Flexible Working: the Impact on Women's Pay and Conditions, *Equal Opportunities Review*, No. 65, January/February.

Equal Opportunities Review (1997a), Minimum Wage Benefits Women and Ethnic Minorities, *Equal Opportunities Review*, No. 73, May/June.

Equal Opportunities Review (1997b), Gender Pay Gap Narrows, *Equal Opportunities Review*, No. 76, November/December.

Evetts, J. (1994), 'Career and Gender: the Conceptual Challenge', in J. Evetts (ed.), *Women and Career. Themes and Issues in Advanced Industrial Societies*, Longman, London.

Fraser, N. (1995), 'From Redistribution to Recognition? Dilemmas of Justice in a Post-socialist age', *New Left Review*, 212, pp.68-93.

Goffman, E. (1959), *The Presentation of Self in Everyday Life*, Penguin, Harmondsworth.

Hartley, J., Jacobson, D., Klandermans, B. and Van Vuuren, T. (1991), *Job Insecurity. Coping with Jobs at Risk*, Sage, London.

Hill Jr., T. E. (1991), *Autonomy and Self-respect*, Cambridge University Press, Cambridge.

Jeffery, M. (1997), 'European Social Policy and the Meanings of Flexibility', *www.britcoun.org/european/ionil.htm*.

Jessop, B. (1994), 'Post-Fordism and the State', in A. Amin (ed.), *Post-Fordism, A Reader*, Blackwell, Oxford.

Kant, I. (1952), 'Fundamental Principles of the Metaphysic of Morals', in R. M. Hutchins (ed.), *Great Books of the Western World*. 42, Kant, Encyclopaedia Brittanica, Chicago.

Konsta, A. (1997), 'The Concept of Flexibility and the European Labour Market', *www.britcoun.org/european/ionil.htm*

Lavalette, M. and Kennedy, J. (1996), 'Casual Lives? The Social Effects of Work Casualization and the Lock Out on the Liverpool Docks', *Critical Social Policy* 48, vol. 16, pp.95-107.

Lewis, S. (1994), 'Role Tensions and Dual Career Couples', in M. Davidson and R. Burke (eds), *Women In Management. Current Research Issues*, Paul Chapman, London.

Leydier, G. (1998), 'Dimensions of Inequality in French and Political Discourse Since the Early 80's', in J. Edwards and J-P. Revauger (eds), *Discourse on Inequality in France and Britain*, Ashgate, Aldershot.

Low Pay Commission (1998), *First Report of the Low Pay Commission*, HMSO, London.

Marx, K. (1954), *Capital: Volume One*, George Allen and Unwin, London. (Originally published 1864).

Pfeffer, J. and Baron, J. N. (1988), 'Taking The Workers Out: Recent Trends in the Structuring of Employment' in B. M. Straw and L. L. Cummings (eds), *Research in Organisational Behaviour*, vol. 10, JAI Press, Greenwich, Conn.

Phillips, A. (1992), 'Democracy and Difference: Some Problems for Feminist Theory', *Political Quarterly*, vol. 63, pp.79-90.

Rawls, J. (1971), *A Theory of Justice*, Oxford University Press, Oxford.

Siddorn, G. (1996), 'Labour Market Insecurity', *Economic Briefing*, Issue 10, www.hm-treasury.gov.uk.

Standing, G. (1986), *Unemployment and Labour Market Flexibility: The United Kingdom*, International Labour Organisation, Geneva.

The Report of the Commission on Social Justice (1994), *Social Justice. Strategies for National Renewal*, Vintage, London.

Townsend, P. (1995), 'Persuasion and Conformity: An Assessment of the Borrie Report on Social Justice', *New Left Review*, 213.

Veneziani, B. (1996), 'Labour Flexibility in Europe', *http://epn.org/iess/ielabo.html*.

Whitton, T. (1998), 'The National Minimum Wage: Pride or Prejudice?', in J. Edwards and J-P. Revauger (eds), *Discourse on Inequality in France and Britain*, Ashgate, Aldershot.

Williams, B. (1964), 'The Idea of Equality', in P. Laslett and W.G. Runciman (eds), *Philosophy Politics and Society*, Basil Blackwell, Oxford.

Young, M. I. (1990), *Justice and the Politics of Difference*, Princeton University Press, Princeton, New Jersey.

12 Flexibility, Economic Security and Social Rights

JOHN EDWARDS

Employment flexibility, as other chapters in this volume demonstrate, represents a change in the socio-economic environment in which those in the labour market and their dependents live. It is a departure from long-established patterns of stable and long-term employment for many employees (though short-term contracts and rapid job succession have of course, been characteristic of some occupations and some sections of the labour market for a very long time), and as such, it will have consequences that go beyond the immediate realm of employment. Employment flexibility is but one of many changes in our socio-economic environment (changes in information technology, periods of inflation, periods of high unemployment, changes in the delivery and effectiveness of welfare and support services and so on), but it stands out, in Europe at least, as being relatively recent, seemingly long term, and as having effects that go to the heart of the way that many individuals and families conduct their lives. It is this last point that motivates the arguments of this chapter.

We have come to assume, whether from habit or principle, a degree of economic certainty in our lives that stems from (generally) long-term and secure employment, and this certainty has been the basis for the way we plan our lines, as individuals and as members of families. Commitments are made, houses bought, expenditure on education is planned (by some), geographical movement made on the back of assumptions about future income, and plans for an economically secure old age are often tied to long-term job stability, employers' pension schemes and so on. Now if these *are* just that - assumptions or expectations - then as we shall see there may be little to be said about what ought to be done about the consequences of employment flexibility, other than that we shall have to adapt to the changed environment and find ways of planning our lives on the basis of less certainty. But there is an argument - which this chapter will elaborate - that social and economic security and stability are not just incidental consequences of the organisation of employment markets, but are part of our social rights (and, possibly, our human rights). In short, so the argument goes, we (every individual) have a right to (some degree of) social and economic stability and security.[1] A good deal of work will need to be done on this bold assertion for it to carry conviction but we can say why it might have significance and why it is worth considering. Whether something is a right, and what sort of right it is will have consequences for what ought to be done (and by whom) if it is threatened. Rights carry duties[2] and depending on the type of right, there is a moral compulsion or at least, a contractual obligation, to see that it is fulfilled (that is, enjoyed in practice). If therefore, we have a right to social and economic stability and security and if these are threatened by employment flexibility, someone or something (most likely the state) has a duty to implement policies to protect the substance of the right. It is not optional for the duty holder to do so; it is a moral requirement. If on the other hand, stability and security are not rights (but their removal no less damaging for that), no-one is under any compulsion to reduce the harm that their removal might cause. States might wish to intervene to reduce resulting hardship but they do not have to do so.

Our concerns therefore are with the consequences of employment flexibility, whether any of these consequences threaten our social rights and what the policy consequences of this would be.

Employment Flexibility and its Consequence

There is general agreement on the components of the 'new' labour flexibility : more self-employment, short term contract work, flexible terms and conditions that differ between the different status of workers, more seasonal employment, more employment mobility and migration, serial skills acquisition, more retraining, and a reduction in the influence of trade unions. All these, in combination, represent a significant change in the social and economic environment. The change will bring benefits (more evident perhaps for employers and economies than for workers and their families) but our concern here lies with the disbenefits that flexibility brings. These, in the absence of quantitative research are easier to identify than to quantify and to the extent that they represent a social concern, it has to be acknowledged that it is one, of the magnitude of which we remain ignorant. The most significant disbenefits and the ones that will most concern us here are, as we have noted, a reduction, for those affected, in the extent of the medium and long-term economic certainty they enjoy, creating greater uncertainty, insecurity and instability which together, may undermine their ability to plan their lives both as individuals and as members of families and households. And the link between the various components of employment flexibility on the one hand and increased insecurity and instability on the other, is direct - as is the consequence - the erosion in people's ability to plan.

We have already asserted that some degree of economic security which provides us with the base from which we can plan our lives (if we wish), has become an expectation, or at least, an assumption for most people particularly in 'advanced' societies. If it is also the case that we have a right of some kind, to stability and security and the ability to plan (and that these are not just expectations), then we shall need to elaborate on the idea of 'planning a life'. It is, after all unwise to assert (or even contemplate) a right to something if we are unclear about what that something is. Firstly however, we need to clarify what the right is *to*, if there is a right. Two possibilities present themselves. The first is that the right is a right to stability and security *per se*. The second is that the right is a right to stability and security as necessary conditions of the ability to plan and that it is the latter that is the fundamental object of the right. Without arguing the case in detail, it would seem more plausible that the second of these alternatives carries more force if only because having a right to stability and security *per se* seems less than compelling. What would it be about these factors that would warrant our having a right to them?

Might it not be possible after all that *uncertainty* in itself could be just as contributive to human autonomy (or whatever is thought to be fundamental of rights) as stability? More compelling is the notion that stability and security are necessary means to the ability to plan and that if we have a right, this would be its object. There will be more to say on this.

What then, do we mean by the ability to plan a life and why should we have a right to it? The second question will be answered in a later section when we consider the nature of social rights. An answer to the first question assumes that it is a part of moral autonomy (or more basically, of being a human) that we do not drift through life devoid of purposes or projects that are partly constitutive of our individual identities (see for example Lomasky, 1984; Benn, 1979; Raz, 1984). Or at least we might say of someone who led their lives through choice always and only in tutelage to circumstances, always reactive, never proactive, that they were hardly 'fulfilling their potential' or leading a life worth leading.[3] And to have projects, to pursue purposes that define our identity requires that we are able, in some degree, at least, to plan our lives; to be able to make a reasonable assessment of our circumstances in at least the medium term; to have a reasonable idea of what next year (or the next five or ten years) may bring. This, in essence is what planning a life means and it is why some degree of stability and security is important. Whether they are important enough to constitute a right or should remain as 'reasonable expectations' will be the subject of ensuing paragraphs.

The Content of Rights

If there is a right to stability and security what sort of right is it? And are stability and security the sorts of things that constitute the content of any particular kind of right?

We cannot adequately deal with these questions without a brief excursion into the realm of rights, confusing as this can sometimes be. For the purposes of policy response (if such were deemed necessary) it will for example be necessary to know what *kind* of right security and stability might be. The list of types of rights seems often to be expanding but the most commonly asserted are civil and political rights, social, economic and cultural rights and, with somewhat less unanimity, the 'third generation rights' to self-governance, development and national and linguistic integrity (see Davidson, 1993; Donnelly, 1989; Galenkamp, 1998, for further discussion). (We need not expand on this last type of right – it is not relevant to our analysis). At a different level of analysis, we may make a distinction between 'human rights' and those rights that are not human rights (there is no term to describe these that comes readily to hand – 'non human rights' conveys the wrong meaning).[4] Examples of rights that are not human rights would include contractual rights between individuals, between individuals and institutions, and between institutions. They are not 'human rights' because they are defined by a contract and cannot apply universally. Most of these – like third generation rights – are of no interest to us except in one important respect. There is a set of substantive rights which might generally be called rights to welfare, that is included in the Universal Declaration of Human Rights and which for that reason, many believe, properly fall within the domain of human rights (but see Cranston, 1976). However, these rights, including rights to education, health care, unemployment benefit and so on, may also be characterised as rights established by contract between the citizen and the state. And it certainly is true that the *amount* of benefit to which you have a right *is* determined by arrangements within states. Now, most of the rights that share this ambiguity are ones that we call social or economic rights (as distinct from civil and political rights) and the ambiguity is of more than semantic importance because it makes possible a dispute about whether social rights (in particular) *are* in fact human rights, notwithstanding their inclusion in the Universal Declaration and the European Convention on Human Rights.

There is an added significance in all this for the concerns of this chapter because if stability and security do form the content of a right then it seems that it is most likely to be a social right.[5] This, we can deduce partly by a process of elimination (they do not constitute part of the content of civil or political rights)[6] but mainly on the grounds of close affinity to other components of social rights and in particular, rights to social security, pensions and unemployment benefit.

However, these remain relatively unconvincing arguments in themselves and we need to examine in more detail the nature and content of a social right both as a human right and as a citizen right. We shall then be better placed to consider security and stability as substantive contents of (some) kind of right.

There is a sense in which the question of the content of a citizen right is uninteresting from the present point of view since it can be whatever is contracted to between a state and its citizens, and this will lie in the domain of political bargaining as much as in the philosophy of rights. There is no reason therefore why any state, but in particular, 'first world' states, should not 'guarantee' their citizens a right of stability and security in their social and economic lives (though the 'guarantee' might last only so long as the democratic process throws up administrations prepared to back it). And in this lies one of the fundamental differences between a citizen right and a human right. Citizens may vote away their citizen rights by reducing the content or their notional contract with the state. Human rights, on the other hand, are universal and imprescriptible; you cannot disown them even if you wanted to.[7] So, there is no reason why stability and security should not constitute a part of the contents of social rights insofar as these are citizen rights and no more.

If we consider a social right to be a human right, two methods of establishing their content immediately present themselves. The first is simply to check the lexicon of the Bill of Rights or regional variations such as the European Social Charter or the European Convention on Human

Rights for rights that might be called social rights. The second is the more fundamental approach of deriving what sorts of rights would be prescribed by the need to maintain everyone as a morally autonomous agent – the ultimate bedrock of human rights. Clearly, the results of the positivistic approach and the morally derivational approach may well be quite different; the former didactic (and born of committees), the second, speculative and probably less precise and detailed.

Articles 22 to 26 inclusive, of the International Bill of Human Rights enumerate what may broadly be called social (and economic) rights.[8] These include the right to 'social security'; the right to 'free choice of employment and to protection against unemployment'; to 'social protection' and to 'security in the event of unemployment, sickness, disability, widowhood, old age or other lack of livelihood in circumstances beyond (his) control'. In addition to these (among which we shall look for an interpretation that will include stability and security), others that might be interpreted as social rights are the right to rest and leisure, including periodic holidays with pay, the right to a standard of living adequate for health and well-being and including food, clothing, housing, medical care and social services, and the right to free education.

These then, are the social rights that are given status in the Universal Declaration. They are agreed to by those countries that are signatories to the Covenants. But they are not derived from fundamental principles : they are the work of committees. A very different approach to identifying what might be called social rights is the derivational approach that takes as its starting point the moral character of man that makes certain rights an inescapable part of his make-up. For present purposes, it will not be necessary to give more than a brief sketch of the argument (but see Plant, 1991; Raz, 1982; Golding, 1984; Lindley, 1986, for versions of it). In essence, the argument grounds the idea of a human right in the moral character of man by positing that human group life (including societies and states) cannot exist without some form of moral system. Moral systems, in their turn cannot function unless they are populated by 'moral beings' – that is – people who have moral sense and the ability to distinguish and choose between right and wrong (and any other moral judgements we care to add). Such beings therefore must have moral autonomy which *is* in effect the ability to make moral choices, to be responsible for their actions and so on. It therefore follows (or so the argument goes) that human beings must have a right to those things that are necessary to maintain moral autonomy. Without that, moral systems including societies, cannot exist. It must be the case then, that we have a right to anything that is necessary for moral autonomy.[9] What *is* necessary for moral autonomy is part of another story and will depend on a detailed specification of 'moral autonomy' itself but we can say at the very least that there must be a right to a certain level of well-being that is sufficient to enable us to function autonomously. (A life led in fear, grinding poverty and constant economic uncertainty is probably not one in which moral autonomy and the ability to make free moral judgements are possible).[10] The constituents of social rights are likely to differ (at the margins at least) depending on whether such rights are considered to be positive, legal, citizen rights; the rights incorporated in the United Nations Declaration and other 'regional' charters; or rights to those things that are necessary for moral autonomy. But, in respect of the latter two, we might expect extensive commonality in the things we have a right to particularly as we have assumed a level of well-being to be necessary for autonomy. We turn next then, to a consideration of the effects of increasing employment flexibility, and particularly reductions in economic security and stability in the context of different formulations of social rights. Can economic stability and security reasonably be seen to be part of the content of social rights in any or all of the three forms we have considered – citizen rights, the contents of declarations, and the requirements for autonomy?

Economic Security and Stability and the Contents of Social Rights

Do we have a (social or economic) right to stability and security either in themselves or as pre-requisites to a right to plan a life? If we do, then it must be the case that we have a right to those things that are *their* pre-requisites such as a guaranteed income either from employment earnings or social security; a reasonably predictable income not subject to unmanageable fluctuations; guaranteed buffers against periodic employment and a continuity of welfare that evens out the hills and troughs of income from (unstable) employment and permits reasonable plan-making over, at least, the middle-term.[11] (It is worth pointing up here by way of juxtaposition what the alternative formulation would be, namely, that security and stability are not things we have rights to but are simply part of the everyday background noise of life in modern capitalist societies and if we wish to plan a life then our plans must be contingent on insecurity. We shall return to this formulation in another section).

The content of positive citizen rights (a form of contract between the citizen as taxpayer and the state as provider) may in theory, as we have seen, be anything the state or citizens may wish to put into the notional contract. There is no reason therefore assuming due process (such as democratic procedures, proper electoral process and the production of political manifestos), why social and economic security and stability and their pre-requisites should not form part of the content of citizen rights in any given state. They will not be universal rights however (and not human rights); their existence will depend on states' desire or willingness to protect them, and it will be subject to political process. Both states and citizens may decide for whatever reason, to derogate them. To this extent therefore, citizen rights tell us little about the moral standing of security and stability as rights in any more fundamental sense than as contractual rights subject to political process.

We have earlier noted the social and economic rights that are included in the Universal Declaration of Human Rights. Do they, individually or collectively, cover a right to security and stability? Well, if not explicitly, they seem to come close. As we have noted, the social rights content of the thirty articles includes a right to 'social security', to 'protection against unemployment', to 'social protection' and to 'security in the event of unemployment... or other lack of livelihood in circumstances beyond (his) control'. There is little point reading the drafters' intentions into these words (but we might reasonably wonder what a right to 'protection against unemployment' means or how it might be implemented in a market society), and neither can we expect the immediate post-war drafters to have been so prescient as to have foreseen the growth of employment flexibility and its consequences. That notwithstanding, we do not have to be cavalier in our interpretation of the articles to recognise something of what we seek (the preconditions of an ability to plan) in Article 25 – 'security in the event of unemployment ... or (other) circumstances beyond (his) control'. Certainly, there is nothing here about evening out the troughs and hills caused by employment flexibility, nor anything explicit about security and stability as necessary for a right to plan. Nor is there, in the Universal Declaration any mention of a right to plan a life as such. To the extent that we must interpret the articles therefore, we can say that the Universal Declaration intends that there be a right to economic security in times of unemployment and that the purpose of this is to maintain some level of income into households so affected in order to prevent hardship. The Declaration contains nothing about security and stability in the context of employment flexibility (because, as we have noted, drafted as it was between 1945 and 1948, it could hardly be expected to have done so). But more significantly, the Declaration is silent on there being a right to plan a life – something which, if it exists, could not have been constrained by the historical positioning of the Declaration itself. So far as the Declaration is concerned therefore, there is a right to security from hardship but there is no right to plan a life.[12]

The third (deductive) approach requires that we look at what is required for moral autonomy and derive the content of social rights from those requirements. We shall then be in a position to judge whether security and stability constitute a part of social rights as derived from the requisites for autonomy. The process of deduction would look something like this

- if social rights are necessary to guarantee autonomy, and
- if autonomy requires stability and security and the ability to plan, then
- *prima facie*, stability and security must be component parts of our social rights.

The 'autonomy argument' says that since moral autonomy is fundamental of moral and social systems then the people who inhabit those systems must have moral autonomy which requires in turn that they have a right to those things that are necessary for its maintenance. Specifying what those things are is made difficult by the want of any clear definition of 'autonomy'. We are working with concepts that do not lend themselves easily to a concrete formulation with a common understanding. However, the present task is a more limited one and will be better achieved by circumventing the more speculative questions involved. It will be necessary then to assert what was earlier supposed, that there are things, necessary for maintaining moral autonomy, that fall in the realm of what, in either contexts, would be called social rights. It was conjectured for example, that we cannot perform as morally autonomous agents with the ability to distinguish between right and wrong, to make moral judgements, to weigh evidence, to participate in the life of our society if we are shackled by poverty, deprivation, lack of education, untreated illness, worry and uncertainty. If we need to be free of these constraints in order to be autonomous agents then we must have a right to those things that will guarantee freedom from such constraints – some degree of income security, education, available health care, a reasonable domestic environment and so on. These are all things that elsewhere would be called social rights. Social rights are necessary for autonomy.

The second part of our 'syllogism' requires that stability, security and (hence) the ability to plan are necessary conditions of being autonomous agents. In a sense, this must be the point on which the argument turns. Is it reasonable to claim that we cannot operate as fully autonomous agents unless we have some degree of certainty, stability and security in our lives and thus the ability to plan a life? It is perfectly plausible to argue as we have noted earlier, that uncertainty and insecurity are themselves conducive to an active, busy and productive life in which we are better able to hone our moral sensibilities and act autonomously.[13] History, after all, is well populated by those made morally stronger by tribulation. But I doubt that their example will found a general argument that uncertainty and insecurity are morally good for you. At least, not in respect of we more lowly mortals with mortgages, debts, children, chronic ill health, pending redundancy, dwindling clients, empty order books, ailing parents or grandparents, and family demands for a summer holiday that might not be affordable. We may choose a life of insecurity or we may have it thrust upon us and emerge better for it, but it seems plausible to argue that for most people, most of the time, leading 'ordinary' lives, insecurity and the inability to plan with any degree of confidence are a bane rather than a stimulus. Clearly, our 'historical' examples are evidence that security and stability are not *necessary* conditions of moral autonomy but they do appear to be highly contributive. A life led in chronic financial insecurity (when it is not chosen) is not one in which moral and personal development can thrive. Constant preoccupation with 'making ends meet' may not prohibit moral autonomy, but it will probably hinder its development.

These arguments are necessarily conjectural (their substance is not subject to empirical test), but to the extent that they carry any conviction, they indicate that social rights are necessary for autonomy and that security and stability, whilst not being necessary conditions of autonomy, are highly contributive. It follows therefore that stability and security are likely to be components of social rights. (Logic dictates that since security and stability are not necessary conditions of autonomy, it cannot follow that they *must* be components of social rights. On a balance of arguments however, it seems that their place in the realm of social rights is as strong as that of many of its other components). At the very least then, we can say that security, stability and the ability to plan are components of social rights when these are derived from the conditions necessary for autonomy. In short, there is a strong case for saying that we have a *right* to security and stability.

Putting together the arguments from the three formulations of social rights, it turns out that social rights as citizen (contract) rights may contain whatever might be agreed to in the political process (a not very revelatory conclusion). The 'social right' articles of the Universal Declaration yield a strong indication that security and stability would be included but a 'right to plan a life' would not. And social rights as derived from the demands of moral autonomy carry a strong likelihood of including in their content, security, stability and the ability to plan a life. On balance therefore, a claim can be made that we have a (social) right to (some degree of) security and stability and to the ability to plan our lives. And the implication of deriving this conclusion other than from contractual rights is the possibility (to put it no higher) that they are human rights as well.[14]

Whilst this is not the place to enter an extended discussion of the relationship between social rights and human rights and the difference between human rights as catalogued in international and regional charters on the one hand and as moral (that is derived) rights on the other, we should at least entertain some argument about the standing of security, stability and the ability to plan, as *human* rights. Firstly, if Articles 22, 23 and 25 of the universal Declaration *are* deemed to include security and stability (but not, we have supposed, the right to plan), then they must definitionally be human rights in the context of the Declaration. Secondly, the purpose of deriving rights from foundational moral characteristics such as autonomy must be to derive universal human (or moral) rights.[15] Rights so derived cannot be differentially distributed across mankind. The implication of the foregoing arguments therefore is that security and stability (and the ability to plan if foundationally derived) are human rights. If we temper argument with intuition however, it behoves us to ask whether we really believe that there is a universal human right to security, stability, (and to the ability to plan). It is not necessary to agree all the way with Cranston's well known argument against the inclusion of social rights in the pantheon of human rights (Cranston, 1976) to see the point of what he says particularly in respect of 'paramount importance'. To provide perspective on the question, Cranston compares some of the social rights included in the Universal Declaration with the more fundamental rights to life and liberty and the right not to be tortured (amongst others). And the same can be done in respect of the rights to security, stability and the ability to plan. Do they belong in the same company with rights to life, liberty, property and so on? Some of the arguments against Cranston tend to rely on reasoning that would justify some social rights (such as the right to education) on the basis that they are necessary for the fulfillment of other, 'fundamental' rights – in this case, the ability to exercise ones civil and political rights (see for example, Plant, Lesser and Taylor-Gooby, 1980, p.73 et sec; Weale, 1983, Ch.7). The same sorts of reasoning could be applied to security, stability and the ability to plan as a means of bringing them more securely into the realm of rights. It is a line of reasoning that has been used in earlier sections of this chapter to clarify the contributive nature of security and stability to the ability to plan a life and in respect of having rights to whatever is necessary for moral autonomy. Implicit in such reasoning is the assumption that some rights exist in order to serve others (or at least some fundamental concept as autonomy) – an assumption that seems to apply to social rights rather more than to other types. And, it is worth noting, that it is a line of reasoning which requires some revision of the view widely held among rights practitioners that all rights are of equal standing, indivisible, absolute and imprescriptible (a stance formally adopted in respect of all the articles in the Universal Declaration for example). If some rights such as education, and in a different context, security and stability, exist as preconditions of, or to service other rights, then it will be necessary to acknowledge some conception of a hierarchy of rights and that some rights are more fundamental than others. This is not a discussion that can be carried further here. Whether or not stability and security are human rights can only be answered as part of a much larger debate. What we can say however, is that there is a strong case for including them among what are called social rights and as such, their existence will impact on the requirements for, and content of, policies in respect of employment flexibility.

Rights and Their Consequences

The overarching question in relation to policy is whether and how, governments should respond to changes in the socio-economic environment of their populations such as those brought about by increases in employment flexibility. The first point to note is that governments do respond in rather *ad hoc* ways as other chapters in this collection show. But because governments cannot intervene in employment markets directly to affect increasing flexibility, the responses must necessarily be reactive. It does not follow that they have to be piecemeal however (though that is what has tended to happen).

Three types of response to the question of whether there ought to be a policy response to flexibility present themselves from the analysis of rights given above. The first supposes that we do not have any kind of right to stability, security and an ability to plan and that if insecurity and instability have increased as a result of employment flexibility, then that is simply a part of the 'background noise' in market societies. Tradition and convention may have created a 'reasonable expectation' of security (an expectation now rudely shattered by increased flexibility) but it remains only an expectation and not a right. Rights entail duties (usually) but reasonable expectations do not. On this reading therefore, states have no duty to correct for the insecurity and instability created by employment flexibility. They may wish to do so and they may in fact do so, to the extent of creating contractual rights to security. But such rights and provisions, as we have noted, may be of tenuous duration, subject as they may be to the vicissitudes of political popularity.

Secondly, if stability and security (but not the ability to plan) are interpreted as being component parts of the social rights enshrined in the Universal Declaration or other 'regional' charters, then it follows that someone, or something, has the duty of fulfilling the right. This duty will normally fall on the state and it will be a duty to fulfil the right or to see that it is fulfilled[16] (by for example non-government-organisations). In practice however, social rights of this kind take on the character of benchmarks or aspirations.

The third type of response would be entailed by the conclusion that stability, security, and the ability to plan were moral rights entailed in our human character as autonomous moral agents (but not components of the Universal Declaration or if they were, that this was secondary to their standing as moral rights). The duty entailed in this case would be a moral one but because the right is a moral right not a legal or positive one, a failure to protect (or fulfil) the right would incur no sanctions. But this third 'reading' of rights and security takes us out of the realm of positive rights (be they contractual rights or the rights enshrined in declarations) with its moderate degree of certainty and into the realm of moral rights where argument must necessarily be more speculative. There are no courts to appeal to if we think our moral rights are trammeled (unless they happen to coincide with positive rights); there are no articles or statutes to point to and no contracts we can claim have been broken. Yet moral rights remain a powerful force not least because they are often the foundation from which positive rights develop.

It may be a more tenuous argument to claim a moral right to security, stability and an ability to plan a life (more tenuous that is, than to be able to point to articles, statutes and contracts) but it tells us more about why we have the right (if we do) and how it is founded. In the long run, it may be more powerful for that.

Notes

1   Perhaps it sounds more compelling as a negative right *viz*: we have a right not to have to lead our lives in constant uncertainty and subject always to caprice.

2   This is not true without exception; there are some rights that do not carry correlative duties but it holds for the vast majority of rights (see Braybrooke, 1972; Bedau, 1984; Feinberg, 1980). Neither does it acknowledge sufficiently the views of communitarians and others who argue that western societies have become obsessed with the rights of individuals to the almost total neglect of their duties; (see Dagger, 1997; Selbourne, 1994).

3   For the purpose of this argument, these do not have to be normative statements; we might think it perfectly good that people do nothing other than stay alive. The argument does assume however that many (most) people have projects that are definitive of what sort of person they are and that it would be 'bad' were they to be prevented from pursuing them.

4   The usual distinction that is made is between 'moral' and 'positive' rights but this does not exactly parallel the distinction we are making here (see Donnelly, 1989).

5   For present purposes, it is adequate to treat social and economic rights as of a similar kind and with closely overlapping content.

6   Except to the extent that some of the content of one right can contribute to another – the proper exercise of political rights for example might seem to depend in some measure on the fulfillment of a social right to education.

7   For a useful analysis of the nature of 'human' and 'natural' rights, see Gewirth, 1984; Hart, 1984.

8   They are not referred to as such in the Bill as adopted in 1948; nor are civil and political rights identified by name. The two Covenants which make the International Bill of Rights legally binding are identified separately as the Covenant on Civil and Political Rights and the Covenant on Economic, Social and Cultural Rights however.

9   What the argument does not tell us of course, is whether there are parallel or subsidiary arguments that justify rights to things that are not necessary for autonomy. Nor does it, by itself, give a prescription for exactly what is (and is not) necessary for autonomy. But these are matters better pursued elsewhere.

10 We shall have cause slightly to qualify this assertion – at least to the extent of acknowledging the possibility that harsh circumstances may be conducive to moral acerbity.

11 A purposely ambiguous phrase that will have to serve for present purposes. Clearly, the desire to plan one's life, one's psychological need to do so, and the length of time one might wish to plan over will all be subject to a wide range of factors.

12 Needless to say some judicious 'reading into' the text of the articles might produce something that could be interpreted as such but this is not a very rewarding task.

13 See Plant, 1991, Chs. 3, 6.

14 For a treatment of the nature of human rights, see Gewirth, 1984; Sumner, 1990.

15 Rights terminology suffers from a surfeit of overlapping names. For some clarification on 'human', 'moral', 'natural', 'universal' rights see Sumner, 1990; Gewirth, 1984. A particularly valuable account is given in Martin, 1997.

16 Terminology varies: if the right is couched in negative terms – the right *not* to be exposed to insecurity – we sometimes speak of the right being 'protected' rather than fulfilled.

References

Bedau, H. (1984), 'Why Do We Have the Rights We Do?', *Social Philosophy and Policy*, vol. 1, Issue 2, pp.56-72.

Benn, S. (1978), 'Human Rights – For Whom and For What?', in E. Kamenka and A. Tay (eds), *Human Rights*, Arnold, London.

Braybrooke, D. (1972), 'The Firm But Untidy Correlativity of Rights and Obligations', *Canadian Journal of Philosophy*, vol. 1, no. 3, pp. 351-363.

Cranston, M. (1976), 'Human Rights, Real and Supposed', in N. Timms and D. Watson (eds), *Talking About Welfare*, Routledge and Kegan Paul, London.

Dagger, R. (1997), *Civic Virtues,* Oxford University Press, Oxford.

Feinberg, J. (1980), *Rights, Justice, and the Bounds of Liberty*, Princeton University Press, Princeton, New Jersey.

Galenkamp, M. (1998), *Individualism Versus Collectivism*, Sanders Instituut and Gouda Quint, Rotterdam.

Gewirth, A. (1984), 'The Epistemology of Human Rights', *Social Philosophy and Policy*, vol. 1, Issue 2, pp. 1-24.

Golding, M. (1984), 'The Primacy of Welfare Rights', *Social Philosophy and Policy*, vol. 1, Issue 2, pp. 119-136.

Hart, H.L.A. (1984), 'Are There Any Natural Rights?', in J. Waldron (ed.), *Theories of Rights*, Oxford University Press, Oxford.

Lindley, R. (1986), *Autonomy*, Macmillan, London.

Lomasky, L. (1984), 'Personal Projects as the Foundation for Basic Rights', *Social Philosophy and Policy*, vol 1, Issue 2, pp. 35-55.

Martin, R. (1993), *A System of Rights*, Clarendon Press, Oxford.

Plant, R. (1991), *Modern Political Thought*, Blackwell, Oxford.

Plant, R., Lesser, H. and Taylor-Gooby, P. *Political Philosophy and Social Welfare*, Routledge and Kegan Paul, London.

Raz, J. (1982), 'Liberalism, Autonomy, and the Politics of Neutral Concern', *Midwest Studies in Philosophy*, no. 7.

Raz, J. (1984), 'Right-based Moralities', in J. Waldron (ed.), *Theories of Rights,* Oxford University Press, Oxford.

Selbourne, D. (1994), *The Principle of Duty : An Essay on the Foundations of the Civic Order*, Sinclair-Stevenson, London.

Sumner, L. (1990), *The Moral Foundation of Rights*, Clarendon Press, Oxford.

Weale, A. (1983), *Political Theory and Social Policy*, Macmillan, London.

13 Citizenship and Work Obligations in Britain and France

ANTHONY REES

Introduction

The literature on citizenship has flourished in the 1980s and 1990s, and writers on the subject, both those concerned with its theoretical and its practical policy aspects, have drawn freely on the work of their predecessors who wrote in the period immediately after the Second World War. As the British sociologist, T.H. Marshall, has been an especially important influence - mainly, it is true, in Anglo-Saxon countries, but not only there - the perspective which was developed in those years may be referred to as 'Marshallian citizenship' (Marshall, 1963). Marshall presented a relatively simple historical progression in which civil rights, political rights and social rights were successively and successfully asserted and established, forming at the end of the process a whole which might be termed modern citizenship. In the hands of later critics, this schema has been adapted as well as adopted, altered as much as it has been admired; Mann (1987), for example, has trenchantly argued that Marshall's ordering of the development of citizenship was drawn up with the British experience in mind, and does not necessarily fit in with what transpired elsewhere: to take but one instance, in Central Europe, especially in Bismarck's Reich, social rights, bestowed from above, preceded rather than followed on from the granting of political citizenship, with very substantial consequences for the attainment of a democratic polity. For Marshall, citizenship yielded a principle of equality, to be set against - and hence modify - the inequalities of a capitalistic class society. In this formulation, access to the benefits and services of the welfare state was regarded as crucial, and one can see why social rights have played such a large part in the British tradition of writing about citizenship.

Marshall and his contemporaries took for granted that citizenship was a matter of membership of a sovereign nation state, and was based upon identities born of a common language, long residence, shared customs, and the like. Since then, however, things have changed a good deal. First, substantial movements of population, often from much poorer countries - in the case of Britain and France mostly from former colonial possessions or dependencies - have made all Western European countries considerably less homogeneous than they used to be: the concept of 'multicultural citizenship', although controversial in some quarters, has been widely accepted (see Kymlicka, 1995a, 1995b). Secondly, in many countries there have been strong moves in favour of greater decentralization and devolution, with an enhanced respect for the rights and cultures of geographically delimited subnationalities. One formerly strongly unitary state, France, has regionalised itself, with a new tier of elected councils; another, Britain, is currently in the process of setting up devolved assemblies in the four countries which have made up the United Kingdom. Whatever may be the case elsewhere in the world, it is difficult to imagine now anywhere in Western Europe the ascent of another Franco who would direct his best efforts to the suppression of the language and culture of the Catalans and the Basques. Thirdly, there has been the establishment of supra-national institutions: 'European citizenship' is now not so much an aspiration as a reality (Meehan, 1993, 1997). Thus, though the nation state is far from being displaced, its monopoly has been and is being eroded from both above and below. Weale, for example, speculates that 'instead of the view that individuals have one basic political identity from which all the others are derivative, we might suppose that individuals can have multiple identities ranging from the neighbourhood through the city and region to the nation state and continental level, and perhaps even to the global level' (Weale, 1997, p.138). In addition, with the rise of social movements, civil society has become a more crowded space, with rights claims being advanced on grounds of gender, sexual orientation, and a variety of other partial identities. Many feminists, for example, feel that the old discourse on citizenship was unreflectingly male-orientated.

However, this paper is more concerned with another persistent theme in the burgeoning literature on citizenship of the past decade and a half. It is some measure of the somewhat messy and contradictory nature of much recent citizenship talk that this view is almost the opposite of that developed in the paragraph above. Far from wishing to see a further proliferation of rights, this second group of critics feels that there has been too much emphasis on them already - perhaps especially on the social rights which guarantee entry to the benefits and services of the welfare state - and too little on commensurate obligations. This standpoint has been adopted by some who have been identified with the New Right, like Lawrence Mead, even though his avowed paternalism is perhaps more redolent of a considerably older form of conservatism. Indeed, in many respects we are dealing here with a standing rebuke to prevailing trends in modern liberalism, economic liberalism most certainly included. The critique of David Selbourne - not a thinker whom it is easy to pigeonhole - is especially full-blooded: he writes of 'corrupted liberal orders dominated by claims to dutiless right, demand satisfaction and self-realization through unimpeded freedom of action'. (Selbourne, 1994, p.5). So it may not be surprising that this view, less swingeingly expressed, is also found in the works of more left-wing commentators - social democratic, or liberal in the American sense - such as Barbalet (1988), Roche (1992) and Janoski (1998). Particular stress has been placed on the (very traditional) obligation of able-bodied recipients of benefit to seek and retain paid work, but one can also see a tendency to extend this analysis to those whose dependencies have hitherto exempted them from the requirement to register for employment. Mead says of his preferred policy option, which he calls the 'enforcement option', that it:

... represents a return to a citizenship rationale, but this time with the emphasis on obligations rather than rights. The argument is that, if nonwork and other incivilities have weakened the welfare state, then work and other duties should be enforced. If the dependent poor become better citizens, especially by working, then the Marshallian case for aiding them is restored (Mead, 1997a, pp. 220-21).

And, of course, this line of argument has struck many chords with governments, again of varying political complexions, in Britain, France, the USA , indeed throughout the Western world.

Thus the purpose of this chapter is to discuss whether the concept of common citizenship provides an adequate justification for the highlighting of these obligations. There will also be some consideration of how far and in what ways this revived perspective has influenced the actual course of social policy in Britain and France, before and after the election of left-wing governments in both of them in 1997. The primary focus of attention is work requirements, although Mead's mention of 'other incivilities' serves as a reminder that there has also been much anxiety about 'bad neighbours', particularly those living on depressed estates of social housing, and about various sorts of criminal behaviour - drugs, burglaries, assaults, etc. - especially but not solely on the part of juveniles.

The Constitutional Background

As is well known, France is a country with a written constitution. French citizenship was triumphantly invented in the aftermath of the French Revolution, with the proclamation of the Universal Declaration of the Rights of Man in 1789 and the adoption of the first French Constitution. However, unlike the United States, France has operated not through continuous amendment of a founding document, but by scrapping and replacing the entire constitution: Cairns and McKeon (1995, p.101) note that this has occurred no fewer than seventeen times since 1790. However, there is a good deal of continuity between successive French constitutions, particularly so far as civil liberties are concerned. The current document, for example, adopted in 1958 as the Constitution of the Fifth Republic, in its Preamble pledges the French Government to uphold the Universal Declaration of 1789, and incorporates the social and economic rights which were contained in the Preamble to its predecessor of 1946. The European Convention on Human Rights has also been incorporated into the French Constitution. However, it should be noted that the individual French citizen has no direct access to the body charged with ascertaining whether proposed laws are compatible with the Constitution, the Conseil Constitutionnel, reference to which has to be triggered by a limited list of highly-placed notables.

On the surface at least, the situation in Britain could not be more different.[1] For a start, Britons have traditionally been subjects of a constitutional monarchy, not citizens. The word 'citizen' first appeared in statute in the British Nationality Act of 1948, when the category of 'citizen of the United Kingdom and Colonies' was invented - while the phrase 'British citizen' did not appear until 1981. Secondly, the United Kingdom has no written constitution, although it has an unwritten one, which is sometimes seen as rather like a string bag - of uncertain perimeter, but yielding and capacious enough to accommodate quite a few of the things which might be put into it. The word 'right' is often used quite loosely in Britain, it being freely accepted that many 'rights' are subject to, or tinged with, discretion: 'droit' may have rather different connotations. This is partly a matter of the importance of common law in England and Wales: (there are also significant differences between the English and the Scottish and the Northern Irish judicial systems, a complication which need not be explored here). Statute law prevails over common law, but there are many areas in which statute law is silent, thereby allowing much scope for legal precedents built up over the centuries, and for the judicial interpretation of such precedents. According to the lapidary formulation in Malone V. Commissioner of Police for the Metropolis (No. 2, 1979, 2 All ER 620, 630, *per* Sir Robert Megarry V-C) 'England is not a country where everything is forbidden except what is expressly permitted: it is a country where everything is permitted except what is expressly forbidden'. Thus the common law tradition works via negative liberties rather than positive rights: the 'right' to stand as a candidate in an election, for example, is the freedom of anyone not otherwise disqualified to do so.

In the law of England and Wales, there are actually four sources from which rights and duties may be derived: statute; common law; public international law; and the law of the European Community or Union. According to standard constitutional practice, international treaties to which Britain is a signatory are only enforceable through domestic courts if they have been incorporated in British law by statute. This is already the case with European Community legislation, and will at some point in the presumably near future also be happening with the rights contained in the European Convention on Human Rights. The Human Rights Bill completed its passage through the House of Commons on 21 October 1998, but at the time of writing the Home Secretary has not indicated when the Act will be brought into force. When it is, British courts may find themselves grappling with such questions as whether the 'right to life' imposes fresh responsibilities on the National Health Service (Griffith, 1999): hitherto, a series of judicial decisions has determined that patients and their relatives are not entitled to require medical practitioners (or the health authorities that pay them) to perform particular surgical operations or prescribe particular courses of drugs or other treatments.

Nevertheless, despite the differences in historical experience and in current constitutional arrangements, the two countries have a good deal in common so far as matters relevant to this paper are concerned. First, they are two ex-colonial powers whose populations contain many with origins in former imperial possessions or protectorates: their citizenship regimes reflect this history, being based more on place of birth (jus soli) than on descent (jus sanguinis), as has been the case in Western Germany. (Although under Balladaur and Major legislation was enacted which moved their nationality laws more towards the German pattern, while the Federal Republic has been contemplating changes in the opposite direction). Secondly, as has already been noted, both Britain and France have been experimenting with greater constitutional and administrative devolution.

Thirdly, despite this, the two countries possess governmental arrangements which evince a pronounced tilt in favour of the executive. Nevertheless, fourthly and perhaps most important, both Britain and France, as liberal democracies, guarantee, or try to purport to guarantee, a wide and very similar list of civil and other liberties.

Rights, Obligations and Citizenship

The chapter will now proceed by setting out six propositions about citizenship:-

1st proposition

That rights - to be rights - must be in some sense enforceable, and similarly with obligations. This means that rights and duties must be backed up by courts of law or legally constituted tribunals, including the possibility of judicial intervention in, and review of, administrative decisions. It should be noted that this may go further than Marshall himself intended, at least if Plant is right when he says that 'what Marshall meant by social rights was not that these would be individually enforceable but that the state had a *general* duty to provide *collective* services in the fields of health, education and welfare'.(Plant, 1991, p.57, emphases in original). However, as Plant goes on to argue, 'rights' which lack the means of enforcement must inevitably be something of a sham.

2nd proposition

That all rights necessitate a commitment of resources. Rights are needs or interests which are judged to be so important that they require special protection. Therefore rights to be rights must be publicly affirmed and maintained - which means by government. It has long been recognised that social rights are claim rights: that is to say, they impose an obligation upon someone else, the state or some other public agency, to provide the resources necessary to meet the claim. However, the same is also true of other kinds of right - for example the civil rights which uphold property. These involve many kinds of public expenditure. There must be title, systems for the recording of title, and rules for the transfer of title. Providers of financial services have to be regulated, to guard against fraud and misrepresentation. Land and buildings are protected again flood and fire. Probably most important of all, there is the expense of policing. And there are many other exercises of public power, most of them long accepted and uncontroversial, which should be added to the account. The idea that no rights are costless, and that they are, in effect, demands for slices of revenue gathered through taxation, has recently been comprehensively worked out, in an American context, by Holmes and Sunstein (1999). Rights are priority claims, but the fact that the availability of resources does indeed enter into the equation means that they must be relative rather than absolute. Even the richest of citizens cannot -or at least should not be able to - determine the precise amount of police effort that is devoted to guarding his property (although he will have the advantage denied to his less affluent fellow-citizens, of being able to pay for the services of private security companies). Rights may also conflict with one another: there may be clashes between different rights, or the same right may be claimed by different individuals in circumstances where only one of them can be satisfied. Trade-offs are necessary. This situation provides a space for political choice, but it leaves many liberals, including liberal conservatives and liberal socialists, feeling uneasy. Surely rights must be mandatory and inalienable? Are they not, in Dworkin's famous phrase, trumps? This is a point which I shall take up again.

3*rd* proposition

That very few rights (or obligations) are those of citizenship, if by that is meant that they are claimable by citizens alone. International law treats civil rights as human rights rather than rights of citizenship: torture is not rendered any more acceptable if a regime restricts it solely to non-citizens. Perhaps less obviously, it also accords human rights status to social, economic and cultural rights. In both legal and practical terms, the granting of a right to residence is of more importance than formal membership of a national community by reason of birth, descent or naturalization. Access to the principal services of welfare state - social security benefits, health care, education, social housing - is generally obtained through residence, and so are many obligations, such as the liability to pay most taxes. Thus the relationship between formal membership of a national community and the possession of civil and social rights is less tight and intimate than Marshall supposed. Since he wrote, the coming of the European Union has altered this situation somewhat: various categories of Community national - workers, the self-employed, the retired, students and the economically self-sufficient - have the right to enter, reside in, remain in, and leave the territory of another member-state. However, only nationals of a country have the unqualified right to reside in that country.

Furthermore, there are some other rights, almost exclusively of a political nature, which *are* restricted to citizens. Here again the European Union has made some difference. The 1992 Maastricht Treaty granted citizens of member states who were resident in other member states the right to vote and stand as a candidate in European and local elections. This caused some consternation in France: the granting of voting rights in local elections was one of the provisions of the Treaty which the Conseil Constitutionnnel declared was contrary to the French constitution, and there was a fear in some (mainly right-wing) quarters that it might prove to be the prelude to the awarding of full citizenship to all resident aliens. However, voting and standing in *national* elections remains everywhere a right enjoyed only by citizens of the country in question. Obligations like the liability to perform military or other forms of national service are also normally only conferred upon citizens.

4th proposition

That many rights are based on rationales which are other than that of citizenship. The last proposition broadened the classification of rights by showing that they were enjoyed by more people than citizens; this proposition narrows it by noting that rights may rest on other grounds than formal membership of a polity (or, indeed, residence). National insurance entitlements provide a clear example. These are certainly rights and relatively strong ones at that: but they depend on a pre-existing employment relationship, not on citizenship as such. If it is not a contradiction in terms, poor law rights - those found in services derived from the Poor Law - may actually be closer to being rights of citizenship. (The right to supplementary benefit - now income support - was actually only conceded in Britain in 1966: before that, the legislation was couched in terms of the obligation of the public authorities to supply, not of the right of the eligible claimant to receive). The idea behind Basic Income schemes is closer still to a pure right of citizenship, and indeed they are often called Citizens Income schemes, but they have never yet caught on as a serious political proposition.

The situation in France is even more complicated, since not only unemployment insurance (assurance-chomage) but also assistance (le regime dit de solidarite) requires a minimum antecedent period of paid work, which excludes newcomers to the labour market and also 'beaucoup de travailleurs precaires' (Freyssinet, 1998, p.95). To cater for their needs, the RMI (Revenu Minimum d'Insertion) was invented a mere ten years ago: in 1998 it provided sustenance for one million applicants (two million persons including dependents) (L'Express, 5.3.98).

5th proposition

That obligations are fewer, are typically less well-defined than rights, and tend to vary more from country to country. The priority of rights is evidenced by the fact that a European Convention on Human Obligations is almost inconceivable! At present, there are only two obligations which are universal in Western democracies, a duty of allegiance and the duty to pay taxes (and national insurance contributions). However, although a non-citizen who seeks and obtains naturalization is required to swear an oath of allegiance to the British sovereign, both of these, like most rights, accompany residence rather than follow on from formal citizenship. To these two might be added the obligation to serve on a jury, if summoned: since, in both Britain and France, selection of jurors is made from the names on the electoral roll, this may be regarded as a duty of citizenship. However, in both countries, there are many citizens who are either debarred from jury service for one reason or another, or who may successfully claim exemption. Another duty which is generally restricted to citizens is the requirement to register for and perform military service. Although National Service ended in Britain nearly forty years ago, and the current French Rendez-vous Jeunes is a pale reflection of the previous conscription into the armed forces, such potentially onerous obligations could be reactivated at any time that a suitable threat to national security is perceived.

An example of the variation in the duties which may be exacted by the public power is the French obligation alimentaire. An aged indigent person in France may apply to their local tribunal d'instance for an order against some or all of his or her children. The judge, after having ascertained that the plaintiff is without resources, and having investigated the circumstance of the child or children, may then require that the latter pay the parent a pension alimentaire. There is no parallel to this in the United Kingdom.

6th proposition

That the notion of a right contains an essential element of unconditionality. There are some obligations which can reasonably be regarded as correlative with particular rights: the most obvious example is the duty of allegiance which may be seen as the reverse side of the promise to give protection.

However, more generally, where 'rights' come with strings attached, then the less are they genuine rights - and this applies even when the restrictions are morally justifiable or are popularly accepted. A case in point, of course, is the exaction of work requirements in exchange for benefits; this is, however, considered more fully later in this chapter.

A considered argument to the contrary, to the effect that rights always carry with them concomitant obligations, has recently (1998) been put forward by the American sociologist, Thomas Janoski. To T.H. Marshall's trilogy of civil, political and social rights he adds a fourth category, participation rights, identifies a particular genre of right as typical of each category, and, with an interesting use of exchange theory, lists obligations under the four headings. In Tables 13.1 and 13.2, I bring together and place side by side the rights and obligations which he includes in the 'social' and 'participation' columns, both of which feature work-related obligations. In the original, rights and duties appear in different chapters.

This is valiant attempt to link the rights and duties of citizenship, but it poses some problems, two of which need to be taken up here. First, the obligations are vague. True, the rights also are only items in a summary list, but with most of them it would be possible to spell them out precisely enough to satisfy the criterion of enforceability. Almost all the obligations, however, fall several hundred metres short of that target. Janoski has taken care to distil the experience of the major European democracies as well as of the USA, and he cannot fairly be charged with having submitted an arbitrarily chosen list of rights and duties. Nevertheless, his obligations in particular, worded as they are, could be read as pious endorsements of the predilections of patriotic Americans with mildly progressive opinions.

Secondly, the rights and duties do not fit together at all closely. It is often difficult to be sure which obligation is intended to be coupled with which right. Janoski would not regard this as a criticism, since he holds that relatively few rights and duties are attached to one another by means of what he terms 'restricted exchange' (as in a contract). Janoski is rather suspicious of restricted exchange, because he fears that viewing things in this way invites calculating citizens to see their relationship with public authorities and the community like the balance in a personal account - so many obligations performed for so many rights and benefits received. Instead, he prefers 'generalized exchange': 'people', he says, 'do not expect immediate and reciprocal returns from the people they help, but they do expect to see their returns materialize over time in building a decent life in a more or less just society' (Janoski, 1998, p.61). In the next section I shall

209

explore further the various ways of construing the relationship between rights and duties with regard to the special problem of work obligations.

The Requirement to Seek and Keep Paid Employment

All countries set conditions for the receipt of benefit by the able-bodied unemployed. Here, and throughout this section, I shall give British illustrations, but French parallels are often close. First and foremost, they have to register, and be available, for employment (although in Britain, at least for the present, women and lone men with child-care responsibilities are exempted from this requirement until the youngest child has reached the age of sixteen). Then they may be debarred from benefit, or have their benefits curtailed, if they are held to have misbehaved in some defined way: left a job voluntarily 'without just cause'; committed 'misconduct' which led to their dismissal by an employer; failed to apply or attend for interview for a post deemed appropriate for their circumstances; refused a place on a training course, or ceased to attend it; and so on. Most of these sanctions - and the quaint language in which they are couched - have their origins in the National Insurance Act of 1948, and lasted largely unchanged until the 1980s. Since then, however, they have been progressively tightened. For example, the maximum period of disqualification has been raised from six weeks to six months, and those disqualified lose all of their Job Seeker's Allowance instead of merely a proportion of their benefit (although they may be able to obtain Hardship Payments). Benefit claimants are also now required to produce detailed evidence of the assiduity of their job search activities. There have been similar developments in France, and, indeed, all Western European countries (Freyssinet, 1998).

Earlier, I pointed to a case where rights and obligations dovetail in a relatively straightforward way - the citizen's duty of allegiance is the other side of the state's responsibility to provide protection. (This has the rather awkward implication, not least for a Hobbesian, that if the public power seriously failed to supply protection, then the obligation of the allegiance withers and perhaps fails). Social and economic rights and obligations are, however, not quite like that, even in the case of national insurance relationships, which are a fairly clear case of restricted exchange - the worker or ex-worker obtains guaranteed entitlements in exchange for

Table 13.1 Social rights and obligations, according to Janoski

Social Rights	Social Obligations
A. Enabling & Preventive Rights	*A. Enabling & Preventive Obligations*
1. Health services	1. Pursue prudent health care
2. Family allowances	2. Raise a loving family
3. Personal and family counseling	3. Maintain a safe and clean
4. Physical rehabilitation	environment
B Opportunity Rights	*B Opportunity Obligations*
1. Pre-primary education	1. Pursue education to the best of
2. Primary and secondary	one's ability
education	2. Pursue career to the benefit to
3. Higher education	society
4. Vocational education	3. Tolerate social diversity
5. Educational assistance for	
special groups.	
C Distributive Rights	*C Sustenance/Economic Obligations*
1. Old age pensions	1. Recipients of unemployment or
2. Public assistance	public assistance should look for
3. Unemployment compensation	work.
	2 Respect other's social rights and
	the need for transfer payments.
D Compensatory Rights	*D Enforcement and Implementation*
1. Work injury insurance	1. Provide resources for social rights
2. War injury pension	2. Help less fortunate by voluntary
3. War equalization	government and association
4. Rights infringement	service.
Compensation	

Source: Janoski (1998), table 2.2, p.31; table 3.1, p.55

Table 13.2 Participation rights and obligations, according to Janoski

Participation Rights	Obligation Rights
A Labour Market Intervention Rights	*A Labour Market Obligations*
1. Labour market information programs	1. Duty of those receiving services to actively pursue work
2. Job placement programs	2. Duty of employers to co-operate with government and unions to provide programs
3. Job creation services	
B Firm and Bureaucracy Rights	*B Firm and Bureaucracy Obligations*
1. Job security rights	1. Ensure equity and productivity in the organisation
2. Workers councils or grievance procedure rights	2. Safeguard firm competitive information
3. Client participation in bureaucracy or self-administration	3. Respect all groups in participatory process
4. Affirmative action and comparable worth	
5. Collective bargaining rights	
C Capital Control Rights	*C Capital Participation Obligations*
1. Co-determination rights	1. Protect and promote the economy
2. Wage earner and union investment funds	2. Provide for capital funds through savings
3. Capital escape laws	
4. Anti-trust laws	
5. Regional investment and equalisation programs	
	D Enforcement & Implementation
	1. Provide resources for programs
	2. Invest in national industries

Source: Janoski (1998) table 2.2, p. 31; table 3.1, p.55

defined obligations. Rather, their form is triadic, as three stages can be delineated. First, the citizen has to possess a right, which will need to be expressed or activated in some appropriate way. Then, some duly appointed public agency has to supply the resources which will make the right meaningful. After that, the beneficiary may have to comply - or, more realistically, make his or her best efforts to comply - with conditions set by the agency in exchange for the benefit. Furthermore, with work requirements, a fourth stage has to be added: someone else, namely an employer, who was most likely not a party to the original agreement, has to come up with a firm offer of a suitable job.

The question is, what does this further stage - and the third one, too - have to do with citizenship? Some commentators, foremost among whom is Lord Dahrendorf, reply: very little indeed. Dahrendorf writes:

> Citizenship is a social contract, generally valid for all members: work is a private contract. In societies in which the private contract of labour does not exist there is no citizenship either. This is true for feudal relations of dependence and for some versions of really existing socialism. It is no accident. For when the general rights of citizenship are made dependent on people entering into private relations of employment, they lose their private and fundamentally voluntary character. In an indirect but compelling manner, labour becomes forced labour. It is imperative that the obligations of citizenship are themselves general and public as it were (Dahrendorf, 1988, p.33).

One way of completing the circumference of this particular circle is for the state itself or other public agencies to undertake to supply the required jobs, or at least to adopt a fallback role, in the absence, that is, of other willing (and subsidised) suppliers. Such arrangements would not meet the objection that workfare is a species of corvee, incompatible with any conception of a free citizenry, but it would help to answer the charge that it is an evasion of governmental responsibility. However, the difficulty with guaranteed employment of this kind is twofold. First, given the large scale of the programmes which would be needed, it could have malign consequences for the efficiency of participating public authorities and for the productivity of public sector workforces. Secondly, it is likely to be enormously expensive in terms of public expenditure: indeed, the flagship schemes in Britain, France and other European countries, with participants experiencing (so far) no more compulsion than a certain deepening of the sanctions referred to above, are also very expensive. In the USA the original Clinton Welfare Plan envisaged a substantial expansion of federal and state employment in order to realise its objective of welfare into work without too much pain and uncertainty for those affected: its less ill-fated replacement, PRWORA (the Personal Responsibility and Work Opportunity Reconciliation Act) does not possess this feature, but nonetheless is proving costly for those states who are taking their new obligations seriously, and do not just regard it as an invitation to cut welfare rolls without worrying too much about what happens to those who get cut. Wisconsin is usually taken as an exemplar in this regard: Mead describes it as a state possessing both 'a tradition of generosity and innovation in social policy' and 'a superlative bureaucracy' (Mead, 1997b, pp. 45-6). Although he calculates that the state has saved $68 million through welfare reform since 1986, this is entirely due to a sharp reduction in the caseload. 'The state has spent millions on work programmes', he says, and much of that investment has gone into the bureaucracy itself' (Mead, 1997b, p. 46).

Moreover, there must be a question-mark over the availability of paid work as such, private sector or public sector. Zygmunt Bauman has expressed with his usual eloquence the view that work is now a scare commodity, and that for the first time since the Industrial Revolution a group has been created – a so-called 'underclass' – which is literally surplus to requirements, and will remain so in foreseeable circumstances:

> The apotheosis of work as simultaneously the highest human duty, the condition of moral decency, the guarantee of law and order and the cure for the plague of poverty, chimed in once with the labour-intensive industry which clamoured for more working hands in order to increase its product. The present day streamlined, downsized, capital- and knowledge-intensive industry casts labour as a constraint on the rise of productivity. In direct defiance of the once canonical Smith/Ricardo/Marx labour theories of value, excess of labour is viewed as an anathema, and any search for more rationalization (i.e. more profit on the capital invested) focuses first on further possibilities to cut down the number of employees. 'Economic growth' and the rise of employment are, for all practical intents, at cross-purposes; technological progress is measured by the replacement and elimination of labour. Under such circumstances the commandments and blandishments of the work ethic sound increasingly hollow (Bauman, 1998, p. 65).

This kind of argument has a growing basis in fact: but it can easily be exaggerated. In Britain, the number of adults in full-time employment has not changed much over twenty years, and the labour market has shown itself capable of accommodating a considerable increase in female activity rates, sometimes via part-time, sometimes full-time, jobs. The average duration of a job has not changed much either: it has fallen by only a few months, and is still nearly seven years. Advocates of stricter work requirements, however, have been particularly heartened by the apparent success of the American economy in generating a continuous stream of jobs, many of them low-paid admittedly, but also ready to be occupied by people with fairly minimal skills. The work is there they say: if the vacancies are not taken up, it must be because of other reasons or constraints than deficient availability.

A particularly full-blooded approach can be found in the latest publication of David Green (1999). Green advocates an eccentric liberalism in which the prime value to be maximised seems to be self-sufficiency – not freedom, nor justice (social or any other kind), nor the utilitarian trinity of social utility, individual flourishing and beneficence. It is not immediately obvious how this fits in with Green's excoriation of dutiless rights, since the assertion of rights is also an assertion of independence. However, he has only one kind of right in his line of fire, welfare rights, and only one kind of dependence, dependence on state benefits. True, he recognises that there are some adults who are genuinely incapable of work, and hence that there are some legitimate dependencies: but they are astonishingly narrowly drawn. He holds, for example, that single mothers should be required to re-register for employment three months after the birth of a child, and that the State Retirement Age should be raised to 75. The thought of 74 year olds being assessed by the Department of Social Security's Medical Service to see if they satisfy the 'all work' test almost beggars belief; but this change is to be phased in over twenty years, so conceivably by then general opinion might have moved in Green's direction.

Mercy occupies a very lowly position in the institute of Economic Affairs' list of virtues, so one would perhaps not expect its leading lights to have much patience with hard luck stories. Less hard-line expressions of these general beliefs and policy approaches are, however, now almost commonplace. Simon Jenkins, star columnist of the London Times, and of Conservative but also progressive liberal sympathies, sums up in a recent article (19th May 1999) what he clearly regards as an emergent consensus. After having commended the US workfare experiments, and having noted that 'focus groups love them (such schemes), at least those drawn from the top four fifths of incomes', he continues:

Retargeting the welfare state has bred its own code. It seeks to replace the 'stigma of dependency' with the dignity of work. I would put it more crudely. Any member of the community – be they a King's Cross dosser or a prima ballerina – must justify that request. They must show that they need what someone else has earned. Thatcherism spared them that indignity. Blairism is proving a less soft touch (Jenkins, 1999).

In an article on the Green Paper on welfare reform, *A New Contract for Welfare*, (Cm. 3805, 1998), Alan Deacon provides a very relevant dissection of 'Blairism'. He points out, with copious illustration, the intimate connection between the phraseology and proposals contained within the document and the language used by Blair in speeches before the 1997 election. Probably the most useful aspect of Deacon's article for present purposes, however, is his argument that the green Paper 'draws upon three differing formulations of the role and purpose of welfare'. He summarises these as below:

Welfare as a channel for the pursuit of self-interest. This formulation looks primarily to incentives to induce people to act in ways which promote social well-being.

Welfare as the exercise of authority. This formulation looks primarily to compulsion to require people to act in ways which promote social well-being.

Welfare as a mechanism for moral regeneration. This formulation looks primarily to moral argument to persuade people to act in ways which promote social well-being (Deacon, 1998, p.306).

Deacon grants that these three are not discrete: indeed they can be held simultaneously, even if they appeal (as Deacon maintains) to rather different conceptions of human nature. This is especially true of views number two and three, whose policy implications may be rather similar – at least if the 'moral' option is not to be solely a matter of patrol-leader platitudes and exhortations.

Comparing Work-Oriented Programmes in Britain and France

I now want to return to Janoski's book, since, in addition to his explorations of the concept of citizenship, he has the subsidiary purpose of reconsidering Esping-Andersen's (1990) division of industrialised societies into the 'three worlds of welfare-capitalism. Esping-Andersen distinguishes three types of 'regime-cluster', which he terms 'liberal', 'corporatist' and 'social-democratic'; the geographical significance of this exercise is made plain in the index to his book, where he annotates the three entries as follows: liberal = Anglo-Saxon; 'corporatist = continental European', and 'social-democratic = Scandinavian' (Esping-Andersen, 1990, p.246). (This is actually a simplification of Esping-Andersen's own work, since Switzerland, for example, marches in his 'liberal' column). Janoski introduces a number of new variables, recalculates Esping-Andersen's sums, and in the process largely validates the earlier classification, discovering a still wider variety of systematic differences according to regime type. However, he renames the 'corporatist' type 'traditional' – which will not please French republicans, as France is of course assigned to this category – while Britain is thrown into limbo: because of its stubborn propensity to appear in the middle range of most selected indicators, it is termed a 'mixed case'. Nevertheless, Janoski regards it as 'leaning towards liberalism', and hence not far from being alongside the United States and the countries of the 'old' Commonwealth.

There are certainly some institutionalised differences between the two countries, which run along the lines to be expected from their failure to appear in the same category of welfare-state regime, and which are relevant to the concerns of this paper. First, there is no doubt that tax-supported means-tested benefits have historically been much more important in British social policy than in its counterpart over the Channel. Secondly, in France the unemployment compensation scheme was set up in 1958 by agreement between the employers and the trade unions, who are organised into locally based Associations pour l'Emploi dans l'Industrie et le Commerce (ASSEDIC) which administer the insurance funds and the benefits, (Milner and Mouriaux, 1997). At national level, these organisations are co-ordinated by the Union Nationale pour l'Emploi dans l'Industrie et le Commerce (or UNEDIC) and not run by Ministries of Labour or Social Security. In Britain neither employers nor unions play any direct role in the administration of unemployment insurance, apart from the former collecting contributions. However, this story could have been very different, had the British trade unions made anything of the subsidies and other inducements dangled before them by Lloyd George in 1911 in order to tempt them into taking a large, and expanding, part in the administration of his Unemployment Insurance Scheme (Gilbert, 1966; Gilbert, 1970).

Neither of these differences is quite what it seems. So far as means-tested benefits are concerned, France has been catching up fast. The RMI is only one of eight currently extant minima sociaux. If the others (minimum vieillesse, allocation adulte handicape etc.) are added in, then together they had 3.3 million beneficiaries in 1998, 6 million counting dependents. (L'Express 5.3.98). One should also note that, because of the stringent work conditions attached, the RMI has often been condemned on the French Left as a species of workfare.

The semi-private structure of UNEDIC and ASSEDIC have restricted the possibilities for direct governmental involvement, but entitlements have nevertheless not been protected. The seemingly inexorable rise in unemployment in the 1970s and 1980s placed great strains upon the insurance funds, and the scheme has frequently been amended – indeed, no fewer than seven times between 1984 and 1995 (Milner and Mouriaux, 1997). In Britain, one of the principal arguments in favour of the somewhat sleight of hand mechanisms of National Insurance has always been that their rights based nature should similarly stay the sticky hand of government. This has not been very successful, either. In April 1994 the Major administration cut the maximum duration of NI Unemployment Benefit from one year to six months, and later that same year it brought both it and means-tested income support for the unemployed together in the Job Seekers Allowance (JSA) which came complete with a pantechnicon of new work-related requirements demanded of its beneficiaries. Earlier than that, in the mid 1980s, whole benefits – the Death Grant, the Maternity Grant – were removed from the National Insurance system and added to the ranks of means tested benefits. Admittedly, they had been so eroded by failure to update in line with inflation and rising incomes that they were not worth a great deal when their general availability was withdrawn, but contributors had been paying in for them over the years. It is a curious form of contract which permits one party to it to alter the terms of entitlement unilaterally and without compensation, or, often, consultation. At the time of writing this is a matter of acute controversy because of the decision of the Government both to impose new eligibility conditions for incapacity benefit, and to means test it

The almost simultaneous advent of centre-left governments in Britain and France in 1997 can be interpreted in much the same way. There have sometimes seemed to be quite considerable differences in general philosophical orientation and policy stance, the Jospin administration being seen – and seeing itself – as more 'old Left' or 'socialist' than the Blair

218

one. Martine Aubry, the French Minister of Labour, apparently regretted contributing a preface to a book by Tony Blair: 'J'ai donne mon accord sans avoir lu le texte. Je le croyais beaucoup plus a gauche', she has explained (L'Express 28.8.97). It is true that the Jospin government has been more interested in the conservation of existing employment and in work-sharing than its British counterpart: Blair has, for example, actively opposed in EU circles the 35-hour week as being more likely to destroy job opportunities than to preserve or create them. However, it is worth reflecting that, in a British context, the establishment of a National Minimum Wage is in some ways the equivalent of the French shortened working week, and certainly business interests have objected to the two policy initiatives on very much the same grounds. One also has to take account of differences in the balance of social forces in the two countries. Once, long ago, in the 1970s, British ministers might have pondered, just occasionally, on the potential for disruption represented by Claimants' Unions — but never thereafter. The wave of occupations of ASSEDIC offices in support of a large increase in the RMI during the winter of 1997/98 would be an almost inconceivable event in Britain. They would make any Prime Minister pause for thought. Nevertheless perhaps the most important thing about these disturbances is that they were summarily put down by the troops of the CRS (Compagnie Republicaine de Securite) without significant concessions by the Government.

It is actually arguable that the French socialist government has produced a more glaring breach with the universalistic principles of the twentieth century welfare state than anything so far attempted in Britain. The Jospin administration — and Mme. Aubry herself — are responsible for the introduction of an income ceiling for receipt of allocations familiales. So far it only affects about 9 per cent of families, those that are best off, and has been justified on the grounds that under successive right-wing governments the child-care aspects of the scheme had become a bonanza for the richest of parents. Bauman, who has spotted this policy change (Bauman, 1998, p.57), is certainly not necessarily correct in his suggestion that the ceiling will gradually edge its way down the income-scale until only poorer families are beneficiaries and the middle classes lose interest in the benefit: this has the defect of all thin end of the wedge arguments, namely, that it very probably won't happen. Nevertheless, the injection of means-testing into one of the proudest and most sacred bastions of the French welfare state is an astonishing policy departure on the part of a left-wing administration.

I will end this section with a brief comparison between the French Emploi-jeunes (for 18 to 26 year olds) and the British New Deal for the Young Unemployed (aged 18 to 24). Both are, as has been said, flagship schemes, the French one will eventually cost billions of francs, while its British equivalent is meant to be paid for out of the up to £3 billion proceeds of the once and for all windfall tax on the profits of the privatised utilities. The British scheme is also only the first and biggest of an ambitious host of New Deals – the New deal for Single Parents, the New Deal for the Long-Term (older) Unemployed, and so on. Both programmes have 'partners' although in France they are listed as 'ministries, collectivities territoriales and associations', while in Britain they are more likely to be voluntary organisations and private sector firms. Both operate via contracts, and offer rebates and subsidies to participating organisations. Both emphasise training, though not to a terribly high level.

Here, however, the similarities end. Emploi-jeunes is much more of an old-fashioned job-creation scheme; 350,000 jobs have been promised in the three years from 1998 onwards. These openings are mainly in public sector employment. By far the largest tranche of jobs announced so far has consisted of posts in the national education service: 70,000 young people are being recruited as 'Aides-educateurs' in schools, colleges, lycees and higher education. (The French young unemployed are on average rather more highly educated than their British counterparts). They will be used on surveillance duties, helping with languages and information technology and in cultural and recreational activities. They will receive five year non-renewable contracts and will be paid at the level of the minimum wage (SMIC). Two hundred hours of professional training are included.

Other possibilities of direct employment are limited, not least because of the challenge to the public purse, but the police are taking on 20,000 security assistants (including 1,500 to be employed in 'sensitive zones': they will be engaged in community policing, reception of the public etc.). However, Ministries have been activating their 'reseaux' of associations, and jobs are being found in the areas of sport, culture, the environment and social care. Public transport and the utilities are also playing a part.

By contrast, the British scheme is much more oriented towards private sector employers. The Department of Education and Employment has issued a host of press releases, detailing the various major companies who have signed up for the New Deal. ('Employer sign-ups: Week 1-30, Week 4-700, Week 8-1,486, Week 12-4,294, Week 16-7,116, Week 18-7,538'. (DfEE press release, 13 May 1998 entitled 'New Deal Sign-ups Accelerate

– 7,550 and still continuing'). The Department has also set up an advisory New Deal Task Force, chaired (unpaid) by Sir Peter Davies, the Group Chief Executive of the Prudential, and with many representatives of industry and commerce among its members.

The New Deal offers the young unemployed four options:

- A job with an employer, including at least one day a week or its equivalent in education or training designed to meet an accredited qualification. Employers receive £60 a week for up to 26 weeks to cover the costs of recruitment and initial employment.
- A job for six months with the Government's Environmental Taskforce, which also includes day release education or training towards an accredited qualification.
- A job for six months with a voluntary sector employer. This has the same education or training requirements as the others, and there is a possibility of receiving a direct wage from the employer, as in the first option, but with the alternative that the participant may continue to receive his or her Job Seekers Allowance, plus a grant of £400 paid in instalments over the six months.
- The opportunity, for those who do not have good prospects of employment without it, of taking up full-time education or training on an approved course leading to a recognised qualification.

The Government is adamant that there is no fifth option of continuing on benefit, and new sanctions (recently tightened) have been introduced for non-compliance.

A very distinctive feature of the New Deal is the emphasis on counseling and mentoring (the latter after employment has been found). Here one can detect the influence of Lawrence Mead. Each entrant to the New Deal is required to pass through a 'gateway'. The identification of suitable employment opportunities and training needs will be for many young people a relatively simple affair, but for those in whose cases significant barriers to employment have been discovered this stage may last up to four months. Such participants will be accorded the services of a 'dedicated caseworker', who will review the options with the participants, explore with them their capacities, aspirations and training requirements, encourage them to attend job interviews, and sometimes refer them on for more specialised help and guidance. How the regular officials of the Employment Service are meeting the challenge of this deepening of their role is not known, but Mead concluded from his various researches that they were often the best people to perform such tasks, as they knew the ropes. However, in a new situation the old ropes may not provide the needed support.

Conclusion

Citizenship has emerged, especially on the left and in the centre of politics, as a key concept in the search for intellectual underpinnings for large-scale state welfare. It is hoped that it can be pressed into service to hold the past, present and future trajectory of social policy together, and allow it to continue – or resume – its role as part of the bandaging which also holds modern societies together. Anxiety about 'social exclusion' is shared by all the countries of the European Union, and is an important current manifestation of this feeling. It is evidenced in Britain by the establishment of the Social Exclusion Unit and in France by the 'loi contre l'exclusion'.

It may be doubted whether citizenship is a strong enough, or suitable enough, concept to perform this role. There are three main reasons for this view. First, it is itself a categorisation which leads to exclusions – that is, of non-citizens. At a time when the position in society, and the rights, of aliens, asylum seekers, and indeed those with an ethnic minority background generally (whatever their precise legal statuses) are in dispute in many countries this is potentially dangerous.

Secondly, the language of citizenship is incoherent, and is open to all. On the far right, it may be adopted precisely because it leads itself to rationales for being nasty to the groups specified in the previous paragraph. Mainstream British Conservative politicians have vaunted the 'active citizen' (who engages in a-political good works among his or her neighbours) while Jacques Chirac has made much of the notion of 'concitoyenete'. Anti-monarchists use the term in Britain to disavow the status of subject. French republican citizenship is different again. The word conjures up a variety of images which may be pleasing to different people, and from which they can select at will.

Thirdly, as we have seen, when used literally, as a legal concept, citizenship is a space sparsely furnished with rights and pretty well empty of entitlements to benefit. It is the basis for consular assistance to persons living abroad, but internal to a country social protection rests much more on the granting of the right to residence.

Neverthless, in spite of these objections, the concept of social citizenship continues to be valuable, for the old Marshallian reason that it is so closely tied to the possession of rights. (Marshall's own understanding of this relationship is an interesting question, but whatever it may have been it is in no way binding on his successors). The idea that the assertion of rights is necessarily – or even usually – a selfish endeavour, seems to me plain wrong, rather in the same way as it is incorrect to assume that because one can class something as a market transaction it must mean that the parties to it are striving to maximise their individual advantage or profit. Concern for others – indeed generosity – is one of the most ubiquitous of all motivations, while a belief in fairness is an essential ingredient of a market or any other system. Respect for persons entails respect for them as rights-holders.

The belief that rights and obligations are in a zero-sum relationship, so that if society has more of one, it must necessarily have less of the other, seems to have been gaining ground in recent years. It is hard to see what warrant there is for it. Neither is there merit in a parallel proposition applied to individual citizens, that the more people feel that they have rights, and the more they aim to realise them, so the more will they be dismissive or neglectful of duties. Both suppositions lack empirical grounding: both are also entirely illiberal. Furthermore, the argument of this paper has been that the relationship between rights and obligations is usually indirect. This does not mean that the latter are less important in some general sense for the functioning of society than are the former, merely that the two do not come neatly wrapped together in packages, but instead need to be analysed separately. Nevertheless, it *is* maintained here that rights are more central to an understanding of the good things which have commonly been subsumed under the title of citizenship than are duties. Rights have not necessarily 'worked': as has been noted, under pressure, governments of all political complexions have frequently proved only too ready to erode them, and there are also plenty of respects in both Britain and France in which the citizen has always been imperfectly protected against the executive power. But the answer to that is more and better rights, not fewer of them. Over a long period of time, rights may sometimes need to be renegotiated and redefined to fit in with changed philosophies and conditions – the American right to bear arms may be a case in point – but in lifetime span terms we ought to be able to count on our rights. In other words they are, or at least they should be, trumps.

I must now turn to work obligations, and here it is necessary to confront the issue of dependence. In a recent New Statesman article, Richard Sennett (1999) makes a case for its virtues: 'If we deny people the right to depend on others', he writes, 'we diminish their capacity to hold others accountable'. This is probably rather too idiosyncratic a view, all the more so since he begins his article with an example unlikely to appeal to a European readership, citing the little packets of money by which city bosses in early twentieth century America 'valued' the loyalty of their voters. Nevertheless, Sennett's argument contains more than a grain of sense: we are all dependent in multitudinous ways, and not merely as children or in old age, or only on other members of our immediate family, but also on employers and on the ability of a whole panoply of institutions, public and private, to perform their tasks fairly, efficiently and reliably. When governments talk about 'ending dependency' they are frequently being deeply duplicitous, since this is so often a smokescreen behind which they can wriggle out of their own obligations, shifting them sideways to whomever will relieve them of cost and responsibility. This will often mean passing them over to the family: the Victorians were adept at dunning relatives, and at writing begging letters to those among the fortunate with whom they could claim a 'connection', but this is not an aspect of Victorian values to which most people would want to return.

There are certainly some trends in the labour market in both countries which discourage the entering into of long-term commitments – obviously, since part of the problem is that employers are becoming more reluctant to enter into long-term commitments themselves. Right-wingers, such as those who write for the Institute of Economic Affairs, deplore the tendency to enter into 'easy come, easy go' relationships when they are discussing single mothers or the increase in cohabitation, but they do not extend this analysis to, or indeed see the connection with, the deteriorating behaviour of many employers and the precarious situation which more and more in the work-force are now experiencing at least partly as a consequence. It might be added that many public sector institutions, such as the British universities, who have employed people on long skeins of temporary contracts, need to be included among those which are badly behaved.

No-one disputes that there are many adults who, because of long-term sickness or for some other reason, are incapable of earning their own crust. One of the troubles with promises to end welfare dependency, and with such slogans as the British New Deal's 'A hand up, not a hand out', is that they may send messages which are demeaning to those who are in this situation. Furthermore, there are many others, particularly among the disabled, whose capacity to earn is genuinely in doubt. To give a 'helping hand' to such people is desirable – work might make all the difference to the quality of their lives, and not merely, or even primarily, in terms of providing income. However, counseling of this kind requires considerable skill and sympathy, which may or may not be forthcoming. How does one guard against the helping hand becoming the yanking hand – pestering, pressing and pincering? As in any paternalistic endeavour, the line between helping and coercion is likely to be thin.

In summing up the common features of the three formulations which he finds in the Blair Government's Welfare Green Paper, Alan Deacon remarks that: 'Each sees the prime task as the creation of a social order in which people behave differently rather than one in which resources are distributed differently'. (Deacon, 1998, p.306). The importance of poverty, he suggests, is thereby downplayed, and so are structural factors generally: 'There is no mention of those who are unable to work because no jobs are available'. (Deacon, 1998, p. 307). The British New Deal and the French Emploi-jeunes are the most ambitious undertakings in this area which their governments have ever attempted, but they follow in the footsteps of many previous programmes, the results of which have generally been disappointing to those of their progenitors who had not always intended them to be largely cosmetic. The British example, in particular, is a testament to the faith of those who believe that labour markets really do clear at present, and will also do so in the future.

Note

1 This account of the legal rights and obligations of citizenship draws on the White Paper 'The Hallmarks of Citizenship' presented at a conference held in London on 8 November 1996 and jointly arranged by the Institute for Citizenship Studies and the British Institute of International and Comparative Law.

References

Barbalet, J.M. (1988), *Citizenship,* Open University Press, Milton Keynes.
Bauman, Z. (1998), *Work, Consumerism and the New Poor,* Open University Press, Buckingham.
Cairns, W. and McKeon, R. (1995), *Introduction to French Law*, Cavendish, London.
Dahrendorf, R. (1988), *Modern Social Conflict*, Weidenfeld and Nicolson, London.

Deacon, A. (1998), 'The Green Paper on Welfare Reform: A Case for Enlightened Self-interest?', *The Political Quarterly*, vol. 69, no. 3, pp. 306-11.

Esping-Andersen, G. (1990), *The Three Worlds of Welfare Capitalism*, Polity Press, Cambridge.

Freyssinet, J. (1998), *Le Chomage*, Editions la Decouverte, Paris.

Gilbert, B.B. (1966), *The Evolution of National Insurance in Great Britain*, Michael Joseph, London.

Gilbert, J.J. (1970), *British Social Policy 1914-1939*, Batsford, London.

Green, D.G. (1999), *An End to Welfare Rights: The Rediscovery of Independence*, IEA, Health and Welfare Unit, London.

Griffith, J. (1999), 'Not Getting it Right', *The Guardian*, 9 April 1999.

Holmes, S. and Sunstein, C.R. (1999), *The Cost of Rights: Why Liberty Depends on Taxes*, Norton, New York.

Janoski, T. (1998), *Citizenship and Civil Society*, Cambridge University Press, Cambridge.

Jenkins, S. (1999), 'We're Off the Sick at Last', *The Times*, 19 May 1999.

Kymlicka, W. (1995a), *Multicultural Citizenship*, Clarendon Press, Oxford.

Kymlicka, W. (ed.) (1995b), *The Rights of Minority Cultures*, Oxford University Press, Oxford.

Mann, M. (1987), 'Ruling Class Strategies and Citizenship', *Sociology*, vol. 21, no. 3, pp. 339-354.

Marhsall, T. H. (1963), 'Citizenship and Social Class', in *Sociology at the Crossroads and Other Essays*, Heinemann, London.

Mead, L.M. (1997a), 'Citizenship and Social Policy': T.H. Marshall and Poverty', *Social Philosophy and Policy*, vol. 14, no. 2, pp. 197-230.

Mead, L.M. et al (1997b), *From Welfare to Work: Lessons from America*, IEA Health and Welfare Unit, London.

Meehan. E. (1993), *Citizenship and the European Community*, Sage, London.

Meehan, E. (1997), 'Political Pluralism and European Citizenship', in P.B. Lehning and A. Weale, (eds), *Citizenship, Democracy and Justice in the New Europe*, Routledge, London.

Milner, S. and Mouraiux, R. (1997), 'France', in H. Compston (ed.), *The New Politics of Unemployment*, Routledge, London.

Plant, R. (1991), 'Social Rights and the Reconstruction of Welfare', in G. Andrews (ed.) *Citizenship*, Lawrence and Wishart, London.

Roche, M. (1992), *Rethinking Citizenship: Welfare, Ideology and Change in Modern Society*, Polity Press, Cambridge.

Selbourne, D. (1994), *The Principle of Duty*, Sinclair-Stevenson, London.

Sennett, R. (1999), 'How Work Destroys Social Inclusion', *New Statesman*, 31 May 1999.

Weale, A. (1997), 'Majority Rule, Political Identity and European Union', in P.B. Lehning and A. Weale (eds), *Citizenship, Democracy and Justice in the New Europe*, Routledge, London.

14 Labour Market Flexibility in Relation to Citizenship

INA DOORNWEERD

Introduction

A more flexible labour market has been envisaged as a possible solution for rising unemployment in Europe in the 1970s and 1980s. The recession was characterised by stagnation, increasing unemployment and inflation and the rigidity of the labour market was considered to be one of the main factors responsible for the economic malaise. The Japanese and American labour markets were more flexible and seemed to perform better in the recession than their European counterparts. By making the labour market more flexible therefore it was thought that the recession could be more efficiently dealt with.

The labour market was considered to be rigid in 'terms of prices of labour, conditions of employment and the quantity and quality of manpower' (Lagos, 1994). By reducing unduly rigid regulations it would be possible to adapt quickly to new technological techniques, to compete well and to absorb the labour supply, and this would arguably further economic growth and reduce unemployment.

The European Commission and the Organisation for Economic Co-operation and Development (OECD) recommended labour market flexibility as a way to get out of the recession and this was combined with a renewed emphasise on supply-side economics and the role of the private sector, as for example, in the Dahrendorf Report (see Ploughmann , 1991).

Partly in response to these pressures, the number of citizens engaged in part-time contracts, short-term contracts, in self-employment and citizens working under flexible terms and conditions has risen significantly and whilst it is argued that the upgrading of labour market flexibility will benefit economic growth and create more employment, some studies (e.g. Lagos, 1994; Standing, 1997) show that the effects of labour market flexibility can be detrimental particularly in respect of insecurity.

These trends have given rise to several questions about what 'citizenship' means in relation to labour market flexibility. What are the effects of increasing labour market flexibility on citizenship? Should citizens for example have a citizenship right to a certain degree of employment security? If so, does this mean that citizens should have this right simply because they are citizens, i.e. because they have a passport of the country they reside in?

Before discussing these and other questions, the concept of citizenship will be defined and the meaning and development of citizenship will be discussed. This will be followed by an analysis of the concept of labour market flexibility. Finally labour market flexibility will be explored in terms of citizenship and questions concerning this relation will be discussed.

Citizenship

Citizenship has been defined in various ways and how it has been defined has been a determining factor in the development of a theory on citizenship. The choice of definition is therefore of crucial importance when analysing citizenship and its relation to labour market flexibility.

Defining Citizenship

As already mentioned, citizenship has been defined in a variety of ways. Dahrendorf (in Dercksen, 1991; Engbersen, 1993) approaches Marshall's definition whereby he describes citizenship as 'the whole of rights and duties that is linked to a full membership of a community'. Roche (1987) added a political dimension to this type of definition whereby 'a full membership of a community' becomes 'a full membership of a political community'.

According to Somers (1993) most sociologists tend to agree on citizenship as being a personal status consisting of a body of 'universal' rights (i.e. legal claims on the state) and duties held equally by all legal members of a nation-state. Somers herself questions this definition in which citizenship is considered to be a personal status. She argues that citizenship is an 'instituted process', i.e. a 'set of institutionally embedded social practices'. Somers considers citizenship, instead of a set of 'ready-made' rights offered by the state to individuals, as 'only one potential outcome of a configuration of natio-nal membership rules'. Likewise Turner (1994) does not consider citizenship to be a personal status, but a set of practices.

In my view the institutionalising of which Somers and Turner speak is purely the process which precedes the accomplishment of the final citizenship rights and duties. The status of citizenship is reflected in the rights and duties citizens have. Naturally this is an outcome of (social) practices, but these social practices in themselves are just the process of establishing rights and duties. Contrary to Somers and Turner it seems preferable to speak about citizenship as an individual status.

Roche, on the other hand, is right to emphasise the political aspect in a definition of citizenship since in contemporary Western society, rights and duties continue to be inextricably linked to a political unit (for example the European Union or the nation-state). I will therefore use the following definition as my starting point for this chapter: 'Citizenship is an individual status consisting of all those rights and duties of all legal members of a political community'.

The Development and Meaning of Citizenship

From most definitions of citizenship we can conclude that citizenship describes a relation between the individual and the political community. We can distinguish three elements: the individual, the nation-state/community and the relationship between the two. The character of these elements is not static, but changes over time: the national state/community has changed with changes of state institutions, new citizens have been excluded while others have been included and new institutions arose which change the relation between the state and the individual (Wiener, 1996).

Our preferred definition tells us that a citizen is entitled to several citizenship rights and has certain duties to fulfil. Often in the past the rights-aspect of citizenship has been emphasised, but recently the duty-aspect has been given more attention. Citizenship rights and duties thus cover a range of different areas. Marshall (1950) distinguished civil, political and social citizenship rights. Later, others have distinguished for example cultural (e.g. Rosaldo, 1994), sexual (Bell, 1995), economic (e.g. Beus, 1992) and ecological (Van Steenbergen, 1994) citizenship rights and duties. However, many of these will fall outside the scope of our discussion of flexibility.

The question of which rights and duties should be included in a status of citizenship is complicated in contemporary societies by the very heterogeneity of their populations. Citizenship must therefore provide a common basis 'from which the claims on the state can be judged'. Thus different identities come to share a common legal status and a formally-defined set of rights and duties (Miller, 1995).

The question remains however of how citizenship should be shaped. Four important conceptions can be distinguished: the liberal-individualistic concept (based on the idea of the calculating citizen pursuing maximal benefit), the communitarian concept (based on the idea of citizens belonging to a community), the republican concept (the public community is central in this concept) and fourthly the neo-republican concept (consisting of elements from the previous three traditions) (Van Gunsteren, 1988). Other distinctions have also been made, for example by Miller (1995), who distinguishes liberal, libertarian and republican conceptions of citizenship.

Most studies of citizenship start by referring to Marshall's paper on citizenship (1950). Marshall described the development of civil citizenship in the 18th century, political citizenship in the 19th century and finally social citizenship in the 20th century. Mann (1987) however rejects Marshall's evolutionary conception of citizenship which he substitutes with the representation of five different strategies which the development of citizenship can follow. Mann shows that the ruling class (a combination of the dominant economic class, the political and the military leaders) played an important role in the development of citizenship. He then describes the five possible strategies which developed industrial countries could follow: the liberal, the reformers, the authoritarian monarchist, the fascistic and the authoritarian socialistic strategy.

Turner (1990) augmented Mann's theory by adding two further dimensions. Firstly the dimension of the private-sphere/public sphere. According to Turner, Mann ignores the influence of the private-sphere on the development of citizenship. Secondly Turner distinguishes the active/passive dimension. As Mann argued, citizenship rights can be developed from above, determined by the ruling class and in this development the population plays a passive role (the passive dimension). However, Turner argues that citizenship can also be developed from below throughout the population (the active dimension). Van Steenbergen (1994) has also emphasised the important role of social movements, such as the womens movement, in the development of citizenship rights.

Bringing these various strands together, we might suggest the following 'model' of the internal dimensions of citizenship.

Next to an internal dimension citizenship also has an exclusionary dimension. Turner (1986) for example distinguished several stages in the development of citizenship whereby the degree of inclusion increases. The first stage is the stage in which the original citizens in capitalist society were property owning, male heads of households. During the second stage female participation in the labour force excluded gender from the definition of citizenship. During the third stage citizenship rights also extended to the elderly and children. (Turner also distinguishes a fourth stage in which rights are ascribed to organic elements of the natural environment).

However, many immigrants residing in a nation-state remain excluded from citizenship, either voluntarily or because the conditions of entitlement to national citizenship require a minimum number of years of residence.

Labour Market Flexibility

Beatson (1995) refers to labour market flexibility as 'the ability of markets (and the agents that operate in them) to respond to changing economic conditions' and by the OECD (1986) as '...the ability of individuals and institutions to abandon established ways and adapt to new circumstances...'. Lagos (1994) notes that these definitions are very general and give little information about the content of labour market flexibility. He argues that most discussions are based on more specific and narrow terms such as that formulated by the International Organisation of Employers (1985): 'the capacity to adapt relative labour costs between enterprises and occupations or adaptation of the costs of factors of production to market conditions'.

However, this type of definition is still incomplete as it refers only to certain types of labour market flexibility. A more inclusive definition based in part on the definition used by the International Labour Organisation (1986) might be formulated as follows: Labour market flexibility is the capacity of the labour market to be adaptable to economic, social and technological changes by means of either a combination of or the individual implementation of adapting wages and non-labour costs, adjusting the work force or the working hours and varying the content of the work.

In the OECD study of 1986 several components of labour market flexibility have been distinguished: flexibility of wages, flexibility of working hours, multi-professionalism, part-time working, fixed-term employment contracts, self-employment, mobility within the country, mobility abroad, and unofficial employment (Nyysölä, 1997).

These components can be combined into three strategies: labour costs flexibility, numerical flexibility and functional flexibility. This classification has been designed by Lagos (1994) and covers, compared to other classifications, all forms of labour market flexibility. Because these three strategies have different effects and implications on the labour market it is necessary to discuss them independently and consider their effects individually. Which types of flexibility and to what degree they will be introduced will depend largely on 'the organisational and technological nature of the production process, the degree of product market competition, and the presence of external constraints (such as government regulation)' (Beatson, 1995).

Labour Costs Flexibility

Lagos (1994) describes labour costs flexibility as 'the degree of responsiveness of nominal wage and non-wage costs to changes in economic conditions in general (e.g. inflation, productivity, terms of trade, demand) and/or the performance of individual firms'. Labour cost flexibility consists of two components, wage costs and non-wage costs. Wage costs represent the 'gross remuneration paid to the wage earners'. Non-wage costs refer to the 'mandatory costs and charges paid by the employer (e.g. fringe benefits, payroll taxes, workers' compensation insurance etc.).

Internal and External Numerical Flexibility

Numerical flexibility consists of two elements, internal and external. Internal numerical flexibility refers to the adjustment of working hours. By adjusting working hours, wages are less likely to be reduced and dismissals less likely to be necessary. Adjustment of hours can be done in various ways, e.g. 'fixing of normal or maximum weekly (monthly, yearly) hours of work, various forms of staggered work, organisation of overtime and compensatory leave, work outside authorised hours (weekend work), and entry into retirement from the labour force' (Meulders and Wilkin, 1987; ILO, 1989; OECD, 1989; Rosenberg, 1989 in Lagos, 1994).

External numerical flexibility, refers to the adjustment of the work force. This means that companies can increase or decrease their work force according to changes in the economic or technological situation (Lagos, 1994). Six forms of flexible contracts have been distinguished by Carnoy, Castells and Benner (1997), namely employees hired through temporary employment agencies, direct hiring into temporary or project work, part-time workers, self-employed workers, informally employed workers and labour hired through subcontracted services.

Functional Flexibility

Functional flexibility is described as 'the ability of a firm to use its work force more effectively by varying the work performed in response to changing workloads and the possibilities offered by new technologies' (Meulders and Wilkin, 1987 in Lagos, 1994). It means that employees are mobile within the company. Functional flexibility involves aspects such as job rotation, multiskilling, work units, mutations in the functional division of labour, retaining and upgrading. In addition education and training, the adaptation of new technology and development in the business structure have moulded and fed the need for an increase in functional labour market flexibility and the means for achieving it (Standing, 1988; De Neubourg, 1990; Lilja, Santamaki-Vuori and Standing , 1990 in Plougmann, 1991).

The Effects of Labour Market Flexibility

As we have seen, labour market flexibility is a complex and ambiguous concept. On a micro-economic level the impact of different strategies of labour market flexibility can be researched from either the individual, the firm or the institutions' point of view (Beatson, 1995). Our main concern here will be on the effects of labour market flexibility on individuals. Once the effects of labour market flexibility have been clarified it will be possible to relate such effects to the concept of citizenship.

Some Positive Effects of Labour Market Flexibility

Labour Costs Flexibility

It is sometimes thought that the recession of the 1970s could have been handled better if a higher degree of labour costs flexibility had been introduced. However instead of adjusting wages, unemployment started to rise (a quantity adjustment) and on top of that, non-wage costs increased.

Tackling unemployment was one of the main incentives for the upgrading of labour market flexibility. It has been pointed out that labour costs flexibility could have a positive effect on employment creation, since when minimum wages are lowered or abolished 'wages will reflect individual productivity more accurately' and therefore employment, i.e. low-wage jobs can be created (Lagos, 1994). Likewise, more jobs for young people could be created (Clarke, 1985 in Lagos, 1994). Normally, employing young people may bring more costs for the employer, because they are less experienced, are 'not used to work discipline' and haven't got a high degree of commitment to the company which in turn can result in a higher turnover. Because of these reasons an employer will have higher recruitment, training and screening costs. If the wages do 'not reflect these differences in costs and productive value' an employer will be more inclined to hire adults.

Numerical Flexibility

If external numerical flexibility were to be upgraded, in other words, if for example dismissing employees were to be made easier and cheaper, it is thought that this would reduce labour costs. Instead of substituting labour for capital, capital will be substituted for labour and employment will be created. Moreover, companies who are restrained in recruiting new manpower will be more inclined to employ new workers if regulations for dismissal are less rigid (Rosenberg, 1989 in Lagos, 1994). As a concession to for example the high dismissal costs in Europe, Saint-Paul (1995) notes the possibility of hiring new employees under more flexible terms and introducing a two-tier system.

It is also argued that companies would employ more workers if they could offer them more flexible contracts. As an example of this the hiring of temporary workers in the Netherlands via temping agencies might be mentioned. This has been shown to be profitable and to make employment creation possible. However this seems only to have been the case in knowledge-intensive companies. In less knowledge-intensive companies the effect wasn't found (Kleinknecht, Oostendorp, and Pradhan, 1997).

It is worth noting that some researchers argue that the proportion of employees in non-permanent employment may sometimes be exaggerated. From the British Household Panel Study, for example, it is evident that in Britain 10 per cent of the working population is in flexible labour, of which 50 per cent were in short-time contracts and a third of those in seasonal casual work found permanent jobs between Panel interviews in 1991-1992 (Taylor-Gooby, 1997). Following from these numbers it is argued that flexible work is not common among the majority of the British working population. Taylor-Gooby concludes that only a 'minority' suffers from a more flexible market and from insecurity and emphasises that this insecurity is mainly evident among groups which have always been the more vulnerable ones. Dutch research also concludes that even though temporary work has increased, the percentages of employees who are entering and leaving companies has appeared to decrease as a result of the recession of 1992/1993. It has also been found that for one group of the unemployed, who found work two years after the start of the interviews, 47 per cent found employment in a flexible job and a half of the employees who worked in a flexible job, had found a permanent job two years later. Measurements over a period of two years, show that 32 per cent remained in a flexible job (Kleinknecht, Oostendorp and Pradhan, 1997).

Functional Flexibility

There is more agreement between employers and employees on functional flexibility than there is on labour costs and external numerical flexibility (Meulders and Wilkin, 1987; ILO, 1989 in Lagos, 1994). It is argued that functional flexibility enables employees 'to make better use of their know-how and skills, get more involved in the production process, and eventually, play a more active role in the management of firms' (OECD, 1990).

There is some agreement that functional flexibility will be beneficial for the firm. Regarding profits and turnovers it can be noted that Kleinknecht, Oostendorp and Pradhan (1997) have also found that Dutch companies which are characterised by a high degree of functional flexibility also seem to be able to create a higher turnover (Kleinknecht, Oostendorp and Pradhan, 1997).

Although it has been argued that for economic reasons labour market security sometimes complicates economic growth, in an ILO report on

Finland (Lilja, 1990) has pointed out that labour market insecurity could also encourage functional flexibility because employees will be more inclined to 'accept technological change and internal job mobility'.

Some Negative Effects of Labour Market Flexibility

Flexible labour market strategies can have unintended and negative effects. In this section we shall consider some of these.

Labour Cost Flexibility

Regarding employment levels, some studies have shown that the lowering of wages does not always establish the expected rise in employment (Boyer, 1988 in Lagos, 1994). Some companies, for example, find it acceptable to pay higher wages to some of their workers when they have invested a large amount of money in their training. Lagos also notes that paying higher wages can be positive for the employer as it enlarges their choice in applicants and their quality. Moreover, 'higher wages provide an incentive for higher productivity from the existing work force, thus lowering unit labour costs' (ILO, 1989 in Lagos, 1994).

Furthermore, it has also been noted that if labour costs were to be reduced by abolishing minimum wages, this would be an incentive for companies not to modernise factory machinery which then would lead to less competitiveness, closing down of companies and a rise in unemployment. In Finland the so-called 'Youth Salary Act'(1993-1995) was implemented with respect to the young employed, whereby employees could hire below the minimum wage, but the intended results failed to occur (Nyssölä, 1997).

In an ILO report on the Netherlands (De Neubourg, 1990 in Ploughmann, 1991) it is argued that lowering wages might not be the solution for combating unemployment as the rigidity of Dutch wages might not be the cause of the existing unemployment. Furthermore a Finnish ILO report (Lilja, Santamaki-Vuori and Standing, 1990) also doubts whether the lowering of non-wage labour costs will have a strong effect in combating unemployment.

Furthermore Kleinknecht, Oostendorp and Pradhan (1997) show that in the Netherlands employees in flexible jobs earn on average 20 per cent less than employees in permanent contracts.

Numerical Flexibility

Both the ILO and OECD state that in the Netherlands the proportion of the working population in non-regular, non-full time employment is about 33 per cent (Standing, 1997). (Somewhat higher than the previously quoted figures for Britain).

External numerical flexibility doesn't always seem to result in employment creation: It has been found in the Netherlands, for example, that when many temporary workers are employed in less knowledge-intensive companies, profits do rise, but no rise in employment creation or a higher turnover could be observed. (Kleinknecht, Oostendorp and Pradhan, 1997). Some companies are more inclined to reduce costs by using the positive effects of flexibility on investment and output (Grahl and Teage, 1989). Furthermore in less knowledge-intensive companies in the Netherlands, characterised by a high turnover of employees, higher profits were made, but again no rise in employment or a higher turnover could be observed. In *high* knowledge-intensive companies characterised by a high turnover of employees, employment did slightly increase, but profits and turnover did not. The introduction of temporary contracts in both types of companies may have resulted in a reduction in labour costs, however no increase in profits, turnover or employment creation occurred (Kleinknecht, Oostendorp and Pradhan, 1997).

Other studies, although not conclusive, also seem to show that 'labour flexibility measures in terms of jobs are ...meagre and the most thorough analysis of numerical flexibility even reveals an increase rather than a decrease in unemployment.' (Meulders and Wilkin, 1987 in Lagos, 1994). Furthermore Kleinknecht, Oostendorp and Pradhan (1997) have found no relation between the speed or the degree of introduction of new technological developments and the employment of temporary employees.

From trade unions in Europe there comes the critique that 'social security and retirement schemes still operate on the basis of full-time employment for fixed hours and are incompatible with flexible hours of work' (European Trade Union Institute). And Standing (1997) argues that in many countries, employees 'in most "non-standard" forms of employment are not covered by employment protection, or are not covered to the same extent as those in regular, full-time waged and salaried employment'. An ILO study on Finland also concludes that 'evidence of the actual effects of employment security provisions on labour costs or on the level and forms of employment is scarce' (Ploughmann, 1991).

With regards to job satisfaction, Kleinknecht, Oostendorp and Pradhan (1997) show that work satisfaction increases when employees get a permanent contract, while employees who are staying in flexible jobs or who move from a permanent contract to a flexible one show less job satisfaction. Again, a study among the young Finnish unemployed shows that attitudes towards labour market flexibility are far from positive (Nyyssölä, 1997).

When discussing the negative effects of numerical flexibility the emphasis is generally put on the effects on employees. A high degree of numerical flexibility can however also cause complications for managers. Honeybone (1997), for example, points out that potential problems could include the management of a temporary work force, problems with skill development and with trust and commitment. That a high degree of numerical flexibility can have negative effects for employers is also emphasised by Kleinknecht, Oostendorp and Pradhan (1997) who found that high turnover increases costs for recruitment and the settling in of new staff. A high turnover can be particularly problematic especially in knowledge-intensive companies that must make considerable investment in their staff. A high turnover in this type of company is therefore not considered a sensible development (except perhaps for temping workers via agencies) (see also Carnoy, Castells and Benner (1997) on the Silicon Valley).

Although internal numerical flexibility may be considered to be positive for both sides, there is a fear that a dual labour market will be created this way. Besides this, working outside 'normal' working hours can be difficult to combine with a personal life (Lagos, 1994).

Functional Flexibility

It is argued that functional flexibility, although usually envisaged as positive, can result in job insecurity and skill production insecurity as 'fewer workers have the prospect of a lifetime "occupation" or a long-term career' (Standing, 1997).

Trade unions are also sceptical towards the introduction of functional flexibility if this concentrates on the removal of regulations: 'the reorganisation of production and the introduction of new technologies may serve to intensify the pace of work and increase managerial control over the production process'. Moreover it is feared that a division will emerge between a skilled 'core' work force and an unskilled 'peripheral' work force within the company (Lagos, 1994). Some employees might also benefit less from training than other employees and training for older employees might be regarded as less beneficial than for the younger ones (ILO, 1989).

Labour Market Flexibility in Relation to Citizenship

When analysing the effects of the various strategies of labour market flexibility on 'being a citizen' and 'the meaning of citizenship', several aspects of citizenship can be highlighted. Here, the effects on the rights-aspects of citizenship will be emphasised.

In the foregoing paragraphs we have seen that the negative effects of labour market flexibility considerably outnumber the positive effects. Many of the negative effects take the form of 'non-effects', i.e. envisaged positive effects which largely don't seem to occur. Furthermore it can be noticed that the quoted positive effects are more often based on theoretical statements, while the quoted negative effects tend to a higher degree to be based on recent empirical research.

The most important empirically researched positive effect of external numerical flexibility seems to be the hiring of temporary workers via temping agencies in knowledge intensive companies. This has been shown to be profitable and to make employment creation possible. Furthermore it is important to note that functional flexibility appears to be regarded as more positive than other forms of labour market flexibility.

With regards to labour costs flexibility and external numerical flexibility it can be concluded that many of the envisaged results do not seem to occur, e.g. employment creation and increasing profits. On top of that job satisfaction seems low, pension building is often problematic, lower wages are earned in temporary contracts and so on. And although less emphasised in the quoted studies, the consequence of a high degree of labour costs flexibility and external numerical flexibility is increasing financial and overall insecurity. Moreover, in the OECD countries, on average 33 per cent of the working population is in flexible jobs and researchers have pointed up the possible emergence of a dual labour market as a result.

If the long-term effects of a high degree of external numerical flexibility were overall positive, i.e. high profits and employment creation, then it would perhaps be 'easier' to accept the negative 'side-effects'. However employment creation is minimal and (financial) insecurity grows.

What does this mean for citizenship? In short, it can be stated that in a *technical* sense, none of the three strategies of labour market flexibility have any effect on the status of citizenship as such. After all, all citizenship rights as constituted in law, will stay unaltered.

One can however ask what citizenship means if one aspect of life, a flexible work situation, can rupture the life of some citizens completely. They might still be entitled to all citizenship rights, but it can be disputed whether this has any meaning if a citizen lives in continuous financial insecurity and cannot *plan* any part of his life because of that. Might it be that some strategies of labour market flexibility have such a negative impact on a citizen's life that it would be necessary to develop a citizenship right to a certain degree of employment security? (see Edwards 2000 in this volume).

Donnelly (1989) points out that '... "having" a right is of most value precisely when one does not "have" the object of the right-that is, when one is denied direct or objective enjoyment of the right'. Do any of the effects which labour market flexibility have on citizens give reason for the establishment of a right, and in particular for a citizenship right? Should citizens have a citizenship right to a certain degree of employment security, a right protecting citizens from the negative effects of (mainly) labour costs flexibility and external numerical flexibility? But firstly we need to say more about the nature of citizenship rights.

Rights, Human Rights and Citizenship Rights

Espada (1996) distinguishes between 'rights in a strict or narrow sense' (claim rights) and 'mere liberties' (privileges). If it is said that 'A is at liberty to do X' this then means that 'A has no duty not to do X'. But if it is said that 'A has a right to do X' then this has a much stronger meaning; 'it somehow implies that others have a corresponding duty to respect A's right'. Espada concludes that the 'main distinctions within claim-rights are related to the duties entailed by them'. Distinctions can be made between *in personam* (specific duties of certain individuals) and *in rem rights* (duties of all others towards the right-holder), between *positive* (to something, mostly social rights) and *negative* rights ('to refrain from doing something/having something done', mostly political and civil rights), and between *active* and *passive* negative rights.

As Espada puts it, the distinction between active and passive rights refers to the action of the right-holder, not to the nature of the corresponding duty. He refers to Feinberg who defines active rights as rights to act or not to act as one chooses and he defines passive rights as rights not to be done to by others in certain ways. An active right is for example the right to free speech, while a passive right might be the right to security. Social rights are in general *in rem* positive claim-rights, because they involve duties of all others towards the right-holder and require a duty to act.

Unlike human rights, which by definition apply to all people universally, citizenship rights are only for members of a certain political unit, usually the nation-state. Human rights, however, have often become citizenship rights by being constituted in national law. Citizenship rights are linked to the status of citizenship; only inhabitants of a certain state who have the passport of that country are entitled to them. For example a Moroccan immigrant in the Netherlands who may have resided there for 30 years but without a Dutch passport is not a Dutch citizen and is therefore not entitled to citizenship rights.

However, long-term residents who do not have citizenship may be entitled to most rights which citizens are entitled to. Short-term immigrants may have more limited rights depending on their country of origin; European citizens who migrate to another European country are covered by a number of EU-rights.

Employment Security a Human Right?

Before discussing the possibility of a citizenship right, the support for establishing a right to a certain degree of employment security would be strong if it were referred to in the International Bill of Rights (see also Edwards, 2000). Article 6 of the International Covenant on Economic, Social and Cultural Rights approaches this matter, but not sufficiently: 'The States Parties to the present Covenant recognise the right to work, which includes the right of everyone to the opportunity to gain his living by work which he freely chooses or accepts, and will take appropriate steps to safeguard this right'. This article can be interpreted as that states which have ratified this Covenant should try to safeguard the right that every individual has to the opportunity to gain his living by work, and therefore should prevent unemployment as much as possible. This in turn could be interpreted as that states should protect individuals from becoming unemployed and should therefore try to prevent the creation of a high (numerical) flexible labour market in which the risk of getting unemployed is high. This interpretation might carry some valid argumentation, but might however be a 'too free' interpretation of Article 6 and cannot therefore be used as an argument supporting the establishment of a citizenship right to a certain degree of employment security.

Another important convention, the Employment Policy Convention (ILO, 1964), which a large number of states have ratified again contains no article referring directly to a right to a certain degree of employment security. However the Preamble to the Articles states that '...the Preamble to the Constitution of the International Labour Organisation provides for the prevention of unemployment and the provision of an adequate living wage...' and 'everyone has the right to...protection from unemployment'. Furthermore it states that 'all human beings, irrespective of race, creed or sex, have the right to pursue both their material well-being and their spiritual development in conditions of freedom and dignity, of economic security and equal opportunity'.

'Providing for the prevention of unemployment' and 'the right to economic security' could be interpreted as requiring that regulations should be developed which will prevent individuals as much as possible from becoming unemployed. This might suggest that dismissal regulations should not be relaxed unduly and that an increase in short-term contracts would also increase the possibility of unemployment.

Furthermore the right to pursue material well-being and spiritual development in conditions of economic security could be interpreted as meaning that economic security should be striven for in order to be able to guarantee that individuals can pursue material well-being and spiritual development. It can be argued that for economic security, employment security and income security are necessary. A high degree of external numerical flexibility and wage flexibility however would have the opposite effect.

Although both comments could be interpreted as referring to safeguarding a certain kind of employment security, the content of these commentaries is not actually reflected in the articles. If articles were to be developed, relating more directly to the content of these comments, it could be argued that states that have ratified these conventions should make an effort to prevent employment insecurity.

In conclusion, although both in the ICSCE and in the ILO conventions some articles and commentary could be interpreted as referring to a right to a certain degree of employment security, it has not been explicitly stated. States that have ratified the International Bill of Rights, therefore, need not, on this basis, develop a national citizenship right to employment security.

Are Negative Effects a Reason for the Development of a Citizenship Right?

Referring back to the negative effects of a high degree of external numerical flexibility and labour costs flexibility, it could be argued that it ought to be necessary to protect citizens from these negative effects. Are these effects reason enough to develop a citizenship right, if not a human right?

Sometimes it seems that rights concerning employment security, which have been developed in particular over the last century, are on the rebound in Europe. European employment regulations seem to have become more flexible. Is it necessary to put a halt to this development?

It can be conjectured what citizenship might mean if life is overshadowed by constant insecurity. A high degree of numerical flexibility in the form of flexible contracts, means that unemployment may always be around the corner. A high degree of labour cost flexibility, although not very common in Europe, means that for example wages can, in some circumstances, suddenly be lowered. In this situation it becomes difficult to plan life. Buying a house becomes more risky, as a general condition for obtaining a mortgage is a long-term contract. Pension building is often complicated as other chapters in this collection have shown and necessary expensive purchases may have to be postponed as a result of financial insecurity. Furthermore job satisfaction may be low and one might speculate what the effects of a high degree of insecurity are on mental well-being.

Citizens who's employment is characterised by a high degree of external numerical and wage flexibility, may have the same citizenship status as every other citizen; life however could be completely different. While in this century rights, guaranteeing citizens' security in all kind of areas, have rapidly expanded, the security around employment, one of the most important aspects of life, is decreasing.

A highly flexible employment situation is different from a situation of long-term unemployment, but some similarities can be observed. It can be hypothesised, for example, that a feeling of not being in control occurs in both situations. The difference between a flexible work situation and long-term unemployment is the degree of stability. Long-term unemployment can be considered as a situation in which a certain degree of stability exists, albeit an undesired situation of stability. A flexible work situation can be called unstable, as contracts are temporary and wage levels can alter. This situation of instability might lead both to actual financial insecurity and feelings of insecurity; life cannot be planned.

243

According to Plant (Espada, 1996) 'every moral code has to recognise that persons need certain minimal capacities that allow them to act and pursue the moral goals enshrined in that moral code. The capacity to act as a moral agent then becomes the basic human end that becomes a requirement of all people. And the conditions or means for that action are unqualified human needs'. Plant suggests that physical survival and autonomy (freedom from arbitrary interference, ill-health and ignorance) are basic conditions of moral activity.

If a right to employment security is not developed, it does not mean that a citizen will not be able physically to survive. However, being a 'playball' on the labour market does affect the autonomy of a person. Citizens who are working in an environment which is characterised by a high degree of external numerical and labour costs flexibility, are constantly relying on the decisions and provisions of companies and state. The citizen therefore, looses control over many aspects of life and cannot plan as insecurity and dependence on others come to dominate his life. If autonomy is used as a criterion for the establishment of a social right, a right to a certain degree of employment security, it can be argued that such a right becomes a moral necessity.

When Plant discusses basic goods, he seems to refer in particular to goods which are often provided by the state, e.g. health care and benefits. Should a right to a certain degree of employment security therefore be labelled as a social (citizenship) right? According to Marshall's definition of social citizenship a right to a certain degree of employment security could be considered as a part of social citizenship. Marshall (1950) defines social citizenship as 'the whole range from the right to a modicum of economic welfare and security to the right to share to the full in the social heritage and to live the life of a civilised being according to the standards prevailing in society'. As a right to a certain degree of employment security is clearly related to a right to economic welfare and security, it might be considered to be a social citizenship right.

A Citizenship Right to Employment Security?

If a citizenship right to a certain degree of employment security, protecting citizens from the negative effects of a high degree of external numerical and labour cost flexibility, were to be developed, would this then imply that only citizens will be entitled to this right, just because they satisfy the technical requirement of having a passport of the country they reside in?

244

If we consider rights in general in a particular Western European country then we can observe that the majority of these rights are not solely (or technically) 'citizenship rights'. As mentioned earlier citizenship rights are rights which only citizens are entitled to. Immigrants without the nationality of their host country and thus without the citizenship status of their host country are not technically entitled to citizenship rights. However most immigrants with a valid residence permit who have resided in the host country for a number of years are entitled to most rights in that country. There are only a few rights which only citizens are entitled to (for example, the right to vote in national elections, serve in the armed forces and so on).

We might conjecture therefore why citizenship is still a matter of issue and why it is considered to be so important. Following from the previous argument, citizenship could be interpreted as a concept that has become inadequate for analysing contemporary society, as 'technical' citizenship rights are limited and few. It seems as if a different kind of 'citizenship' has emerged; not a status, (being entitled to rights and duties, based on only having a passport of the country of residence), but also based on the number of years of residence even without a national passport. Should we therefore not instead speak, if we speak about developing a right, about a right for all inhabitants who have resided in the country for a number of years with a valid residence permit whatever their nationality?

Before answering this question we shall note that having the status of citizenship, (i.e. having the passport of the country of residence) is still the main door to entitlement to *all* rights, including the important right to vote in national elections. The status of citizenship also still fulfils an important psychological function, a function which refers to one as a 'first class inhabitant' and which bestows a sense of belonging to the country of residence.

The recent discussion in Germany around (dual) citizenship for immigrants seemed to have caused sufficient tumult to give the CDU, who envisaged a more strict policy regarding the ascription of citizenship to immigrants, the victory in the election in Hessen. Citizenship seems to be rooted deep in the heart of people. It remains a very important good which should not be ascribed to 'others' easily. Hesitation occurs when immigrants want to belong to 'their' group and the same nationality. Formally considered 'citizenship' can be substituted by 'nationality'. The conception of citizenship these citizens hold can however also be substituted by 'having a passport and the same nationality'.

The psychological aspect seems to play the largest role, and although probably not realised and not intended, this seems to be the 'right' conception of citizenship, because officially the rights which non-citizens will become entitled to when becoming citizens will not increase much.

In conclusion, it seems that if rights are to be developed or have been developed, they should not be 'citizenship' rights, but rather rights for any inhabitant who has lived in their country of residence for a number of years with a valid residence permit.

Although most European countries are not characterised by the degree of flexibility as known in for example the USA, there has been a tendency towards the development of a more flexible labour market. Recently in Europe, as negative effects have been recognised, some attempts have been made to develop some sort of regulations which would prevent inhabitants from the negative effects of increasing external numerical flexibility (wage flexibility is not that apparent in Europe). This is for example the case in the Netherlands, where the so-called 'Flexwet' has been introduced. (the duty of the employer to offer their employees permanent contracts after having given them three times running a temporary contract of three months or less).

What may be most at issue in Europe is the avoidance of a dual labour market based on a distinction between 'full citizens' and those who reside in a country with a residence permit but without full citizenship status. If social rights to counter insecurity were to be developed therefore it would be of considerable importance that they were inclusive of both groups.

References

Beatson, M. (1995), *Labour Market Flexibility*, Research Strategy Branch, Employment Department, Sheffield., Bell, D. (1995), 'Pleasure and Danger: the Paradoxical Spaces of Sexual Citizenship', *Political Geography,* vol. 14, no. 2, pp. 139-153.

de Beus, J.W. (1992), 'Economisch Burgerschap: een Ideaal Zonder Beweging', in J.B.D. Simonis, *De Staat van der burger, Beschouwingen over Hedendaags Burgerschap*, Boom, Amsterdam, Meppel, pp. 121-141.

Boyer, R. (1988), 'The Search for Labour Market Flexibility', in R.A. Lagos (1994), *Labour Market Flexibility: What Does it Really Mean?* CEPAL Review, 54 (December).

Carnoy, M., Castells, M. and Benner, C. (1997), 'Labour Markets and Employment Practices in the Age of Flexibility: A Case Study of Silicon Valley', *International Labour Review*, vol. 136, no. 1, pp. 27-48.

Clarke, O. (1985), 'Labour Market Flexibility: Two Sides of the Coin', *Social and Labour Bulletin* 3-4, March, in R.A. Lagos, (1994), *Labour Market Flexibility: What Does it Really Mean?*, CEPAL Review, 54 (December).

Dercksen, W.J. and Engbersen, G. (1993), 'Arbeid en Sociaal Burgerschap', Manuscript, in *Burgerschap in een Europese Context*, Reader, Utrecht University.

Donnelly, J. (1989), *Universal Human Rights in Theory and Practice*, Cornell University Press, New York.

Edwards, J. (2000) 'Flexibility, Economic Security and Social Rights' in J. Edwards and J-P. Révauger (eds), *Employment and Citizenship in Britain and France*, Ashgate, Aldershot.

Espada, J.C. (1996), *Social Citizenship Rights: A Critique of F.A. Hayek and Raymond Plant*, St. Martin's Press Inc., New York.

Grahl, J. and Teague, P. (1989), 'Labour Market Flexibility in West Germany, Britain and France', *West European Politics*, vol. 12, no. 2, pp. 91-111.

Gunsteren, H. van (1988), 'Admission to Citizenship', *Ethics*, 98, pp. 731-741.

Honeybone, A. (1997), 'Introducing Labour Flexibility: The Example of New Zealand', *International Labour Review*, vol. 136, no. 4, (Winter), pp. 493-507.

International Labour Organisation (1964), *Employment Policy Convention*, Geneva.

International Labour Organisation (1986a), 'Labour Market Flexibility – Report of an Expert Group Meeting', Geneva, May, in R.A. Lagos (1994), Labour Market Flexibility: What Does it Really Mean?, *CEPAL Review*, 54 (December).

International Labour Organisation (1989), 'Adjustment, Employment and Labour Market Policies (GB.244/CE/4/3)', Committee on Employment, Geneva, November, in R.A. Lagos (1994), 'Labour Market Flexibility: What Does it Really Mean? *CEPAL Review*, 54 (December).

International Organisation of Employers (IOE) (1985), 'Adapting the Labour Market', Geneva, September, in R.A. Lagos, (1994), 'Labour Market Flexibility: What Does it Really Mean? *CEPAL Review*, 54(December).

Kleinknecht, A.H., Oostendorp, R.H., and Pradhan, M.P. (1997), *Patronen en Economische Effecten van Flexibiliteit in de Nederlandse Arbeifsverhoudingen*, Sdu Uitgevers, Den Haag.

Lagos, R.A. (1994), 'Labour Market Flexibility: What Does it Really Mean?', *CEPAL Review*, 54(December).

Lilja, R., Santamaki-Vuori, T. and Standing, G. (1990), *Unemployment and Labour Market Flexibility, Finland*, International Labour Organisation, Geneva.

Mann, H. (1987), 'Ruling Class Strategies and Citizenship', *Sociology*, vol. 21, no. 3, pp. 339-354.

Marshall, T.H. (1950), *Citizenship and Social Class*, Pluto Press, London.

Meulders, D. and Wilkin, L. (1987), 'Labour Market Flexibility: Critical Introduction to the Analysis of a Concept', *Labour and Society*, vol. 12, 1, January, in R.A. Lagos, (1994), 'Labour Market Flexibility: What Does it Really Mean?', *CEPAL Review*, 54(December), pp. 81-95.

Miller, D. (1995), 'Citizenship and Pluralism', *Political Studies*, XLIII, pp. 432-450.

Neubourg, de (1990), *Unemployment and Labour Market Flexibility: The Netherlands.* International Labour Organisation, Geneva.

Nyyssölä, K. (1997), 'Young People and Flexibility on the Labour Market. The Attitude of Unemployed Finnish Young People Towards Flexible Employment', *Acta Sociologica*, vol. 40, no. 1, pp. 3-15.

Organisation for Economic Co-operation and Development (1986), 'Labour Market Flexibility – A Report by a High-Level Group of Experts to the Secretary-General', Paris, May, in K. Nyyssölä (1997), 'Young People and Flexibility on the Labour Market. The Attitude of Unemployed Finnish Young People Towards Flexible Employment', *Acta Sociologica*, vol. 40, no. 1, pp. 3-15.

Organisation for Economic Co-operation and Development (1989), 'Labour Market Flexibility – Trends in Enterprises', Paris, March, in R.A. Lagos (1994), 'Labour Market Flexibility: What Does it Really Mean?' *CEPAL Review,* 54(December).

Organisation for Economic Co-operation and Development (1990), *Labour Market Policies for the 1990's*, OECD, Paris.

Ploughman, P. (1991), 'Unemployment and Labour Market Flexibility', *Work, Employment and Society*, vol. 5, no. 3, September, pp. 471-473.

Roche, M. (1987), 'Citizenship, Social Theory and Social Change', *Theory and Society*, 16, pp. 363-399.

Rosaldo, R. (1994), 'Cultural Citizenship and Educational Democracy', *Cultural Anthropology*, vol. 9, no. 3, pp. 402-411.

Rosenberg, S. (1989), 'The State and the Labour Market', Plenum Press, New York, in R.A. Lagos (1994), 'Labour Market Flexibility: What Does it Really Mean?', *CEPAL Review*, 54(December).

Saint-Paul, G. (1995), 'Some Political Aspects of Unemployment', *European Economic Review*, vol. 39, no. 3-4, pp. 575-582.

Somers, M.R. (1993) 'Citizenship and the Place of the Public Sphere', *American Sociological Review*, 58, pp. 587-620.

Standing, G. (1988) *Unemployment and Labour Market Flexibility: Sweden*, International Labour Organisation, Geneva.

Standing, G. (1997), 'Globilization, Labour Flexibility and Insecurity: the Era of Market Regulation', *European Journal of Industrial Relations*, vol. 3, no. 1, pp. 7-37.

Steenbergen, B. van (1994), *The Condition of Citizenship*, Sage, London.

Taylor-Gooby, P. (1997), 'In Defence of Second-Best Theory: State, Class and Capital in Social Policy', *Journal of Social Policy*, vol. 26, no. 2, pp. 171-192.

Turner, B.S. (1986), 'Citizenship and Capitalism', Allen and Unwin, London in M. Waters (1989), 'Citizenship and the Constitution of Structured Social Inequality, *International Journal of Comparative Sociology*, vol. 30, nos. 3-4, September-December, pp. 159-180.

Turner, B.S. (1990), 'Outline of a Theory of Citizenship', *Sociology*, vol. 24, no. 2, pp. 189-213.

Turner, B.S. (1994), 'Postmodern Culture/Modern Citizens', in B. van Steenbergen, *The Condition of Citizenship*, pp. 153-168, Sage, London.

Waters, M. (1989), 'Citizenship and the Constitution of Structured Social Inequality', *International Journal of Comparative Sociology*, vol. 30, no. 3-4, September-December, pp. 159-180.

Wiener, A. (1996), 'Rethinking Citizenship: the Quest for Place-Oriented Participation in the EU', *The Oxford International Review*, Summer Issue, pp. 44-51.

15 Conclusion

JOHN EDWARDS

Increasing labour market flexibility is one among a number of socio economic changes taking place in the world of work and superficially at least, it does not appear to be the most important. Unemployment and chronic unemployment would rank among most commentators as being of greater import. But as the contributors to this book reveal, the immediate and potential consequences of labour market flexibility are more far-reaching and more varied than might at first appear to be the case. They also differ – at least in significance – between France and Britain.

The foregoing chapters do not represent a systematic survey of the consequences of, and responses to, flexibility (that was never our intention) but they reveal a number of dimensions in which its consequences require consideration. Firstly, there are the more immediate social policy responses the purpose of which is to help maintain a degree of economic security. Foremost among these will be new designs for pension provision that shift the emphasis from employer-based schemes to other forms of pension building. Other social policy adjustments will occur in relation to social security, unemployment and other benefits, particularly as these will need to accommodate changes due to increased inter-country migration.

More fundamentally however, increased flexibility raises questions about citizenship, rights, and the maintenance of self-respect. In anything other than a liberal individualistic free-market arrangement, changes in employment markets cannot pretend to be insulated from the state and its citizens and the relation between them. Economic, financial, and social, security are not incidental products of economic systems (rather, they may be, but we tend not to think of them as incidental to the way we want to live our lives) and to the extent that employment market changes will affect them, they themselves are too important to allow the consequences to lie where they fall. If people feel that what is entailed in their citizenship, what their rights are, and how their self-respect is sustained, are being compromised by the effects of increasing employment flexibility, what is being touched is something more fundamental than is likely to be put right solely by adjustments to social policies designed simply to fill gaps in provision or to facilitate the search for new jobs. These will help but responses to employment flexibility will need to be cognisant of the deeper consequences. If rights, citizenship and self-respect are at issue, patching-up policies will not work. But the question of how best to take on board these more fundamental issues is likely to differ considerably between the two countries given the different meaning and contents of citizenship and rights that exist.

There is a third dimension to the consequences of flexibility which the foregoing chapters reveal (though it is a concern primarily of French contributors). This represents the wider 'political' ramifications of increasing employment flexibility. The particular topics in this domain covered by two French contributors concern the new forms of social settlement in the work domain that might be generated by an increasingly fissiparous employment market and the 'proxy' involvement in social movements of participants in the cultural industries whose employment status, already precarious by the nature of the sector is being exacerbated by the influence of flexibility. This third dimension of the consequences of employment flexibility is not one that appears to have featured in any British commentaries, notwithstanding that the incursion of 'flexibility' into British employment markets has been greater than in France – and indeed – greater than most countries in the European Union.

If there is to be any form of policy response to the consequences of employment flexibility in France or Britain (or, for the purposes of argument, any other member states of the European Union) they will need at least, to be aware of the broader context represented by the second of these dimensions. (It is doubtful that policy can take account of the political dimensions of shifting social settlements and social movements – at least in any direct and explicit way – though they must form part of the 'deeper' context in those countries in which they occur). And if there is to be any transfer of policies or policy ideas in relation to employment flexibility and its consequences between France and Britain, it can only realistically happen if the context of rights, citizenship and self respect (no doubt among other things not covered here) is fully understood and its impact on policy receptiveness and effectiveness is fully appreciated.

There is one respect in which a form of transferability will be 'imposed'. Increasing standardisation of social policies within the EU will effect a form of transferability though not in the sense that informs this collection. Increasing geographical movement across the EU will require that social security measures are brought into line, or smoothed out. Even then of course, there must be an element of 'suck it and see' until we know what the differential effects of 'standardising' policies will be when implemented in different countries with different cultures, political regimes, social composition, conceptions of citizenship and rights and so on. But if at least standardisation within a 'European Social Area' can reduce discrepancies in the financial welfare of migrants, minorities, the dependant, the workless, and those who must rely on intermittent employment, then some benefit will have accrued, whatever the unforeseen cultural and social side effects.

There is general agreement in EU states that labour market deregulation and greater employment flexibility are economically valuable and (their proponents would argue) necessary, in order to maintain a competitive position in world markets. This was the undertow at the Luxembourg meeting. But as is so often the case, an incremental shift in (employment) market arrangements did not seem to strike anyone as a socio-economic change that might have consequences for people that could not themselves be managed by the market. The social and financial consequences therefore remain to be picked up elsewhere. The market will not have to pay the costs of its actions. It is when employment market flexibility is viewed by this wider perspective – as an item of socio-economic change and not simply a competitiveness-enhancing adjustment to labour market arrangements – that the extent and nature of its consequences begin to be apparent. Until flexibility is seen in this wider context, and its consequences as potentially much more than changes in working arrangements for some people, social policy responses will be piecemeal and, in likelihood, superficial. New ways of pension building may be found; benefits may be amended to take account of serial employment and geographical migration; training and re-training and re-re-training may be introduced, all of which are ameliorative, and some, important, but they take place in isolation from the social and cultural context. To ask 'what does it do to a society if increasing proportions of its workforce have to change the pattern of their employment from career building and/or long-term employment with the same employer to short-term employment, fixed contracts, self-employment and greater insecurity?' is to ask a question at a fundamentally different level of concern than one which looks for social policy adjustments to employment dislocation. Nevertheless, they are connected. The seriousness with which the latter are undertaken ought to be influenced by an appreciation of the significance of social change brought about by employment dislocation. If, for example, employment flexibility is taking place on a minor scale with the changes small and the numbers affected, few, then fairly minor adjustments in social security and pensions provision may be adequate. But the same level of policy reaction may be

251

inadequate – or even irrelevant – if the magnitude of flexibility is sufficiently large to generate wider changes in people's work and domestic arrangements. Such might be the case for example in Britain where much of the growth in casual employment and self-employment may go unrecorded and operate in the 'black economy'. There may be emerging therefore, not just a dual labour market that several contributors to this volume have referred to, but a triple market where the third 'market' goes largely unrecorded. The same is probably not the case in France where the much slower rate and magnitude of growth of employment flexibility has been contained within the formal sector.

The underlying difference here between the two countries lies less with the sorts of social policy that might be put in place (which, as we have noted, may be tending towards standardisation anyway) but rather with the social and political culture within what they must work. Employment flexibility (or dislocation) has found more fertile ground in Great Britain than in France. In France, social institutions have proved to be sufficiently robust to accommodate the consequences of employment flexibility – or at least – with adjustments, will do so. It seems unlikely that flexibility and its consequences will have much impact on social and financial arrangements and that policies in respect of social security, pensions and welfare more generally will, for this reason, be able to work without being subject to the 'warping' effects of the social and cultural environment.

In Britain, governments throughout the nineteen eighties and the first half of the nineties were remarkably successful in changing the social culture to one in which self-interested individualism became respectable and rewarding. The enterprise culture, which in the event, became something of a euphemism for the pursuit of self-interest proved to be a stimulating environment in which any number of forms of 'employment flexibility' could flourish – and none more so than self-employment and, for want of a better term, 'making money' whilst avoiding the inconvenience of paying taxes. At least a third of Britain's workforce is now in 'flexible' employment and that figure is higher by an unknown quantum if those in the informal economy could be included. This is a very different environment for social policy to work in than is the case in France and what may work in France as a means of providing new and various ways of securing pension building, or providing income security during lean periods, may well not succeed in Britain. Britain has a very poor record in selling financial services particularly in the field of pensions and mortgages (probably another manifestation of the enterprise culture) and when such 'mis-selling' is combined with populations who may be most at risk and least well informed about financial matters and with a significant population that is in the informal economy and who may not be inclined to enter any arrangements that require them to declare their employment status and earnings, the prospects of large numbers of people *not* building adequate pensions and who fall through other parts of the welfare net are very considerable.

Social policies to combat the undesirable consequence of employment flexibility that might take hold in a relatively sympathetic environment in France might therefore be destined to make only a piecemeal and partial impact in the more hostile social and cultural environment in Britain.

The role that rights might play in the formulation and transfer of policy in relation to employment flexibility remains complex and as yet relatively unresearched. At Luxembourg, there was little talk of rights, and policy reactions to the consequences of flexibility such as they have been, have not been in response to the authority of rights. However, the question of rights (and the related matters of citizenship and individual self-respect) cannot be dismissed as being of no relevance to the consequences of flexibility. Cranston, among others, has alerted us to the potential dangers of extending the domain of rights too far and too insubstantially. The more inclusive the domain, the greater may be the danger that the compelling nature of fundamental rights (to life, liberty, free speech, not to be tortured) may be diluted by their keeping company with some social and economic rights. There is truth is these strictures but they carry the reverse danger that we are not able to consider new rights because they will always seem *relatively* inconsequential compared with the most basic and fundamental rights. The contributions to this volume make a case that at the least, a right to social and economic security ought to be considered as having some standing in the EU. We have no criteria by which to judge whether a particular condition or social provision is, or is not, a right and hence the too-oft resort to rights-rhetoric. For these reasons, it is more likely to be the case that a consideration of whether we have a right to (some) social and economic security will be as much affected by the 'culture of rights' in any given country as by theoretical rights deliberations.

Whether or not we are considered to have a right to social and economic security and whether or not a policy response is predicated on this, will be matters that may well have a determining effect on the transferability of relevantly ameliorative policies between France and Britain.

Bibliography

Aguiton, C. and Bensaïd, D. (1997), *Le Retour de la Question Sociale*, Cahiers Libres, Lausanne.

Annales de l'Université de Savoie (1991), *L'Europe Sociale à Onze*, Annales de l'Université de Savoie, no. 14, Chambéry.

Annales de l'Université de Savoie (1994), *La Grande Bretagne de John Major : Changement ou Continuité?*, Annales de l'Université de Savoie, no. 17, Chambéry.

Barbalet, J.M. (1988), *Citizenship*, Open University Press, Milton Keynes.

Barbier, J.C. (1997) 'Les politiques de l'emploi en Europe', *Flamarion*. Dominos.

Bauman, Z. (1998), *Work, Consumerism and the New Poor*, Open University Press, Buckingham.

Baumeister, R. F. (1993), *Self Esteem. The Puzzle of Low Self Regard*, Plenum Press, New York.

Beatson, M. (1995), *Labour Market Flexibility*, Research Strategy Branch, Employment Department, Sheffield.

Beattie, R. and McGillivray, W. (1995), 'A Risky Strategy: Reflections on the World Bank Report "Averting the Old Age Crisis"', *International Social Security Review*, vol. 48, no. 3/4.

Bedau, H. (1984), 'Why Do We Have the Rights We Do?', *Social Philosophy and Policy*, vol. 1, Issue 2, pp.56-72.

Beer, S.M. (1920), *A History of British Socialism*, vol II, Bell, London.

Beer, S.M. (1965), *Modern British Politics ; A Study of Parties and Pressure Groups*, Faber, London.

Bell, D. (1995), 'Pleasure and Danger: the Paradoxical Spaces of Sexual Citizenship', *Political Geography*, vol. 14, no. 2, pp. 139-153.

Benjamin, W. (1991), *Ecrits Français, l'Oeuvre d'Art*, Payet, Paris.

Benn, S. (1978), 'Human Rights – For Whom and For What?', in E. Kamenka and A. Tay (eds), *Human Rights*, Arnold, London.

Benoit-Guilbot, O. (1989), 'Quelques reflexions sur l'analyse societale : l'exemple des regulations des marches du travail en France et en Grande Bretagne', *Sociologie du Travail No. 2*, pp. 217-225.

Bernié-Boissard, C. Dreyfuss, L. and Nicolas-Le-Strat, P. (1998), *Ville et Emploi Culturel – le Travail Créatif Culturel dans les Agglomerations de Nîmes et Montpellier*, ARPES, Université de Montpellier III, Montpellier.

Beveridge, W. (1942), *Social Insurance and Allied Services*, Cmd. 6404, HMSO, London.

Beveridge, W. (1944), *Full Employment in a Free Society*, Allen and Unwin, London.

Beveridge, W. (1960), *Full Employment in a Free Society*, Allen and Unwin, London (first published, 1944).

Boyer, R. (1986) 'Modernisation et flexibilité'. *Travail*, No. 11, avril, pp. 54-60.

Boyer, R. (1986), *La Flexibilité du Travail en Europe*, La Découverte, Paris.

Boyer, R. (1987) 'La flexibilite du travail en Europe'. *Editions La Decouverte*, p. 331.

Boyer, R. (1988) 'The Search for Labour Market Flexibility', in R.A. Lagos (1994), *Labour Market Flexibility: What Does it Really Mean?*, CEPAL Review, 54 (December).

Braybrooke, D. (1972), 'The Firm But Untidy Correlativity of Rights and Obligations', *Canadian Journal of Philosophy*, vol. 1, no. 3, pp. 351-363.

Brett, J. M. and Stroh, L. K. (1994), 'Turnover of Female Managers' in Davidson, M. and Burke, R. (eds), *Women In Management. Current Research Issues*, Paul Chapman, London.

Brown, M.B., Coates, K., Fleet, K. and Hughes, J. (eds) (1978), *Full Employment*, Spokesman, Nottingham.

Brunhes, B. (1989), 'La Flexibilité du Travail. Réflexion sur les Modéles Européens', *Droit Social*, mars.

Brunhes, B. (1989). 'La flexibilité du travail. Reflexion sur les modeles europeens'. *Droit Social No. 3*, pp. 251-255.

Buchele, R. and Christiansen, J. (1998), 'Do Employment and Income Security Cause Unemployment? A Comparative Study of the US and the E-4', *Cambridge Journal of Economics*, vol. 22, pp. 117-136.

Cairns, W. and McKeon, R. (1995), *Introduction to French Law*, Cavendish, London.

Calnan, M., Cant, S. and Gabe, J. (1993), *Going Private: Why People Pay for their Health Care*, Open University Press, Buckingham.

Capet, A. (1998), 'L'Ideal Travailliste de Attlee à Blair dans les Manifestes Electoraux', *Annales de l'Université de Savoie*, Grenoble.

Carnoy, M., Castells, M. and Benner, C. (1997), 'Labour Markets and Employment Practices in the Age of Flexibility: A Case Study of Silicon Valley', *International Labour Review*, vol. 136, no. 1, pp. 27-48.

Carraud, M. (1994), *Droit Social Européen*, Publisud, Paris.

Cazal, D. and Peritti, J.M. (1992), 'L'Europe des resources humaines', *Editions Liaisons*, p.257.

Cecchini, (1988), '1992: la Nouvelle Economie Européene: Une Evaluation des Effets Economiques Potentiels de l'Achevement du Marché Intérieur de la Commununté Européene', (The Cecchini Report), *Economie Européene*, mars, no. 35.

Central London Training and Enterprise Council (1997), *Excluded Youths*, FOCUS, London.

Centre de Sécurité Sociale des Travailleurs Migrants, *La Protection Sociale des Française à l'etranger*, État au 1er janvier 1998.

Chassard, Y. (1998), 'Assistance sociale et emploi : les lecons de l'experience britannique', *Droit Social No. 3*, mars, pp. 269-272.

Childs, D. (1995), *Britain Since 1939 : Progress and Decline*, Macmillan, London.

Churchill, W. (1909), House of Commons Debate, 28th April, c388, House of Commons, London.

Clarke, O. (1985), 'Labour Market Flexibility: Two Sides of the Coin', *Social and Labour Bulletin*, 3-4 March, in R.A. Lagos, (1994) *Labour Market Flexibility: What Does it Really Mean?*, CEPAL Review, 54 (December).

Clegg, H. (1979), *The Changing System of Industrial Relations in Britain*, Blackwell, Oxford.

Coates, K. and Topham, T. (1977), *Industrial Democracy in Britain*, Spokesman, Nottingham.

Collinson, M. and Collinson, D. (1996), '"Its Only Dick": the Sexual Harassment of Women Managers in Insurance Sales', *Work Employment and Society*, vol. 10, no, 1, pp.29-56.

Commission Européenne, Emploi et Affairs Sociales: Guide Practique (1997), 'Vos droits de sécurité sociale quand vous vous déplacé dans l'UE'.

Cook, C. and Stevenson, J. (1996), *The Longman Companion to Britain Since 1945*, Longman, London.

Corby, S. (1993), 'How Big a Step is 'Next Steps?', Industrial Relations Developments in Executive Agencies', *Human Resource Management Journal*, vol. 4, pp. 52-69.

Craig, F.W.S. (ed.) (1975), *British General Election Manifestos 1900-1974*, Macmillan, London.

Cranston, M. (1976), 'Human Rights, Real and Supposed', in N. Timms and D. Watson (eds), *Talking About Welfare*, Routledge and Kegan Paul, London.

Cutler, T. and Waine, B. (1998), *Managing the Welfare State: Text and Sourcebook*, Berg, Oxford.

Cutler, T., Williams, K. and Williams, J. (1986), *Keynes, Beveridge and Beyond*, Routledge, London.

Dagger, R. (1997), *Civic Virtues*, Oxford University Press, Oxford.

Dahrendorf, R. (1988), M*odern Social Conflict*, Weidenfeld and Nicolson, London.

Dahrendorf, R. (1996), 'Prosperity, Civility and Liberty : Can We Square the Circle?', *Proceedings of the British Academy*, vol. 90, pp. 223-235, The British Academy, London.

Davidson, M. J. and Cooper, C. L. (1992), *Shattering The Glass Ceiling*, Paul Chapman, London.

Davies, P. and Freedland, M. (1993), *Labour Legislation and Public Policy*, Clarendon Press, Oxford.

Deacon, A. (1998), 'The Green Paper on Welfare Reform: A Case for Enlightened Self-interest?', *The Political Quarterly*, vol. 69, no. 3, pp. 306-11.

de Beus, J.W. (1992), 'Economisch Burgerschap: een Ideaal Zonder Beweging', in J.B.D. Simonis, *De Staat van der burger, Beschouwingen over Hedendaags Burgerschap*, Boom, Amsterdam, Meppel, pp. 121-141.

De Montalbert, M. (1997), 'L'Europe Sociale', in *La Protection Sociale en France*, La Documentation Française, Collection Les Notices, Paris.

Department of Education and Employment (1997), 'Job Creation in the USA and Europe Compared', *Labour Market Trends*, May, pp. 173-4, Department of Education and Employment, London.

Department of Social Security (1998), *A New Contract for Welfare: Partnership in Pensions*, Cm. 4179, Stationery Office, London.

Department of Social Security (1998), *Partnership in Pensions*, HMSO, London.

Department of Trade and Industry (1998), *Fairness at Work*, Cmnd. 3968, Stationery Office, London.

Department of Trade and Industry (1998), *The Government's Response to the First Report of the Low Pay Commission*, Statement by Margaret Beckett, President of the Board of Trade, Thursday 18th June 1998, Department of Trade and Industry, London.

Department of Trade and Industry (1999), *A Detailed Guide to the National Minimum Wage*, DTI, London.

Dercksen, W.J. and Engbersen, G. (1993), 'Arbeid en Sociaal Burgerschap', Manuscript, in *Burgerschap in een Europese Context*, Reader, Utrecht University.

Dickens, L. and Hall, M. (1995), 'The State, Labour Law and Industrial Relations' in P. Edwards (ed.), *Industrial Relations: Theory and Practice in Britain*, Blackwell, Oxford.

Dolado, J., Kramarz, F., Machin, S., Manning, A., Margolis, D. and Tealings, C. (1996), 'The Economic Impact of Minimum Wages in Europe', *Economic Policy*, 23, pp. 317-372.

Donnelly, J. (1989), *Universal Human Rights in Theory and Practice*, Cornell University Press, New York.

Dreyfuss, L. (1998), *Réseaux Culturels et Space Politique*, ARPES, Université de Montpellier III, Montpellier.

Dreyfuss, L. and Marchand, A. (1995), 'Gouvernement Local et Legitimation vers des Républiques Urbaines ?', *Future Antérieur*, no. 29, L'Harmattan, Paris.

Dumont, J.P. (1988), *Les Systèmes Etrangers de Sécurité Sociale*, Economica, Paris.

Dupeyroux, J.J. (1993), *Droit de la Sécurité Sociale*, Dalloz, Paris.

Edwards, J. (2000), 'Flexibility, Economic Security and Social Rights' in J. Edwards and J-P. Révauger (eds,) *Employment and Citizenship in Britain and France*, Ashgate, Aldershot.

Ehrenberg, A. (1998), *La Fatigue d'Etre Soi*, Odile Jacob, Paris.

Employment Department (1988), *Wages Council : 1988 Consultation Document*, December, Employment Department London.

Equal Opportunities Review (1996), Flexible Working: the Impact on Women's Pay and Conditions, *Equal Opportunities Review*, No. 65, January/February.

Equal Opportunities Review (1997a), Minimum Wage Benefits Women and Ethnic Minorities, *Equal Opportunities Review*, No. 73, May/June.

Equal Opportunities Review (1997b), Gender Pay Gap Narrows, *Equal Opportunities Review*, No. 76, November/December.

Espada, J.C. (1996), *Social Citizenship Rights: A Critique of F.A. Hayek and Raymond Plant*, St. Martin's Press Inc., New York.

Esping-Anderson, G. (1990), *The Three Worlds of Welfare Capitalism*, Polity Press, Cambridge.

Esposito, M-C. (1984), 'Le Patronat et le Chomage: Emploi et Chomage en Grande-Bretagne 1979-1983', *Revue Française de Civilisation Britannique*, no's. 2-4, pp.33-48, Université de Provence, Aix-Marseille 1, Aix en Provence.

European Code of Social Security, EC European Treaties ETS No. 48, Strasbourg 1964.

European Code of Social Security (revised), CE ETS No. 139, Rome 1990.

European Commission (1993), *Competitiveness and Employment*, (White Paper on Growth), 5th December, European Commission, Brussels.

European Commission (1996), *Employment in Europe 1996*, European Commission, Luxembourg.

European Commission (1997), *Employment in Europe 1997*, European Commission, Luxembourg.

European Commission (1997), *Eurostat Yearbook*, European Commission, Brussels.

European Commission communication (1997), *Modernising and Improving Social Protection in the EU.*

European Commission (1997a), *Proposals for Guidelines*, 1st October, European Commission, Brussels.

European Commission (1997b), *Presidency Conclusions*, 24th November, European Commission, Brussels.

European Commission (1997c), *An Employment Agenda for the Year 2000: Issues and Policies*, 24th November, European Commission, Brussels.

European Commission (1997d), *Executive Summary*, 24th November, European Commission, Brussels.

European Commission (1998), *Social Action Programme 1998-2000*, European Commission, Luxembourg.

European Convention on the Legal Status of Migrant Workers, Council of Europe (CE), ETS 93, Strasbourg 24th November 1977.

Evetts, J. (1994), 'Career and Gender: the Conceptual Challenge', in J. Evetts (ed.), *Women and Career. Themes and Issues in Advanced Industrial Societies*, Longman, London.

Feinberg, J. (1980), *Rights, Justice, and the Bounds of Liberty*, Princeton University Press, Princeton, New Jersey.

Field, F. (1984), *The Minimum Wage – Its Potential and Dangers*, Heineman, London.

Financial Times, 27th June 1997, 'UK Calls For More Labour Flexibility in Europe', *Financial Times*, London.

Ford, H. (1926), *Aujourd-hui et Demain*, Payot, Paris.

Fouquin, M. et al (1998), 'Le marche du travail britannique vu de France'. *La lettre du CEPII, No. 167*, avril.

Fraser, N. (1995), 'From Redistribution to Recognition? Dilemmas of Justice in a Post-socialist age', *New Left Review*, 212, pp.68-93.

Freeman, R. (1995), 'The Limits of Wage Flexibility to Curing Unemployment', *Oxford Review of Economic Policy*, vol. 11, pp. 63-72.

French Institute of International Relations (1996), *Rapport Annuel Mondial sur le Système Economique et les Stratégies*, (Ramses 96) Dunod, Paris.

Freyssinet, J. (1998), *Le Chomage*, Editions la Decouverte, Paris.

Friedman, M. and Friedman, R. (1980), *Free to Choose*. Secker and Warburg, London.

Froud, J. and Shaoul, J. (1998), 'Appraising and Evaluating PFI for NHS Hospitals', Paper presented at the *CIMA Public Sector Accounting Workshop*, University of Edinburgh, 24-25th September.

Galenkamp, M. (1998), *Individualism Versus Collectivism*, Sanders Instituut and Gouda Quint, Rotterdam.

Gallacher, W. (1936), *Revolt on the Clyde*, Lawrence and Wishart, London.

Gardiner, K. (1993), *A Survey of Income Inequality Over the Last Twenty Years - How Does the UK Compare?* STICERD/LSE, London, Discussion Paper WSP/100.

Gautie, J. (1993), 'Les politiques de l'emploi. Les marges etroites de la lutte contre le chomage', *Vuibert Eco,* p. 208.

Gewirth, A. (1984), 'The Epistemology of Human Rights', *Social Philosophy and Policy*, vol. 1, Issue 2, pp. 1-24.

Gilbert, B.B. (1966), *The Evolution of National Insurance in Great Britain*, Michael Joseph, London.

Gilbert, J.J. (1970), *British Social Policy 1914-1939*, Batsford, London.

Ginn, J. and Arber, S., (1998), 'Prospects for Women's Pensions: the Impact of Privatisation', paper given at the *American Sociological Association Annual Conference*.

Giorgio, R. and Guerre, C. (1996), *Le Spectacle Vivant en Languedoc-Rousillon*, Observatoire Regional de l'Emploi Culteral, Montpellier.

Glennerster, H. (1997), *Paying for Welfare Towards 2000*, Harvester Wheatsheaf, London.

Goffman, E. (1959), *The Presentation of Self in Everyday Life*, Penguin, Harmondsworth.

Golding, M. (1984), 'The Primacy of Welfare Rights', *Social Philosophy and Policy*, vol. 1, Issue 2, pp. 119-136.

Gosling, A., Machin, S. and Meghir, C. (1994), 'What Has Happened to Men's Wages Since the Mid-1960s?', *Fiscal Studies* 15(4), pp. 63-87.

Grahl, J. and Teague, P. (1989), 'Labour Market Flexibility in West Germany, Britain and France', *West European Politics*, vol. 12, no. 2, pp. 91-111.

Green, D.G. (1999), *An End to Welfare Rights: The Rediscovery of Independence*, IEA, Health and Welfare Unit, London.

Gregg, P. (1967), *The Welfare State*, Harrap, London.

Gregg, P. and Wadsworth, J. (1996), 'More Work in Fewer Households?' in, Hills, J. (ed.), *New Inequalities: The Changing Distribution of Income and Wealth in the United Kingdom*. Cambridge University Press, Cambridge, pp. 181-207.

Gregory, M. and Salverda, W. (1999), 'Employment and Wages: Summary Report', in *Wages and Employment*, EC/DG V – OECD/DEELSA Seminar, European Commission, Luxembourg.

Griffith, J. (1999), 'Not Getting it Right', *The Guardian*, 9 April 1999.

Guggenbülh, A. and Leclerc, S. (1995), *Droit Social Européen des Travaillers Salaries et Indépendents*, Bruylant, Brussels.

Gunsteren, H. van (1988), 'Admission to Citizenship', *Ethics*, 98, pp. 731-741.

Habermas, J. (1978), *L'Espace Public*, Payot, Paris.

Hansard (27th November 1997), *Select Committee on European Legislation: Sixth Report.*

Hansard, (3rd December 1997), Mr Ian McCartney, MP.

Hansard, (4th December 1997), Mr Streeter, MP.

Hansard, (15th January 1998), Mr Green, MP.

Hansard, (20th January 1998), Mr Green, MP.

Harris, J. (1977), *William Beveridge: a Biography*, Clarendon Press, Oxford.

Harris, J. (1993), *Private Lives, Public Spirit: Britain 1870-1914*, Oxford University Press, Oxford.

Hart, H.L.A. (1984), 'Are There Any Natural Rights?', in J. Waldron (ed.), *Theories of Rights*, Oxford University Press, Oxford.

Hartley, J., Jacobson, D., Klandermans, B. and Van Vuuren, T. (1991), *Job Insecurity. Coping with Jobs at Risk*, Sage, London.

Henrard, J-C. and Veysset-Puijalon, B. (1997), 'Les Personnes Agées et la Dependance', in *La Protection Sociale en France*, La Documentation Française, Collection Les Notices, Paris.

Her Majesty's Stationery Office (1944), *Employment Policy*, Cmnd 6527, Her Majesty's Stationery Office, London.

Her Majesty's Stationery Office (1997), *Annual Abstract of Statistics*, HMSO, London.

Her Majesty's Stationery Office (1998), *New Ambitions for Our Country: A New Contract for Welfare*, Her Majesty's Stationery Office, London.

Hill Jr., T. E. (1991), *Autonomy and Self-respect*, Cambridge University Press, Cambridge.

Hill, M. (1996), *Social Policy: A Comparative Analysis*, Prentice Hall/Harvester Wheatsheaf, London.

Hills, J. (1993), *The Future of Welfare: A Guide to the Debate*, Joseph Rowntree Trust, York.

Hills, J. (1998), *Thatcherism, New Labour and the Welfare State*, Centre for the Analysis of Social Exclusion, London School of Economics, London.

Hinton, J. (1973), *The First Shop Stewards Movement*, George Allen and Unwin, London.

Holmes, S. and Sunstein, C.R. (1999), *The Cost of Rights: Why Liberty Depends on Taxes*, Norton, New York.

Honeybone, A. (1997), 'Introducing Labour Flexibility: The Example of New Zealand', *International Labour Review*, vol. 136, no. 4, (Winter), pp. 493-507.

Hutton, W. (1996), 'The Stakeholder Society', in D. Marquand, and A. Seldon, (eds), *The Ideas that Shaped Post-War Britain*, Fontana, London.

Income Data Services (IDS) (1996), *Private Medical Insurance* (study no. 593), IDS, London.

Industrial Relations Services (1999), 'Employment Relations Bill Stumbles Out of the Blocks', *Industrial Relations Law Bulletin*, 611, pp. 2-3.

Insight (1998), 'Youth Unemployment – the European Perspective', *Insight*, 42, Summer 1998, p. 28.

Insight (1999), 'Tackling Social Exclusion', *Insight*, 44, Spring 1999, p. 30.

International Labour Organisation (1964), *Employment Policy Convention*, Geneva.

International Labour Organisation (1986a), 'Labour Market Flexibility – Report of an Expert Group Meeting', Geneva, May, in R.A. Lagos (1994), Labour Market Flexibility: What Does it Really Mean?, *CEPAL Review*, 54 (December).

International Labour Organisation (1989), 'Adjustment, Employment and Labour Market Policies (GB.244/CE/4/3)', Committee on Employment, Geneva, November, in R.A. Lagos (1994), 'Labour Market Flexibility: What Does it Really Mean?,*CEPAL Review*, 54 (December).

International Organisation of Employers (IOE) (1985), 'Adapting the Labour Market', Geneva, September, in R.A. Lagos, (1994), 'Labour Market Flexibility: What Does it Really Mean? *CEPAL Review*, 54(December).

Janoski, T. (1998), *Citizenship and Civil Society*, Cambridge University Press, Cambridge.

Jaoui-Pylypiw, E. (1997), 'L'Etat Providence Sous le Gouvernement Conservateur: le Cas des Personnes Agées': L'Etat Providence: Bilan de 18 Années de Gouvernement Conservateur', *Revue Française de Civilisation Britannique*, vol. IX, no. 4, Université de Provence, Aix-Marseille I, Aix en Provence.

Jeffery, M. (1997), 'European Social Policy and the Meanings of Flexibility', *www.britcoun.org/european/ionil.htm*.

Jenkins, S. (1999), 'We're Off the Sick at Last', *The Times*, 19 May 1999.

Jessop, B. (1994), 'Post-Fordism and the State', in A. Amin (ed.), *Post-Fordism, A Reader*, Blackwell, Oxford.

Johnson, C.V. (1991), *The Economy Under Mrs Thatcher*, Penguin, London.

Johnson, R. and Crystal, S. (1997), 'Health Insurance Coverage at Midlife: Characteristics Costs and Dynamics', *Health Care Financing Review* vol. 18, pp. 123-148.

Join-Lambert, M.T. (1997), *Politiques Sociales*, Presses de Sciences-po et Dalloz, Paris.

Kaisergruger, D. (1997), 'Negocier la Flexibilité', *Editions d'Organisation*, p. 237.

Kant, I. (1952), 'Fundamental Principles of the Metaphysic of Morals', in R. M. Hutchins (ed.), *Great Books of the Western World*. 42, Kant, Encyclopaedia Brittanica, Chicago.

Keynes, J.M. (1936), *The General Theory of Employment, Interest and Money*, Macmillan, London.

Kleinknecht, A.H., Oostendorp, R.H., and Pradhan, M.P. (1997), *Patronen en Economische Effecten van Flexibiliteit in de Nederlandse Arbeifsverhoudingen*, Sdu Uitgevers, Den Haag.

Kohli, M. et al (eds) (1991), *Time for Retirement. Comparative Studies of Early Exit from the Labour Force*, Cambridge University Press, Cambridge.

Konsta, A. (1997), 'The Concept of Flexibility and the European Labour Market', *www.britcoun.org/european/ionil.htm*.

Krugman, P. (1995), *Development, Geography and Economic Theory*, MIT Press, Cambridge, Mass.

Kymlicka, W. (1995a), *Multicultural Citizenship*, Clarendon Press, Oxford.

Kymlicka, W. (ed.) (1995b), *The Rights of Minority Cultures*, Oxford University Press, Oxford.

Labour Party (1992), *It's Time to Get Britain Working Again*, Labour Party, London.

Labour Party (1997) *Because Britain Deserves Better*, (The Labour Party 1997 General Election Manifesto), The Labour Party, London.

Labour Party (1997), *New Labour : Because Britain Deserves Better*, Labour Party, London.

Lagos, R.A. (1994), 'Labour Market Flexibility: What Does it Really Mean?', *CEPAL Review*, 54(December).

Laing and Buisson (1998), *Healthcare Market Review 1998-99*, Laing and Buisson, London.

Land, A., Lowe, R. and Whiteside, N. (1992), *The Development of the Welfare State 1939-1951: a Guide to Documents in the Public Record Office*, HMSO, London.

Lavalette, M. and Kennedy, J. (1996), 'Casual Lives? The Social Effects of Work Casualization and the Lock Out on the Liverpool Docks', *Critical Social Policy* 48, vol. 16, pp.95-107.

Leca, J. (1991), *Sur Individualism*, Presses de la FNSP, Paris.

Lee, P., Midy, P., Smith, A. and Summerfield, C. (1998), 'French and British Societies: A Comparison'. *Social Trends*(28), Stationery Office, London, pp. 15-28.

Le Monde (1997), 'Le quinze ébauchent une politique sociale', 21st November.

Lewis, S. (1994), 'Role Tensions and Dual Career Couples', in M. Davidson and R. Burke (eds), *Women In Management. Current Research Issues*, Paul Chapman, London.

Leydier, G. (1998), 'Dimensions of Inequality in French and Political Discourse Since the Early 80's', in J. Edwards and J-P. Revauger (eds), *Discourse on Inequality in France and Britain*, Ashgate, Aldershot.

Liberation (1997), 'Emploi ce que l'Europe peut faire', 20th November.

Lilja, R., Santamaki-Vuori, T. and Standing, G. (1990), *Unemployment and Labour Market Flexibility, Finland*, International Labour Organisation, Geneva.

Lindley, R. (1986), *Autonomy*, Macmillan, London.

Lomasky, L. (1984), 'Personal Projects as the Foundation for Basic Rights', *Social Philosophy and Policy*, vol 1, Issue 2, pp. 35-55.

Lourie, J. (1995), 'A Minimum Wage', *House of Commons Library, Research Paper 95/97*, House of Commons, London.

Low Pay Commission (1998), *First Report of the Low Pay Commission* HMSO, London.

Low Pay Commission (1998), *The National Minimum Wage: First Report of the Low Pay Commission*, Stationery Office, London.

Low Pay Commission (1998a), *The National Minimum Wage*, Cm. 3976, The Stationery Office, London.

Low Pay Commission (1998b), *The National Minimum Wage, Summary Report*, The Stationery Office, London.

Low Pay Commission (1998c), *National Minimum Wage: Monitoring and Evaluation*, Paper presented to the Education and Employment Economics Group, 30th October 1998, The Stationery Office, London.

Luckhaus, L. and Moffat, G. (1996), *Serving the Market and the People's Needs? The Impact of European Union Law on Pensions in the UK*, York Publishing Services, York.

MacGregor, S. and Jones, H. (1998), *Social Issues and Party Politics*, Routledge, London.

Maddox, G. L. (1992), 'Long Term Care Policies in Perspective', *Ageing and Society*, 12, pp. 355-368.

Malthus, T. (1798), *An Essay on Population*, Dent 1914, London.

Mann, H. (1987), 'Ruling Class Strategies and Citizenship', *Sociology*, vol. 21, no. 3, pp. 339-354.

Maquart, B. (1997), 'Les Régimes de Retraite', in *La Protection Sociale en France*, La Documentation Française, Collection Les Notices, Paris.

Marhsall, T. H. (1963), 'Citizenship and Social Class', in *Sociology at the Crossroads and Other Essays*, Heinemann, London.

Marshall, T.H. (1950), *Citizenship and Social Class*, Pluto Press, London.

Martin, R. (1993), *A System of Rights*, Clarendon Press, Oxford.

Marx, K. (1954), *Capital: Volume One*, George Allen and Unwin, London. (Originally published 1864).

McCarthy, Lord (1999), *Fairness at Work and Trade Union Recognition: Past Comparisons and Future Problems*, Institute of Employment Rights, London.

Mead, L.M. (1997a), 'Citizenship and Social Policy: T.H. Marshall and Poverty', *Social Philosophy and Policy*, vol. 14, no. 2, pp. 197-230.

Mead, L.M. et al (1997b), *From Welfare to Work: Lessons from America*, IEA Health and Welfare Unit, London.

Meager, N., Court, G. and Moralee, J. (1996), 'Self-employment and the Distribution of Income' in, Hills, J. (ed.), *New Inequalities: The Changing Distribution of Income and Wealth in the United Kingdom*, Cambridge University Press, Cambridge, pp. 208-235.

Meehan, E. (1997), 'Political Pluralism and European Citizenship', in P.B. Lehning and A. Weale, (eds), *Citizenship, Democracy and Justice in the New Europe*, Routledge, London.

Meehan. E. (1993), *Citizenship and the European Community*, Sage, London.

Menger, P-M. (1997), 'Les Intermittents du Spectacle', *INSEE Premiere*, no. 510 : fevrier.

Metcalf, D. (1981), *Low Pay, Occupational Mobility and Minimum Wage Policy in Britain*, American Enterprise Institute, Washington.

Metcalf, D. (1999), 'The Low Pay Commission and the National Minimum Wage', *Economic Journal*, February.

Meulders, D. and Wilkin, L. (1987), 'Labour Market Flexibility: Critical Introduction to the Analysis of a Concept', *Labour and Society*, vol. 12, 1, January, in R.A. Lagos, (1994), 'Labour Market Flexibility: What Does it Really Mean?', *CEPAL Review*, 54(December), pp. 81-95.

Meyer, J. L. (1996). 'L'Etat et les emplois intermediaries : l'example des CIE et des CES', in *La construction sociale de l'emploi en France*, A. Friot and S. Rose, L'Harmattan, Paris, pp. 87-101.

Meyer, J.L. (1998), 'Intermediaries de l'emploi et marche du travail', *Revue Française de Sociologie no. 3*, pp. 345-364.

Miller, D. (1995), 'Citizenship and Pluralism', *Political Studies*, XLIII, pp. 432-450.

Milner, S. and Mouraiux, R. (1997), 'France', in H. Compston (ed.), *The New Politics of Unemployment*, Routledge, London.

Morgan, J. (1996), 'Labour Market Recoveries in the UK and Other OECD Countries', *Labour Market Trends*, December, pp. 529-539.

Munday, B. and Ely, P. (eds) (1996), *Social Care in Europe*, Prentice Hall/Harvester Wheatsheaf, London.

National Association of Pension Funds (NAPF) (1997), *Annual Survey 1996*, NAPF, London.

Neubourg, de (1990), *Unemployment and Labour Market Flexibility: The Netherlands.* International Labour Organisation, Geneva.

Nicolas-Le-Strat, P. (1998), 'Multiplicité Artistique et Reseaux' in C. Bernié-Boissard, L. Dreyfuss, and P. Nicolas-Le-Strat, (eds), *Ville et Emploi Culturel – le Travail Créatif Culturel dans les Agglomerations de Nimes et Montpellier*, ARPES, Université de Montpellier III, Montpellier.

Nyyssölä, K. (1997), 'Young People and Flexibility on the Labour Market. The Attitude of Unemployed Finnish Young People Towards Flexible Employment', *Acta Sociologica*, vol. 40, no. 1, pp. 3-15.

Obelkevitch, J. and Catterall, J. (1994), *Understanding Post-War British Society*, Routledge, London.

O'Brien, J. and Feist, A. (1997), *Employment in the Arts and Culture Industries : An Analysis of the 'Labour Force Survey' and Other Sources*, ACE Research Reports no. 9, The Arts Council of Great Britain, London.

Offe, C. (1997), *Les Démocraties Modernes à l'Epreuve*, L'Harmattan, Paris.

Office for National Statistics (1998), *Social Trends*, 28, HMSO, London.

Office for National Statistics (1999), *Labour Market Trends*, February.

Ogus, A., Barent, E. and Wikeley, B. (eds), (1995), *The Law of Social Security*, Butterworths, London.

Organisation for Economic Co-operation and Development (1986), 'Labour Market Flexibility – A Report by a High-Level Group of Experts to the Secretary-General', Paris, May, in K. Nyyssölä (1997), 'Young People and Flexibility on the Labour Market. The Attitude of Unemployed Finnish Young People Towards Flexible Employment', *Acta Sociologica*, vol. 40, no. 1, pp. 3-15.

Organisation for Economic Co-operation and Development (1989), 'Labour Market Flexibility – Trends in Enterprises', Paris, March, in R.A. Lagos (1994), 'Labour Market Flexibility: What Does it Really Mean?', *CEPAL Review*, 54(December).

Organisation for Economic Co-operation and Development (1990), *Labour Market Policies for the 1990's*, OECD, Paris.

Organisation for Economic Cooperation and Development (1991), *Economic Survey 1990-91 : France*, Organisation for Economic Cooperation and Development, Paris.

Organisation for Economic Cooperation and Development (1994), *Jobs Study : Evidence and Explanations*, Organisation for Economic Cooperation and Development, Paris.

Organisation for Economic Cooperation and Development (1997), *Implementing the OECD Jobs Strategy: Lessons from Member Countries' Experience*, Organisation for Economic Cooperation and Development, Paris.

Parsons, N. (1998), 'The Welfare State and Labour Market Reform 1979-1997: L'Etàt-Providence : Bilan de Dix-Huit Annèes de Pouvoir Conservateur (1979-1997)', *Revue Française de Civilisation Britannnique* no's 6-4, Université de Provence, Aix-Marseille 1, Aix en Provence.

Pendleton, A. and Winterton, J. (eds) (1993), *Public Enterprise in Transition: Industrial Relations in State and Privatized Industries*, Routledge, London.

Pension Provision Group (1998), *We all Need Pensions - the Prospects for Pension Provision*, The Stationery Office, London.

Pension Provision Group (1999), *Response of the Pension Provision Group to the Green Paper on Pensions*, PPG/AON CONSULTING, Harrow.

Pfeffer, J. and Baron, J. N. (1988), 'Taking The Workers Out: Recent Trends in the Structuring of Employment' in B. M. Straw and L. L. Cummings (eds), *Research in Organisational Behaviour*, vol. 10, JAI Press, Greenwich, Conn.

Phillips, A. (1992), 'Democracy and Difference: Some Problems for Feminist Theory', *Political Quarterly*, vol. 63, pp.79-90.

Pierson, P. (1994), *Dismantling the Welfare State: Reagan, Thatcher and the Politics of Welfare State Retrenchment*, Cambridge University Press, Cambridge.

Plant, R. (1991), 'Social Rights and the Reconstruction of Welfare', in G. Andrews (ed.) *Citizenship*, Lawrence and Wishart, London.

Plant, R. (1991), *Modern Political Thought*, Blackwell, Oxford.

Plant, R., Lesser, H. and Taylor-Gooby, P. *Political Philosophy and Social Welfare*, Routledge and Kegan Paul, London.

Ploughman, P. (1991), 'Unemployment and Labour Market Flexibility', *Work, Employment and Society*, vol. 5, no. 3, September, pp. 471-473.

Pollock, A. and Dunnigan, M. (1998), 'Public Health and the Private Finance Initiative', *Journal of Public Health Medicine*, vol. 20, no. 1, pp. 1-2.

Pollock, A., Dunnigan, M., Gaffney, D., Macfarlance, A. and Azeem Majeed, R. (1997), 'What Happens When the Private Sector Plans Hospital Services for the NHS: Three Case Studies under the Private Finance Initiative', *British Medical Journal*, vol. 314, 26th April, pp. 1266-1271.

Pond, C. and Winyard, S. (1983), *The Case for a National Minimum Wage*, Low Pay Unit, London.

Ravier, J-P. (1981), *Les Syndicats Britanniques Sous les Gouvernements Travaillistes 1945-1970*, PUL, Lyon.

Ravier, J-P. (1985), 'La Montée du Chômage Depuis 1967 : Quelques Explications', *Chômage et Emploi en Grande-Bretagne : Actes du Colloque de Chambéry*, 12-13 octobre 1984, Annales de l'Université de Savoie No. 6/7, Chambéry.

Rawls, J. (1971), *A Theory of Justice*, Oxford University Press, Oxford.

Raz, J. (1982), 'Liberalism, Autonomy, and the Politics of Neutral Concern', *Midwest Studies in Philosophy*, no. 7.

Raz, J. (1984), 'Right-based Moralities', in J. Waldron (ed.), *Theories of Rights*, Oxford University Press, Oxford.

Révauger, J-P. (1986), *L'Idée d'Autoqestion en Grande-Bretagne*, Thèse d'Etat, University de Grenoble III.

Révauger, J.P. (1998) 'Les concepts structurants de la protection sociale en Grande-Bretagne et en France : divergences et convergences', *Revue Française de Civilisation Britannique*, Université de Provence Aix-Marseille I, Aix en Provence.

Reynaud, E. (1997), 'France: A National and Contractual Second Tier' in Rein, M. and Wadensjö, E., *Enterprise and the Welfare State*, Edward Elgar, Cheltenham.

Ritzer, G. (1998), *The Macdonaldization Thesis*, Sage, London.

Roche, M. (1987), 'Citizenship, Social Theory and Social Change', *Theory and Society*, 16, pp. 363-399.

Roche, M. (1992), *Rethinking Citizenship: Welfare, Ideology and Change in Modern Society*, Polity Press, Cambridge.

Rosaldo, R. (1994), 'Cultural Citizenship and Educational Democracy', *Cultural Anthropology*, vol. 9, no. 3, pp. 402-411.

Rosenberg, S. (1989), 'The State and the Labour Market', Plenum Press, New York, in R.A. Lagos (1994), 'Labour Market Flexibility: What Does it Really Mean?', *CEPAL Review*, 54(December).

Rowlands, O., Singleton, N., Maher, J and Higgins, V. (1997), *Living in Britain: Results from the 1995 General Household Survey*, Stationery Office, London.

Saint-Paul, G. (1995), 'Some Political Aspects of Unemployment', *European Economic Review*, vol. 39, no. 3-4, pp. 575-582.

Selbourne, D. (1994), *The Principle of Duty : An Essay on the Foundations of the Civic Order*, Sinclair-Stevenson, London.

Selbourne, D. (1994), *The Principle of Duty*, Sincliar-Stevenson, London.

Sennett, R. (1999), 'How Work Destroys Social Inclusion', *New Statesman*, 31 May 1999.

Sewill, B. (1995), 'Reflections on the Demise of Full Employment', *Contemporary Record*, vol. 9, no.3, pp. 651-656.

Shanks, M. (1961), *The Stagnant Society*, Penguin, Harmondsworth.

Siddorn, G. (1996), 'Labour Market Insecurity', *Economic Briefing*, Issue 10, www.hm-treasury.gov.uk.

Simmel, G. (1914), *L'Art Pour l'Art*, Editions Rivages, Paris.

Smith, A. (1776), *The Wealth of Nations*, Dent 1910, London.

Smith, D. (1998), 'Don't look now but the big bad euro is coming up behind you', *The Sunday Times*, 26 April.

Social Trends 1996, HMSO, London.

Somers, M.R. (1993), 'Citizenship and the Place of the Public Sphere', *American Sociological Review*, 58, pp. 587-620.

Spencer, P. (1996), 'Reactions to a Flexible Labour Market' in, Jowells, R. (ed.), *British Social Attitudes Survey 13th Report*, Dartmouth, Aldershot.

Spender, H. (1912), Preface to: Snowden, P., *The Living Wage.*

Standing, G. (1986), *Unemployment and Labour Market Flexibility: The United Kingdom*, International Labour Organisation, Geneva.

Standing, G. (1988), *Unemployment and Labour Market Flexibility: Sweden*. International Labour Organisation, Geneva.

Standing, G. (1997), 'Globalization, Labour Flexibility and Insecurity: the Era of Market Regulation', *European Journal of Industrial Relations*, vol. 3, no. 1, pp. 7-37.

Stationery Office (1998a), *New Ambitions for our Country: A New Contract for Welfare*, Cm. 3805, The Stationery Office, London.

Stationery Office, (1998b), *A New Contract for Welfare: Partnership in Pensions*, Cm 4179, The Stationery Office, London.

Steenbergen, B. van (1994), *The Condition of Citizenship*, Sage, London.

Sumner, L. (1990), *The Moral Foundation of Rights*, Clarendon Press, Oxford.

Sutherland, H. (1998), *A Citizen's Pension*, Microsimulation Unit, Department of Applied Economics, University of Cambridge.

Taverne, D. (1995), *The Pension Time Bomb in Europe*, Federal Trust, London.

Taylor-Gooby, P. (1997), 'In Defence of Second-Best Theory: State, Class and Capital in Social Policy', *Journal of Social Policy*, vol. 26, no. 2, pp. 171-192.

The Report of the Commission on Social Justice (1994), *Social Justice. Strategies for National Renewal*, Vintage, London.

The Treaty of Rome, 1958.

Thorpe, K. (1997), 'The Health Care System in Transition: Care, Cost and Coverage', *Journal of Health Politics, Policy and Law*, vol. 22, pp. 341-361.

Townsend, P. (1995), 'Persuasion and Conformity: An Assessment of the Borrie Report on Social Justice', *New Left Review*, 213.

Treasury (1999), *The Modernisation of Britain's Tax and Benefit System. Number Four. Tackling Poverty and Extending Opportunity*, The Public Enquiry Unit, London.

Treasury Select Committee (1998a), *Report on the Mis-Selling of Personal Pensions, Ninth Report*, Session 1997/8, vol 1, HC 712-1, The Stationery Office, London.

Treasury Select Committee (1998b), *Report on the Mis-Selling of Personal Pensions, Minutes of Evidence and Appendices, Ninth Report*, Session 1997/8, vol 1, HC 712-2, The Stationery Office, London.

Turner, B.S. (1986), 'Citizenship and Capitalism', Allen and Unwin, London, in M. Waters (1989), 'Citizenship and the Constitution of Structured Social Inequality', *International Journal of Comparative Sociology*, vol. 30, nos. 3-4, September-December, pp. 159-180.

Turner, B.S. (1990), 'Outline of a Theory of Citizenship', *Sociology*, vol. 24, no. 2, pp. 189-213.

Turner, B.S. (1994), 'Postmodern Culture/Modern Citizens', in B. van Steenbergen, *The Condition of Citizenship*, pp. 153-168, Sage, London.

Veil, S. (1997), *Report of the High Level Panel on the Free Movement of Persons*, presented to the Commission on 18th March 1997.

Veneziani, B. (1996), 'Labour Flexibility in Europe', *http://epn.org/iess/ielabo.html.*

Vincent, J-M. (1996), 'La Déstabilisation du Travail', *Futur Antérieur*, no 35-36, L'Harmattan, Paris.

Viossat, C-C. (1997), 'Protections et Institutions Sociales', in *La Protection Sociale en France*, La Documentation Française, Collection Les notices, Paris.

Waine, B. (1995), 'A Disaster Foretold? The Case of the Personal Pension', *Social Policy and Administration*, vol. 29, no. 4, pp.317-334.

Waine, B. (1996), 'Security in Retirement: the Case of the Personal Pension', *Benefits*, 17, pp. 14-17.

Waters, M. (1989), 'Citizenship and the Constitution of Structured Social Inequality', *International Journal of Comparative Sociology*, vol. 30, no. 3-4, September-December, pp. 159-180.

Watson Wyatt Partners (1998), *Pension News: Green Paper: UK Pension Reform*, www.watsonwyatt.com.

Weale, A. (1983), *Political Theory and Social Policy*, Macmillan, London.

Weale, A. (1997), 'Majority Rule, Political Identity and European Union', in P.B. Lehning and A. Weale (eds), *Citizenship, Democracy and Justice in the New Europe*, Routledge, London.

Westergaard-Nielson, N. (1998), 'Wage Dispersion, Employment and Unemployment : Possible Trade Offs', in *Wages and Employment*, EC/DG V–OECD/DEELSA Seminar, European Commission, Luxembourg.

Whitton, T. (1997a), 'The national minimum wage : Pride or prejudice?', in, J. Edwards, and J-P. Révauger (eds), *Discourse on Inequality in France and Britain*, Ashgate, Aldershot.

Whitton, T. (1997b), 'Labour's national minimum wage', *Revue Française de Civilisation Britannique*, 9-3, pp. 115-117, Université de Provence, Aix-Marseille 1, Aix en Provence.

Whitton, T. (1998), 'The National Minimum Wage: Pride or Prejudice?', in J. Edwards and J-P. Revauger (eds), *Discourse on Inequality in France and Britain*, Ashgate, Aldershot.

Wiener, A. (1996), 'Rethinking Citizenship: the Quest for Place-Oriented Participation in the EU', *The Oxford International Review*, Summer Issue, pp. 44-51.

Wigham, E. (1963), *What's Wrong With the Unions?*, Penguin, Harmondsworth.

Williams, B. (1964), 'The Idea of Equality', in P. Laslett and W.G. Runciman (eds), *Philosophy Politics and Society*, Basil Blackwell, Oxford.

Williams, B. and Nicholl, J. (1994), 'Patient Characteristics and Clinical Caseload of Short Stay Independent Hospitals in England and Wales, 1992-3', *British Medical Journal*, vol. 308, pp. 1699-1701.

Williamson, J. (1997), 'Should Women Support the Privatisation of Social Security?', *Challenge*, vol 40, no.1, pp 97-108.

World Bank (1994*)*, *Averting the Old Age Crisis*, Oxford University Press, New York

Young, M. I. (1990), *Justice and the Politics of Difference*, Princeton University Press, Princeton, New Jersey.